Triumph of the Image

Critical Studies in Communication and in the Cultural Industries

Herbert I. Schiller, Series Editor

———————————◆———————————

Triumph of the Image: The Media's War in the Persian Gulf—A Global Perspective, edited by Hamid Mowlana, George Gerbner, and Herbert I. Schiller

Mass Communications and American Empire, Second Edition, Updated, Herbert I. Schiller

The Persian Gulf TV War, Douglas Kellner

FORTHCOMING

The Panoptic Sort: The Political Economy of Personal Information, Oscar Gandy, Jr.

Intellectual Property in the Information Age: A Political Economy of Film and Video Copyright, Ronald Bettig

The Communications Industry in the American Economy, Thomas Guback

Media Transformations in the Age of Persuasion, Robin K. Andersen

The Dallas Smythe Reader, edited by Thomas Guback

The Social Uses of Photography: Images in the Age of Reproduction, Hanno Hardt

Introduction to Media Studies, edited by Stuart Ewen, Elizabeth Ewen, Serafina Bathrick, and Andrew Mattson

A Different Road Taken: Profiles of Five Critical Communication Scholars, John A. Lent

Hot Shots: An Alternative Video Production Handbook, Tami Gold and Kelly Anderson

Music Television, Jack Banks

Triumph

of the Image

The Media's War in the Persian Gulf— A Global Perspective

edited by
Hamid Mowlana, George Gerbner,
and Herbert I. Schiller

Westview Press
Boulder • San Francisco • Oxford

Critical Studies in Communication and in the Cultural Industries

Copyright © 1992 by Westview Press, Inc.

Published in 1992 in the United States of America by Westview Press, Inc., 5500 Central Avenue, Boulder, Colorado 80301-2877, and in the United Kingdom by Westview Press, 36 Lonsdale Road, Summertown, Oxford OX2 7EW

Library of Congress Cataloging-in-Publication Data
Triumph of the image : the media's war in the Persian Gulf—a global
perspective / edited by Hamid Mowlana, George Gerbner, Herbert
I. Schiller.
      p.   cm. — (Critical studies in communication and in the
cultural industries)
    Includes bibliographical references.
    ISBN 0-8133-1532-8 — ISBN 0-8133-1610-3 (pbk.)
    1. Persian Gulf War, 1991—Journalists—Public opinion.
2. Persian Gulf War, 1991—Public opinion.   3. Public opinion—
history—20th century.   4. Press—History—20th century.
I. Mowlana, Hamid, 1937–   .   II. Gerbner, George, 1919–   .   III. Schiller,
Herbert I., 1919–   .   IV. Series.
DS79.739.T75   1992
956.704'3—dc20   92-7254
                                                                            CIP

Printed and bound in the United States of America

 The paper used in this publication meets the requirements
of the American National Standard for Permanence of Paper
for Printed Library Materials Z39.48-1984. Printed on recycled paper.

10   9   8   7   6   5   4   3

Contents

Preface

THE TRIUMPH OF IMAGE over reality and reason is the theme of this book. New communication technologies made it possible to transport images and words about the war in the Persian Gulf in real time to hundreds of millions of people around the world. But the studies in this book show that what was in fact witnessed was media imagery success-fully orchestrated to convey a sense of triumph and thus to realize results that reality and reason could never have achieved.

Part One explores the social, political, and economic context of that orchestration. Part Two shifts the focus to the international scene; studies from many nations document the domination of one image and the struggle for alternative perspectives. Part Three probes the dynamics of image making and poses some challenges for the future.

These studies, essays, and media samplings provide a unique glimpse at how the world outside the United States as well as many people in the United States viewed the war in the Persian Gulf. There are thirty-four authors and eighteen countries represented. Most of them are critical of the images conveyed by the dominant media and of the conduct of the war itself. This book should, in some small measure, balance the trium-phalist image of what happened in the Gulf and how it was represented to the world at large.

The Persian Gulf War should settle any argument about the near-total Western control of news about international conflict. Typical is P. Sainath's comment that despite a good number of Indian publications editorially taking a position against the war, the *content* of the news columns that were published in the same papers, almost without exception, were the reports of Western news agencies and journalists. In the case of India, there was an additional obstacle to obtaining alternative views: Indian reporters were excluded from the conflict region. And so papers were compelled to carry Western accounts, regardless of their own editorial opinions.

The contributions to this book offer abundant evidence that there were many more substantially divergent views and social movements than those conveyed by the dominating press. But those views and regions most adamant in their opposition to the U.S.-led war were the most tightly shut out of the global information networks.

The need for some balancing and plurality also derives from the disappearance of the dialectical polarity of worldviews from the world's press. Since the breakdown of the Soviet system as well as the weakening of the nonaligned movement of African, Asian, and Latin American nations, there is no longer any force to question or to contest the dominant viewpoint of a few global media conglomerates. Their accounts of what happened in the Persian Gulf, or anywhere else for that matter, are couched mostly in self-serving formulations that leave out essential information.

A critical eye focused on the activities of the global media machine is needed now more than ever because we are experiencing a monopolization of the definition and content of history. To an ever-increasing extent, what is happening is being told to us by a single narrator with a very powerful voice indeed. That narrator has long demonstrated a special talent for erasing as well as distorting history.

Already the Gulf War, despite hundreds of Pentagon-arranged and -funded victory parades and the efforts of thousands of TV and radio talk-show enthusiasts, is a distant event. How could the situation be otherwise when the war is succeeded by a never-ending preoccupation with events, trivial and important, hardly distinguished from one another, paraded across the screen (or the page), and sandwiched between omnipresent commercials? How can history coexist alongside call-in shows, sound-byte news, and pageants recreating a past that never existed—the bicentennial, Columbus's "discovery" of America, and the centenary of the Statue of Liberty?

But outside the media, history does exist, and it is not the story seen from the dominating heights. That constructed world, with its colonial stereotypes, is coming apart, but the media history machine daily works steadily, if vainly, at restoring it. In the Gulf War, there were more than a few throwbacks to this imagery. A powerful, industrialized state organized a subservient "coalition" to support its pulverization of a poor country with a relatively tiny population that had, admittedly, an unattractive and unsavory government. As Noam Chomsky points out in Chapter 4, a war requires at least two participants. But the Gulf War was, in his words, "a massacre." It was the destruction of people who were not considered fully human and therefore did not count. As if to emphasize the point, U.S. commanders pointedly mentioned their total lack of interest in how many Iraqis were killed or wounded.

Yet it was a massacre with a purpose: to send an unmistakable message to most of humanity—its poorest part in particular—that no challenge to existing privilege would be tolerated. In the following pages, we hope to offer an admittedly limited view of how this message was received in several places around the world.

The image cannot triumph indefinitely over the realities it conceals. We hope that what this book reveals about the dynamics of image making and information control will help make global communication freer to serve diverse perspectives and human cooperation instead of domination.

Hamid Mowlana
George Gerbner
Herbert I. Schiller

Acknowledgments

WE HAVE BEEN ASSISTED in the preparation of this book by the careful and dependable efforts of Kim Buermann, Ginger Smith, Elizabeth Fox, Danielle Vierling, and Amy Tully.

We thank them.

H. M.
G. G.
H.I.S.

───────◆───────

Image and Reality

CHAPTER ONE

◆

A Third-World War:
A Political Economy of
the Persian Gulf War and
the New World Order

Andre Gunder Frank

THE GULF WAR may be termed a Third-World War in two senses of this phrase: First, this war aligned the rich North, the rich oil emirates or kingdoms, and some bribed regional oligarchies against a poor Third World country. In that sense, the Gulf War was a Third-World War by the North against the South. It was massively so perceived throughout the Third-World South, not only in Arab and Muslim countries but also elsewhere in Asia, Africa, and Latin America.

Second, the Gulf War may mark the brutal beginning of the Third World War, following on the First and Second World Wars. Not only was the tonnage of bombs dropped on Iraq of world war proportions, but also the Gulf War and the new world order it was meant to launch signified the renewed recourse by a worldwide "coalition of allies" to mass destruction of infrastructure and mass annihilation of human beings. Moreover, in so doing the allies, led by the United States, clearly signaled their threat to build the new world order on repeated recourse to military

---

This chapter is abridged from a much longer and more documented version published as "Third World War in the Gulf: A New World Order Political Economy," *Notebooks for Study and Research* (Amsterdam), no. 14 (June 1991); *ENDpapers* (Nottingham) 22 (Summer 1991); *Economic Review* (Colombo) 17, nos. 4–5 (July-August 1991); *Sekai* (Tokyo), no. 560 (September 1991); and *Bush imperator: Analyses de la crise de la guerre au golfe,* ed. Jean Naudin (Paris: Editions la Breche, 1991).

force and annihilation against any other recalcitrant country or peoples—
as long as they are poor and weak and in the Third-World South.

With the conclusion of the cold war, the Third-World War is to be
fought, not between East and West or West and West, but between North
and South. Since the Second World War, West-West wars have been
obviated, and the East-West cold war has been fought out in regional hot
wars in Korea, Vietnam, Angola, Nicaragua, and other parts of the Third
World. Now, West-West cold conflicts are also to be transmuted, as in the
Gulf War against Iraq, into the ever-existing North-South conflict and
into a Third-World War at the expense of Third World peoples on Third
World soil.

This chapter examines the Gulf War and the new world order in this
global context. It also concentrates on the political economic motives,
actions, and their consequences of the major actors in the unfolding of
this tragic drama.

False Western Pretexts for War in the Gulf

The violation of international law through the invasion and occupation
of Kuwait by Iraq under the presidency of Saddam Hussein is beyond
dispute. But the allegation that the purpose of the Gulf War was to protect
the "principle" of world order, international law, and the Charter of the
United Nations from lawless might-is-right violation is a lie. Many similar
aggressions and violations of both the U.N. Charter and U.N. resolutions
have gone without any such response or often even without any notice.
Indonesia invaded and ravaged East Timor and Irian Jaya with the world
taking hardly any notice. Apartheid in South Africa, but less so South
Africa's continual aggressions against its neighboring front line states in
southern Africa, led to embargoes by the United Nations and its members;
but no one ever suggested going to war against South Africa. The Soviet
invasion of Afghanistan merited condemnation and opposition, albeit not
by the Security Council; but certainly no counterinvasion of the Soviet
Union was proposed. The Iraqi invasion of Iran received, but did not
merit, de facto political and even military support by the same coalition
of allies that then waged war against Iraq's invasion of Kuwait.

Indeed, among the very same states who allied themselves in a
coalition to "liberate Kuwait" from aggression, several today occupy the
territory of other peoples and nations. For instance, Israel invaded and
still occupies the Golan Heights, the West Bank, and the Gaza strip in
violation of U.N. Resolution 242: Israel also invaded Lebanon and still
exercises de facto military control over its southern part. Syria invaded
and still exercises military control over parts of northern Lebanon. Turkey
invaded Cyprus in 1974 and still occupies part of it militarily. Morocco

invaded and took over the Western Sahara. Significantly, hardly anyone except some Latin Americans—not even President Saddam Hussein and certainly not President George Bush—made the obvious linkage of the Iraqi occupation of Kuwait with the U.S. one of Panama.

Unfortunately, lying cynicism is not limited to Presidents Hussein or Bush and their immediate supporters. No Security Council resolutions were passed or even proposed to protect President Bush's new world order from his own violation of the sovereignty of Panama. On the contrary, President Bush received only acquiescence or even outright support for his violation of international law and human rights in Panama. So had President Ronald Reagan when he invaded and occupied sovereign Grenada (which is still administered by the United States). Indeed, the entire European Community (EC), not to mention the United States, supported Prime Minister Margaret Thatcher when she escalated her war against Argentina and its military junta (notwithstanding that she torpedoed all efforts in Lima to defuse the situation and prevent war in the South Atlantic and that she threatened to nuke the Argentine city of Córdoba). The Falklands War was the first major war of the entire West against a single Third World country. The latter received no support from any other country in the North and only moral support, regardless of ideology, from its regional partners in Latin America.

Immediate Economic Reasons for War

The most obvious economic reason for the Gulf War was oil. The real price of oil had again declined, especially with the renewed decline of the dollar. Iraq had some legitimate demands, both on its own behalf against Kuwait and on behalf of other Arab states and oil producers. In pressing these demands by resort to invasion, Saddam Hussein threatened some other oil interests, clients of the United States, and the success of the U.S. divide et impera policy.

Another economic reason for the war was to counter domestic recession or at least its political consequences at home, as Secretary of State James Baker suggested. Indeed, both Presidents Hussein and Bush started this war to manage their own domestic political economic problems in the face of a new world economic recession. The timing, however, of the U.S. response abroad was immediately related to economic needs and political conflicts at home. President Bush's failure to deliver on his electoral promise of a domestic renewal program was eating into his popularity ratings, and the oncoming recession reduced them further.

President Bush reacted with much historical precedent. Harry S. Truman's massive response in the Korean War in 1950 followed postwar demobilization and the first recession in 1949, which many feared might replay the Depression of the 1930s. During the 1953–1954 recession, the United States intervened in the military overthrow of the constitutionally elected Arbenz government in Guatemala. The 1968 Vietnamese Tet Offensive and the 1969–1970 recession were followed by renewed U.S. escalation in Indochina, including in Cambodia. The 1973–1975 recession also resulted in further escalation of the war in Vietnam. The 1979 recession and President Jimmy Carter initiated the second cold war. The two-track decision to install cruise missiles in Europe and to negotiate with the Soviet Union from strength as well as the 3 percent yearly increase in North Atlantic Treaty Organization (NATO) budgets, occurred *before* the Soviet Union invaded Afghanistan in December 1979. The unexpectedly strong U.S. response, which was not expected by the Soviets or perhaps anyone else, *followed* not only the invasion but also the 1979 recession. The 1981–1982 recession brought on Reagan's military Keynesianism and massive arms buildup, not to mention his Nicaraguan contra policy and perhaps his overreaction in Grenada.

World Geopolitical Economic Reasons for War

The recession started in the United States but was soon a worldwide phenomenon. France, Spain, Italy, the Netherlands, Sweden, and even Switzerland were experiencing reduced or negative growth rates. Africa was in a depression. In Latin America, gross national product declined .5 percent and per capita income went down 2.4 percent in 1990, on top of a 10 percent decline in the 1980s. Eastern Europe experienced an overall 20 percent economic decline in 1990; statistics for the Soviet Union were equally dismal. The People's Republic of China (PRC) was worried about growth, as was India, which the recession had largely bypassed in the 1980s.

Were Japan and Germany exceptions? The answers to this question were ambiguous, as could be seen in these newspaper headlines: "Without World Recovery, Bonn Fears a Slowdown," "Germany's East: Bleaker Yet," "Economy Feels Strains as Price of Unity Mounts," and "German Trade: No Moscow Miracles Foreseen." The Bundesbank president, Karl Otto Pohl, declared the economic consequences of German unification a "catastrophe" and drove the deutsche mark down several pfennings the next day.

Japan's stock market declined 40 percent in 1990, real estate prices plummeted, and Japanese investors and speculators transferred funds from abroad to help them cover their losses at home. In 1990, for the first time since 1986 and now that the United States needed it most, the net flow of Japanese capital was from the United States back to Japan. The prospects for a severe recession in Japan and the East Asian newly industrializing countries were quite real. Thus, the threat that world recession in the early 1990s would be even more severe than in the early 1980s was quite real.

At the same time, U.S. economic and geopolitical interests worldwide were under siege. The primary threats to these interests—competition from Japan and Germany or from a Japanese-led Asia and a German-led Europe—were intensified by the virtual elimination of the Soviet threat. The cold war was over, and Japan and Germany had won! The United States was now economically dependent on continued capital inflows from its principal economic rivals, which the Japanese had already begun to withdraw. In response to even deeper recession and/or with greater deliberation, the Japanese now intended to pull the financial rug out from under the United States and its dollar altogether. And other trade and economic disputes were growing ever deeper, including the General Agreement on Tariffs and Trade Uruguay rounds. Japan was distinctly uncooperative, and Europe refused to budge more than a few percent on the issue of agricultural subsidies. The road to "Europe 1992" was made more difficult by the 1989–1990 events in Eastern Europe and by Great Britain's intransigent foot dragging.

"BRAVO FOR AMERICAN POWER" celebrated the "serious" *Sunday Telegraph* (London) in a five-column January 20, 1991, editorial: "Bliss is it in this dawn to be alive; but to be an old reactionary is very heaven. . . . Who matter are not the Germans or the Japanese or the Russians but the Americans. Happy days are here again." The *Telegraph* also made its own the observation of the aptly named U.S. journal *National Interest:* "The fact [is] that the military power of the United States was the only thing capable of mounting an effective riposte—when the economic power of a Japan or a Germany was virtually irrelevant." The United States was not able to use its military might *against* Japan and Germany; and it could no longer do much *for* them either, now that the Soviet military threat was waning.

Since 1945, world economic conditions have shaped international and national politics and social movements. In particular, the economic conflicts and opportunities generated by the world economic crisis since 1967 have proved more important in shaping international relations and domestic policy than has the ideological and political cold war between the United States and the (former) Soviet Union. Many East-West conflicts have been a sham and a cover for always real North-South contradictions. None of the fourteen "revolutions" in the South since 1974 has been what it appeared to be or has turned out as was hoped or feared. The United States still has the military power and the political ambitions to try defending its place in the world order—now all the more so at the expense of the Third-World South.

The escalation of the Gulf crisis was marked by three important new departures in recent international political economic relations:

1. The energetic U.S. response in the Gulf was visibly over an economic issue—oil. This issue was absent any cold war ideological overtones. The conflict about oil and the massive U.S. response were barely masked behind appeals to the "defense" of small states in international "law."
2. This mobilization occurred without any pretense of an East-West ideological cover.
3. There was near unanimity and alliance of the North against the South. The lineup against Iraq from West to East included the United States, Western and Eastern Europe, the Soviet Union, and the PRC and Japan as well as U.S. client states and governments whose arms were easily twisted, as in Egypt and Pakistan. This new alignment was a major difference, a new departure, and an ominous threat for the future of "international" relations.

Economic Buildup and Political Escalation in the Gulf

The Iraqi invasion of Kuwait was not an unexpected bolt of lightning out of the blue. Its utilization by the United States as a pretext to launch a new world order through the most destructive war since World War II appears increasingly as malice aforethought.

> Stealing Kuwait was not simple greed or national hatred. Theft on a national scale [of what had been Iraqi before the British created Kuwait] had become the only possible access for war-devastated Iraq to . . . the modern standard of living that Western nations and small oil-producing emirates of the Gulf enjoy today as a matter of right. . . . The strength of this almost suicidal drive to emerge from poverty and backwardness . . . was the motor. (Jim Hoagland, *International Herald Tribune*, March 5, 1991)

"The Americans were determined to go to war from the start," and Saddam Hussein "walked into a trap," according to the former French Foreign Minister Claude Cheysson (*International Herald Tribune*, March 11, 1991). "State Department officials . . . led Saddam Hussein to think he could get away with grabbing Kuwait. . . . Bush and Co. gave him no reason to think otherwise" (*New York Daily News*, September 29, 1990). Former White House Press Secretary Pierre Salinger wrote at length about how this trap was set. Other aspects of the trap emerged elsewhere, and some may be summarily put together here. The belatedly publicized July

25 interview between President Hussein and U.S. Ambassador April Glaspie was only one piece of a largely hidden trap.

At the State Department, Secretary James Baker had promoted John Kelly to assistant secretary of state for Middle Eastern Affairs. Kelly visited Baghdad in February, "the records of which he is desperately trying to deep-six" (William Safire, *International Herald Tribune,* March 26, 1991). Kelly told President Hussein that "President Bush wants good relations with Iraq, relations built on confidence and trust." Moreover, Kelly then rebuked the Voice of America and countermanded the Defense Department on statements he considered too unfriendly to Iraq. On April 26, Kelly testified to Congress that Bush administration policy toward Iraq remained the same and praised Saddam Hussein for "talking about a new constitution and an expansion of participatory democracy." On July 31, only two days before the invasion of Kuwait, Kelly again testified to a congressional subcommittee that "we have no defense treaty with any Gulf country."

Evidence suggests that the Persian Gulf war was the result of a long process of preparation, much more so than was the case with the Tonkin Gulf incident in Vietnam. For a decade during the Iran-Iraq Wars, Saddam Hussein's Iraq had enjoyed U.S. and Western military, political, and economic support, including $1.5 billion in sales approved by the U.S. government. George Bush had been a key figure in the Reagan administration's support for Iraq. After the conclusion of Iraq's war with Iran and the accession of George Bush to the presidency, U.S. policy toward Iraq became increasingly confusing and/or the product of a downright Machiavellian strategy to deceive Iraq and set a trap for Hussein.

President Hussein may also have had reasons for the invasion that were additional to his oil-related grievances with Kuwait. The stalemate in his war with Iran may have incited him to try once again for a realignment of the regional balance of power. It is useful to recall that Mesopotamia (Iraq), Persia (Iran), and Egypt, and occasionally the Arabian Peninsula as well, have been disputing, without resolution, hegemonial regional overlordship since the Sumerian Sargon tried to achieve it around 2500 B.C.

Between the Iraqi invasion of Kuwait on August 2, 1990, and the start of U.S. bombing on January 17, 1991, President Hussein gave clear indications of his willingness to negotiate an Iraqi withdrawal on at least six occasions. Three times, he unilaterally took steps that could have led to withdrawal. President Hussein made repeated statements indicating that he was serious about withdrawal, which would include Iraqi "sacrifices" for a negotiated package deal. On more than one occasion, President Hussein and his foreign minister, Tariq Aziz, also told Secretary General Javier Pérez de Cuellar of the United Nations of their desire for a negotiated solution. All these Iraqi and other initiatives came to naught because the Bush administration wanted and arranged for them to fail.

Fighting and Lying to Win the War

Two propaganda blitzes dominated the war. One was that it was valiantly waged against "the world's fourth largest army" with a highly trained "elite Republican Guard." The other one was that coalition forces there-fore had to put on history's first high-tech "Nintendolike" electronic war with "smart bombs"—at least courtesy of U.S. and U.K. military command videotaped briefings for CNN and other TV networks around the world. Hardly anyone then noticed that these two features of the war were mutually contradictory in principle and empirically false in practice. Claude Cheysson, did, however, declare, "I categorically reject notions about avoiding unnecessary damage. The allied goal of annihilating Iraq's economy was bound to involve civilian casualties . . . 200,000—a massacre, with a terrifying impact. . . . Why don't you ask why the air war lasted 40 days instead of the 15 as planned" (*International Herald Tribune,* March 11, 1991).

Only after it was all over did a bit of truth emerge about what the *International Herald Tribune* headlined "Desert Mirages: In the War, Things Weren't Always What They Seemed. U.S. Overestimated Size and Ability of Iraq's Armed Forces." The United States did so deliberately to help justify the carpet and terror bombing of both the military and civilian "assets" of this Third World country with a population of only 17 million souls. The Pentagon presented sanitized images of a new kind of high-tech war between machines, not men. We saw videos of outgoing Patriot missiles destroying incoming Iraqi Scud missiles. Only later did we learn that the Patriots hit only the Scud propulsors and did not destroy the warheads, which still hit buildings and killed people. We also were not shown that both types of missiles fell back to the ground to cause damage. Indeed, only on April 18 did the *International Herald Tribune* reveal that "the Patriot may have caused as much damage as it prevented."

The military commands also released many videos of precision-guided smart bombs taking out hard targets in Iraq. But they neglected to show that these bombs still missed 10 percent of their targets. Still less did the military commands mention that the smart bombs accounted for only 7 percent of the tonnage dropped. The other 93 percent were not smart enough to get on TV. Of the total bombs dropped by the new Stealth bombers, 3 percent accounted for 40 percent of the target hits, which included roads, bridges, power plants, and irrigation works. The *New York Times* editorialized a bit belatedly on March 25, 1991 (cited in *International Herald Tribune,* March 25, 1991): "The bulk of the damage found by the U.N. team was not accidental or collateral, but the intended consequence of the successful air campaign to destroy Iraq's war machine by attacking its industrial base and urban infrastructure. The findings raise questions about how much of that bombing was needed, or justified. That debate will go on."

The *New York Times* and other "responsible" media, however, did precious little to start the debate before or during that bombing, when it should have been avoided, limited, or stopped. When U.S. targeters hit the only powdered milk and infant formula factory in the country and then a civilian air raid shelter, the Pentagon insisted that they had correctly hit military targets. CNN and its Peter Arnett were hounded as traitors to the cause for sowing doubts after having loyally aired hundreds of hours of war propaganda. In a case of the pot calling the kettle black, the U.S. commanding general, Norman Schwarzkopf, said, "I did resent CNN aiding and abetting an enemy who was violating the Geneva Convention" (*International Herald Tribune,* March 28, 1991).

The United States also violated U.N. International Energy Commission regulations that prohibited bombing nuclear facilities because of the danger of uncontrollable contamination. Despite this ban and danger, U.S. bombs were dropped on Iraqi nuclear facilities anyway. "In one of these cases, the bombardment resulted in what Iraq described as 'radiation contamination of the region.' . . . Thousands of Iraqi weapons have been described by Baghdad as buried beneath the contaminated debris of Iraqi storage sites and production factories" (*International Herald Tribune,* May 2, 1991). Contrary to allied assurances, bombs also damaged ancient Sumerian and Assyrian archeological treasures (*International Herald Tribune,* May 6, 1991).

Human and Material War Damages and Costs

No one knows, or probably will ever know, how many Iraqi casualties resulted from this unnecessary war that could and should have been avoided. The world's "fourth largest army," from a country whose entire population was not even one and a half times that of New York City, was decimated from the air before the long heralded but brief allied ground offensive even started. (The offensive lasted one hundred hours.) Only after the war did several press sources repeatedly report U.S. military and CIA estimates of between 100,000 and 250,000 Iraqi dead, most of them military. In his televised interview with David Frost, General Norman Schwarzkopf reported "50,000 or 100,000 or 150,000 or whatever of them to be killed." A Saudi military commander told CNN of 100,000 Iraqi troops dead and 200,000 wounded. A French military intelligence source told the *Nouvelle Observateur* that 200,000 were killed. Greenpeace estimated more than 150,000 dead, including 100,000 to 120,000 troops and 5,000 to 15,000 civilians. At least 5 million people lost their homes or jobs (*International Herald Tribune,* May 30, 1991). The Muslim Institute referred to "up to 500,000 Iraqi civilians killed or injured by Allied bombs" in the April 12 *International Herald Tribune.* At war's end in Iraq, a U.N. commission of inquiry found a country in "near-apocalyptic" conditions of catastrophe, with its economy, society, and people bombed back into the preindustrial age.

The U.S. war planning, execution, and finale (wanton massacre and burial alive of retreating troops and civilians) violated all standards of civilized conduct and several international conventions to which the United States was signatory. These included the 1907 and 1923 Hague, the 1948–1950 Geneva, the Nuremberg, and the Genocide conventions on rules and crimes of war as well as the U.N. Declaration of Human Rights (sponsored by Eleanor Roosevelt). These violations were detailed in Representative Henry Gonzalez's January 1991 House Resolution 34 to impeach George Bush and in the May 1991 "initial complaint" against him and other high-ranking members of his administration presented before the Commission of Inquiry for the International War Crimes Tribunal, organized by former U.S. Attorney General Ramsey Clark.

Even before the first shot was fired, the Gulf crisis had produced many casualties: Millions had become refugees and/or had lost their livelihoods because of the occupation of Kuwait and the embargo against Iraq. The many Third World countries from which guest workers came lost the remittances of foreign exchange from these workers. Moreover, they were returning home penniless to augment the masses of unemployed. The price of petroleum temporarily skyrocketed for the old Third World countries in the South and the new Third World countries in Eastern Europe. Hundred of millions of people around the world saw their most urgent problems (such as renewed famine in Africa) even more neglected as attention focused on the Gulf.

Another casualty of the war was the environment. But even here the Western propaganda used ecological damage to extend and intensify the war and in the process increased ecological costs still further. For example, the Pentagon blamed the oil spills of the Gulf on the Iraqis. In support, the media showed heart-rending images of dead oil-soaked birds, the effect of which was to whip up even more anti-Hussein sentiment to justify the escalation of the war. As it turned out, these pictures were taken during earlier oil spills elsewhere, and ecological damage was less than advertised. Wildlife conservationists now estimate that .5 percent of the birds in the area were affected. As for the oil slicks, Claude-Marie Vadrot of the *Paris Journal de Dimanche* (February 3, 1991) wrote, "None of the existing slick in the Gulf have resulted from voluntary action or piracy, and four out of five are the responsibility of allied forces."

The five hundred burning Kuwaiti oil wells may indeed have been set afire by the Iraqis, who had announced from the very beginning that they would have to use this measure. It was one of the few available to them to defend themselves from superior force in general and from threatened amphibious attacks across Gulf waters in particular. Moreover, having been incited into this war by Kuwaiti oil competition and duplicity, Iraq now assured itself of a long respite from this competition by setting fire to the Kuwaiti oil wells. But the Commission of Inquiry for the International War Crimes Tribunal charged that "attacks by U.S. aircraft . . . and helicopters dropping napalm and fuel-air explosives on oil wells, storage tanks, and refineries caused oil fires throughout Iraq and many, if not most, of the oil fires in Iraq and Kuwait." The resulting human-made environmental damage from smoke was unprecedented, at least in its regional impact.

Political Costs of the Gulf War

The Gulf War fought against a ruthless dictator in the South by the great democracies in the West violated or subverted the most important bases and institutions of democracy. The will of the vast majority of the people in the West was violated. Freedom of the press was actively censored, and the free press, the guardian of democracy, censored itself. As much by omission as by commission, the media deliberately misled the public. Participant democracy was bypassed and neutralized or sterilized. At the same time, racism and chauvinism flourished and were used to aid and abet the war effort on the home front. The Gulf War was falsely fought in the name of "democracy." The war witnessed one of the sorriest days for real democracy in the West, not to mention the newly democratic East.

The major institutional casualties of the Gulf War were the U.S. Congress and other parliaments. The constitutional mandate of Congress to keep the president in check and balance, especially in the exercise of his authority to declare war for good cause, was subverted. President Bush skillfully outmaneuvered almost the entire U.S. political establishment, including eight out of nine secretaries of defense who opposed the war. Bush also used deceit and blackmail against Congress in a manner reminiscent of and functionally analogous to the Tonkin Gulf affair. Congress would most likely have refused to vote Bush war powers in November or perhaps even in December, which was surely why President Bush did not send his war resolution to Congress before he had crossed so many Rubicons. Congress could hardly have denied its support to the men and women whom the president had sent to the front.

Only after the war did General Schwarzkopf publicly admit to eighteen month's prior planning of his campaign and did Chief of Staff General Colin Powell refer to the related computerized war games developed in 1989.

President Bush made his decision to go to war against Iraq in August. A crucial step was to double the number of troops in Saudi Arabia by bringing in two hundred thousand more U.S. NATO troops from Germany in November. He brought them not to rotate them (as initially announced), but to add them to those troops already there. In the process, the mission of the U.S. troops was changed from the supposed defense of Saudi Arabia against a possible attack by Iraq to the "liberation" of Kuwait through a planned U.S. attack on Iraq itself and a defeat of its military forces. In view of this commitment by President Bush, the ever-astute Henry Kissinger then observed that any withdrawal without victory "would lead to a collapse of American credibility, not only in the area but in most parts of the world" (*International Herald Tribune,* January 17, 1991). These far-reaching decisions were made before the November 6 U.S. congressional elections, but they were deliberately withheld from the public and Congress before the elections and were implemented only thereafter. It's unlikely that the U.S. public and the U.S. Congress would have agreed to this deliberate escalation toward war by President Bush if they had been given a choice. That is why President Bush gave them no choice but instead deceived them and pursued his covert policy of faits accomplis.

Thus, President Bush won. The U.S. Congress was denied its constitutional mandate to exercise checks and balances on the president, especially on his ability to wage war. Because of this deceit, the two major institutional safeguards against war, the United Nations and the U.S. Congress, became major casualties before the first shot was even fired in the Gulf War.

Other parliaments in the West were also bypassed and/or bamboozled into supporting and paying for a war whose real reason and purpose were never explained to them or their voter constituencies. The easiest task was perhaps in Britain, where all substantive discussions of the matter in the House of Commons were avoided and attention was focused on the change of parliamentary and government leadership. President Bush's most enthusiastic foreign support did come from Britain, first under the leadership of Prime Minister Margaret Thatcher and then under that of her successor, John Major. The *Telegraph* (January 20, 1991) offered an interpretation in a column entitled "To the Point": "Britain goes up in the world" again thanks to its support for President Bush in the Gulf, which "suggests that Britain, not Germany, is the more natural leader for a Europe aspiring to greater political unity." In support of this thesis, the same paper also cited "so influential an American organ of opinion" as the *Wall Street Journal*. Moreover, by February 14, the *International Herald Tribune* was reporting that "Britain has a new credibility within the EC that has been bolstered, for the time being at least, by the Gulf crisis, officials said." Unmentioned, but perhaps not irrelevant, was the fact that the recession-ridden British economy and the London financial "City" still needed the continued financial support of the Kuwaiti and other oil sheiks and that the unpopular Tory government was in dire need of a political boost. A jingoist war in the Gulf offered both. In Japan, in Germany, and even in France, the heads of government had more trouble bypassing their parliaments and/or twisting their arms to exact support for Bush's war.

The Gulf War was accompanied and indeed prepared by the biggest media blitz in world history. But when war breaks out, the first casualty is the truth, as was said during the Crimean War. Poor Joseph Goebbels. The Nazi minister who made the management of racist and totalitarian war propaganda synonymous with his name would have to start in kindergarten to learn how today's high-tech news management functions to brainwash a global population via instant satellite TV. All semblance of democratic procedures was thrown to the wolves during the war. FAIR (Fairness and Accuracy in Reporting) monitored 878 on-air sources on the U.S. ABC, CBS and NBC networks during the war and found only one of these to represent a peace organization (*International Herald Tribune,* May 25–26, 1991).

The Pentagon-managed press pool was the most successful military weapon used in the war. The pool was designed to permit a military monopoly on gathering, assembling, and disseminating information; this monopoly was accomplished through commission *and* omission. Far from denying military secrets to the military enemy in Iraq, however, the pool foreclosed or neutralized potential civilian enemies of the war on the home front. Very few newspeople left the region on their own account, as a CNN reporter apparently did rather than forsake her integrity. The self-censorship by the press at home probably exceeded even the military's blackout of battlefield news and its analysis, which might have fed the citizen at home with even a modicum of the information he or she might have used to question the aims and prosecution of this war.

In fact, the home front witnessed much dissatisfaction with the press for failing to contribute enough to the war effort! Once the shooting started, barrages of letters, phone-ins, interviews, and public opinion polls in the United States and Great Britain gave vent to the public demand for even more news censorship and management. In the former country, 80 percent of the public supported the restrictions on the press, and 60 percent wanted even more military control over the press and information (*International Herald Tribune,* February 1, 1991). So where then was the denial of democracy? Was it in the management of public opinion? Or was it in the brainwashing of people who for the second half of 1990 knew little about the basis for such a war or wanted it to be fought?

Little wonder that Anthony Lewis could belatedly make the following contention in the *New York Times* under the title "Docile Media Hawked the Official View of the War":

> Most of the press was not a detached observer of the war, much less a critical one. It was a claque applauding the American generals and politicians in charge. In the press I include television, its most powerful component now and the most egregious lapdog during the war. For the most part the networks simply transmitted official images of neat, painless war. Or worse: put a gloss of independent corroboration on those false images. And they were false. . . . Perhaps the most dangerous shortcoming of the press was its failure to keep asking whether the war was necessary or wise. (Cited in *International Herald Tribune,* May 7, 1991)

The decisions to go to war were made at the highest national and international levels. The government leaders involved not only failed to consult their populations and voters but also, as I noted previously, President Bush even deliberately avoided putting the issue to the people's elected representatives in Congress until long after the congressional elections and his subsequent doubling of U.S. Gulf troops in November 1990. In so doing, these government leaders also pulled the rug out from under the social movements in civil society both in the United States and Western Europe after these movements had already been bypassed in Eastern Europe. The mobilization of civil society around myriad local, national, and international issues of gender relations, environmental issues, and peace received a brutal blow. Even the director of that old cold war think tank, the International Institute of Strategic Studies, observed in the *International Herald Tribune* (February 11, 1991), "The current collapse of pacifist movements in Western countries, not the least Germany, is one of the notable features of the war."

In Europe, the media confronted people with a choice between the Iraqi Saddam Hussein and the American George Bush. With *that* choice, the men in the street and in front of their TV sets chose the white American. More women, fortunately or wisely, refused that false Hobson's choice and opted for peace instead. Nonetheless, Western European civil society rapidly became infected with rabid racism and chauvinism directed against any and all Arabs and Turks—in total disregard of the fact that many Arabian countries as well as Turkey (which also has its eye on some Iraqi petroleum producing territory) were loyal active members of the allied coalition. Thereby, these Western Europeans may have also demonstrated a preference for replacing cheap non-European labor from the South with newly available cheap European labor from the East. Perhaps it was not altogether accidental that half a dozen countries in Western Europe chose that time to lift visa requirements for entry by Poles, who came by trains and buses to look for work. Meanwhile, all around the equator not only Arabs and Muslims but also other peoples in Asia, Africa, and Latin America demonstrated against the United States and its war against the Third World.

Thus deliberately or not, the Gulf War bypassed, undermined, violated, subverted, and otherwise seriously damaged the most precious democratic institutions and processes in the very democracies that supposedly went to war to defend democracy against tyranny. This sacrifice of democracy, in addition to the negation of peace and threat of future wars, was a terrible price to pay for the new world order.

International Political Costs of the War

The most important and most obvious international political cost of the war was peace. This sacrifice of peace, however, had several dimensions, not all of which have received the attention they merit. Perhaps the most significant one was the cancellation of the "peace dividend" expected, perhaps naively, from the end of the cold war. The hoped-for peace dividend was not limited to the conversion of military production to civilian use or the diversion of military budgets to social needs. More importantly, the peace dividend promised a transition from the cold war and its associated hot wars in the Third World to a new era of peace, such as that which broke out in several Third World countries in 1988–1989. (The United Nations successfully intervened to that effect in Afghanistan, Angola, Cambodia, Iran-Iraq, and Namibia, if not Nicaragua; and its blue helmets were awarded the Nobel Prize for Peace.) The end of the cold war and its associated stalemate between the superpowers in the Security Council held out hopes that the United Nations could finally begin to meet its chartered responsibilities to keep the peace. Most importantly, however, the peace dividend was to be the de facto renunciation of war as an instrument of foreign policy in the settlement of international disputes, as enshrined forty-five years previously in the U.N. Charter.

The first and most important institutional cost to peace was the perversion of the United Nations. Secretary General Pérez de Cuellar declared outright that this was a U.S., not a U.N., war and that the Security Council was in the hands of the United States, Britain, and France.

The conservative U.S. columnist William Safire wrote under the title "Consider These White Lies and The Truths They Veil":

> This is not a U.N. enforcement action; that part of the U.N. Charter has never been invoked. Instead this is a collective defense authorized by the Security Council, similar to the Korean defense, which means that the resolutions . . . cannot be revoked without American concurrence. . . . America shows obeisance to the UN, but obedience is a white lie." (*International Herald Tribune,* February 26, 1991)

The Security Council violated the U.N. Charter on several particular counts and shirked its general responsibility to the world to keep the peace. Instead, the Security Council and the institution and prestige of the United Nations were used to legitimate war. Under the U.N. Charter, the Security Council mandate is to preserve the peace, not to authorize or legitimatize war. Moreover, the charter enjoins or bars the resort to war under Article 42 until the Security Council (not the president of the United States) determines under Article 41 that *all* peaceful means to resolve a dispute have been exhausted. Clearly, this was not done before this war. Resolution 678 setting the January 15 deadline for military action violated both Articles 41 and 42 as well as the Security Council vote regulating Article 27 of the charter.

The Gulf War dashed all these peace dividend hopes and set a precedent for a renewed resort to war, this time by a coalition of allied Western powers with some southern and eastern support, to uphold the new world order. This linkage of war to a new order demonstrated for all to see that this order was being initiated and constructed, and then maintained, through the wanton destruction of the weak by the military force of the powerful and through the subversion of the world's most precious institutions. This war clearly announced that military might is right in all senses of the word. Ominously, this war also threatened the repeated resort to similar wars in the future.

The integrity of NATO was another of the war's international costs. The Western allies diverted or converted NATO into an offensive instrument against the Third-World South. This diversion of the NATO alliance and institution from East-West conflicts to North-South ones was portentious for the world as a whole. Indeed, President Bush had already set a very serious precedent in November when he sent to the Gulf the U.S. NATO troop contingents that had been stationed under U.S. NATO command in (West) Germany. President Bush used NATO facilities and U.S.-supplied military hardware—and no doubt software—for deployment to the Gulf and asked his NATO allies in Europe to do the same. This quiet diplomacy and the de facto Bush policy for transforming the function and direction of NATO threaten to become one of the most dangerous legacies of the Gulf War for the rest of the world. (The peace dividend from the end of the cold war was another major casualty of President Bush's Gulf War policy even before the first shot was fired.)

Far from settling any of the long-standing political problems in the Middle East, the Gulf War exacerbated them and then made them even more difficult to address and solve. The strengthened recalcitrance in and by Israel through its nonparticipation in the Gulf War and the political weakening of the Palestine Liberation Organization (PLO) leadership, as well as that of King Hussein of Jordan, were only the most visible and interrelated problems. So were the postwar Shiite and Kurdish rebellions in Iraq. Even the mildest success of the Iranian-supported Shiites was not in the interests of the United States and its European or Arab allies, for whom the mullahs in Iran were more than enough. Neither the Iraqi Shiite nor the democratic opposition in Iraq received any Western or other allied support or publicity.

De- and Downgrading Europe, Japan, and the Soviet Union

In the Gulf crisis, Western Europeans gave up all pretense at a unified and independent European foreign policy. In particular, the relatively more constructive and progressive European policy toward, and goodwill in, the Middle East was sacrificed. European intervention in favor of a more reasonable settlement of the Palestine-Israeli issue receded beyond the visible horizon. The Gulf War participation by and consequences for the Soviet Union were less clear, but for that perhaps even more danger- ous. Mikhail Gorbachev's government sought to be on its best behavior and caved in and/or sold out to the United States and its Western allies. This concession, of course, was essential in constructing the charade of the U.N. cover for the U.S. war plan. Even an opportune Soviet abstention, not to mention a veto, at the Security Council would have tipped the balance and would probably have changed the votes of the PRC and France as well. But President Gorbachev went along with President Bush, except for Gorbachev's and his envoy's vain efforts to shore up the waning Soviet role in the area. As it turned out, the USSR's role in the Gulf War sacrificed Soviet influence over other Arab nations, the war further increased sympathy among Soviet Muslims for their Islamic brethren abroad, and Soviet military leaders had to witness the miserable defeat of the Soviet weapons systems and the military strategy of the USSR's client army in Iraq.

Putting the Third World in Its Place

Perhaps the clearest gulf in this war was between the rich and the poor. The Western powers in this war represented above all, the interests of the rich in the world. (Perhaps the Texans, President Bush, and Secretary of State Baker represented the rich Texas oil interests more than they would like to admit.) And Saudi Arabia (the original dispatch of troops was for its protection), the United Arab Emirates, and Kuwait were also among the oil rich, who are reputed to have placed some $670 billion worth of investments abroad (*Economic and Political Weekly,* January 5–12, 1991).

Of course, these investments and relations also afforded the Kuwaitis continued income and political influence in the West even without drawing up another drop of oil at home. Suffice it to ask whether the rich West would have sent more than half a million troops to defend any other poor country or people in Africa or elsewhere. The other Arabs in the coalition were U.S. client governments representing the rich in their respective countries. The poor populations of these same Arab countries were massively on the other side of this conflict in support of Iraq, whose president opportunistically declared himself their spokesperson as well as that of poor Palestinians and other Muslims. As we have observed, throughout the Third-World South masses of people understood that this Gulf War was designed and executed to put them in their place in Bush's new world order.

It is no joke that the April 1, 1991, cover of *Time* asked whether the U.S. "Globo Cop. [was] Coming Soon to Your Country." *Time* took the trouble to send its reporters around the Third World and elsewhere to ask how people viewed the new world order. The introductory summary of *Time*'s findings remarked that "critics protest that Bush's proclaimed new world order conjures up misty and dangerous visions of a militaristic American Globo-cop on the march." In affirmation, President Bush said at the June 9 commemoration of the war dead at Arlington cemetery that "although we hope this is the last time, we are ready to respond again if there is a new aggression" (*El País,* June 9, 1991).

Finally, the Pentagon and its associated military-industrial complex has already announced a major campaign of tens of billions of dollars of new arms sales for the wholesale replenishment and extension of military arsenals in the Middle East. First the United States and its Western European allies armed the shah of Iran to the teeth. Then they sold their arms to President Hussein to cut Iran's successor regime down to size. Then the same allies bombed Hussein's war machine to smithereens. Now they propose to provide more arms to their next client in the region. It is living dangerously indeed to be a U.S. client state in the Middle East (or for that matter in Panama and Central America), but to build these states up and then abandon them are also profitable for the United States.

The United States in the New World Order

The long-term question remains whether the Bravo for bravado of President Bush's new world order will really save the United States or even himself. Or will President Bush's adventurism bankrupt and sink the United States even further than his mentor Ronald Reagan did? He promised to make "the United States number one again" and nearly bankrupted it instead. It may well go bankrupt, especially in the face of the new world economic recession and the virtually irrelevant economic power of Japan and Germany—to which countries Bush had to send Secretary of State Baker, hat in hand, to help finance the war in the Gulf.

This recession/war is not likely to turn out as previous ones did. World War II pulled the United States out of the Depression and made it hegemonic. The Korean War pulled the United States out of the recession of 1949 and launched the military Keynesianism that helped ward off the feared economic stagnation. The Vietnam War was enough for the United States to avoid the recession that hit West Germany and Japan in 1967. It was not enough, however, to prevent the recession of 1970 or ward off the first severe postwar recession of 1973–1975. On the contrary, the Vietnam War weakened the United States relative to its Japanese and West German rivals. The costs of that war obliged the United States to abandon the fixed exchange rates and the institutional mechanisms established at Bretton Woods and then to devalue the dollar.

The Gulf War offers no lasting political or economic benefits; indeed it holds several more dangers. Probably more important than the wartime or postwar consumer confidence in the United States is the confidence of international capital and of allied governments elsewhere in the West. The more important effects of the recession and war will play themselves out via the reactions of private capital and the decisions by governments and central banks in Europe and Japan. Without an adequate economic base, military power is insufficient to keep a great superpower afloat. On the contrary, the foolish use of its military power may instead sink that power. It is not by accident that Paul Kennedy became a best-selling author (apparently not in the Bush White House or the Pentagon) when he wrote that foolish military overextension beyond the economy's means to support it is the basis of the rise and fall of the great powers.

CHAPTER TWO

◆

Manipulating Hearts and Minds

Herbert I. Schiller

FOR NEARLY A HALF A CENTURY American editors and government officials have lectured the world on the virtues of a free press, the desirability of the free flow of information, and the necessity to avoid governmental domination of the informational system.

How have these principles fared in the seven months beginning with the invasion of Kuwait in August 1990? There is a rich record from which to judge. Here only a tiny sample will be taken, but this demonstrates the essential practices of media performance in this period. What has been revealed? Along with providing a living laboratory for an assessment of the high-tech weapons the Pentagon has been building and stockpiling for decades, the Gulf War offered a spectacular opportunity for information and opinion management.

In retrospect and on balance, the remarkable control of American consciousness during and after the war must be regarded as a signal achievement of mind management, perhaps even more impressive than the rapid military victory.

After all, Iraq has only 18 million people. It is essentially a poor, not heavily industrialized society which was temporarily the possessor of a sizable arsenal. Its quick capitulation before overwhelming force was foretold.

But the informational assault against the American people is an altogether different affair. Here was "the information society," capable of the most dazzling capabilities for making information available instantaneously to the entire population. Did it meet the challenge? Actually, a

This chapter was originally published in *Le Monde Diplomatique* (Paris) (May 1991).

simple truth emerged: Dazzling information technology is no substitute for, and can obscure, elemental bread-and-butter information.

For, in fact, the United States, with its enormous media system operating with state-of-the art technologies, has been as closed as a society could be to information, facts, and opinion which in the slightest challenged the national war policy. As one journalist put it, after the war was over and the censorship straitjacket somewhat loosened, "the real, and dangerous, point is that the Bush Administration and the military were so successful in controlling information about the war they were able to tell the public just about what they wanted the public to know. Perhaps worse, press and public, largely acquiesced in the disclosure of only selected information" (Tom Wicker, "An Unknown Casualty," *New York Times,* March 20, 1991, p. A17).

The main theater of operations for the information war was television. The print press was a secondary front and not quite as carefully guarded.

As Ronald Reagan's deputy chief of staff in charge of imagemaking, Michael Deaver, put it: "Television is where 80% of the people get their information," and what was done to control that information in the six weeks of war "couldn't [have been] better" (*New York Times,* February 15, 1991, p. A9).

What happened then to the principles of free speech and free flow of information, to say nothing of information pluralism, between January 15 and March 1, 1991, in the American media?

In short, the control process exercised through an amazing coordination of voluntaristic efforts by hundreds of media gatekeepers (editors, broadcasters, disc jockeys, sports announcers, talk-show hosts, etc.) succeeded in presenting the Gulf War, again according to Michael Deaver, as "a combination of Lawrence of Arabia and Star Wars"—i.e., heroic Western leadership of the Arab world joined with mouth-gaping demonstrations of advanced weaponry.

Accomplishing this end took painstaking effort. At home, the faces and views of only a very select group of individuals appeared on living room screens. Night after night, as well as throughout the day, nearly all commentary about the crisis and the war was restricted to military questions. Not surprisingly, every retired general found a new career as a consultant to one or another of the national networks. When civilians appeared, they were the politically certified think-tank experts or D.C. politicos with impeccable establishment credentials.

A former assistant editor of the *Washington Post* writing on Gulf War coverage for the *Columbia Journalism Review* ([March-April 1991]: 25–28) notes that "during the crucial first two weeks of the crisis [in August

1991] 76 percent of all references to Bush [on the networks] were favorable."

Yet even more significant in contributing to the American public's information deficit was what *was kept off television*. Far and away the most glaring informational omissions at the beginning of the crisis were the views and testimony of the U.S. ambassador to Iraq, April Glaspie.

According to an Iraqi transcript of a conversation between Glaspie and Saddam Hussein, only a few days before the invasion of Kuwait, Glaspie, in effect, said that the U.S. was indifferent to the Iraq-Kuwait dispute and considered it an intra-Arab matter.

Seven months later, this is denied by Glaspie, who claims that the transcript had been tampered with. But where were the media in that interval to explore this remarkable episode? Glaspie, in fact, was held incommunicado in Washington, under State Department order not to speak with the press.

Yet a diligent and truth-seeking press corps—which had no problems, ethical or otherwise, surrounding former Senator Gary Hart's Washington home to nail him for an interview about a weekend liaison—was suddenly impotent to find a U.S. ambassador in the nation's capital.

When Glaspie finally emerged on March 20 to tell her completely unconvincing story ("Needed the Glaspie File," *New York Times,* March 23, 1991), members of Congress treated her deferentially and asked no embarrassing questions. But Congress's abdication of responsibility for scrutinizing Bush's war policy is another story for another time.

The shocking refusal of the media to report vitally relevant domestic events and perspectives about the crisis and the war extends well beyond the Glaspie affair, important as that was. Ralph Nader noted that the January 26 peace march in Washington "was probably the biggest citizen demonstration ever . . . in winter." CBS gave it a four-second scan.

Nader also pointed out that "a senior member of Congress, Henry Gonzalez, the chairman of the House Banking Committee . . . put in a resolution to impeach Bush on the war; he's virtually shut out [of the news]" (*Columbia Journalism Review,* [March-April 1991]: 27).

Another instance, Jesse Jackson's experience with the media during the crisis, reveals the emptiness, or at least the arbitrariness, of the revered journalistic principle of newsworthiness—to say nothing of the degree of news control that was being exercised at the national level.

Jackson reported: "Since August 2nd, I have talked with Saddam Hussein for six hours, two hours on tape. Longer than any American. I met Tariq Aziz [Iraq's foreign minister] for almost ten hours. I took the first group of journalists into Kuwait, negotiated for the release of hostages.

"And when we got back, there was not one serious interview by a network. A categorical rejection. Now why is there no interest in what we saw, observed, and got on tape?" (*Columbia Journalism Review* [March-April 1991]: 28).

Jackson's legitimate question has not been answered, and it should be noted that his comment was published in a relatively insignificant periodical with a circulation of about thirty-thousand—hardly a competitor for one of the national news magazines which sell in the millions.

The total control of the news at the war front at least was more straightforward. The Pentagon decided what would be reported, and that was that.

A lawsuit was filed by the Center for Constitutional Rights against the Department of Defense, and Richard Cheney, Colin Powell, and George Bush in particular, on behalf of several small nonestablishment media (*Nation, In These Times, Guardian, Harper's, Progressive, Mother Jones, L.A. Weekly, Village Voice, Texas Observer,* and Pacifica Radio News).

In contrast, the networks and national papers' editors and publishers hardly protested their exclusion from independent reporting of the war. The war was over before the lawsuit against the government could be acted upon.

While the bombings and the ground war were under way, television screens for hours on end carried little but Pentagon briefings: Pentagon-released footage and reporters' censored stories, most of which came from the armed forces information sources to begin with.

One reporter, *Newsweek*'s correspondent in the Gulf and a decorated war veteran, complained, "I had more guns pointed at me by Americans or Saudis who were into controlling the press than in all my years of actual combat." And another reportorial comment added, "Desert Storm was really two wars: The Allies against the Iraqis and the military against the press." (Both quotes are from Bob Sipschen, "The Media Rewrite, Review the Gulf War," *Los Angeles Times,* March 7, 1991, p. E2.)

Some could say that the rigid military control of the American media was hardly necessary. With few exceptions, the media did their own self-censorship and did it thoroughly.

This was most observable in the foreign opinion coverage—what there was of it. The foreign voices that supplemented the American generals and think-tank experts were no less carefully selected. John Major, the British prime minister, was the preferred spokesperson on almost all developments that seemed to call for an overseas commentary. Occasionally, François Mitterrand or a supportive German leader was summoned to reassure the American public that the war was truly an international effort.

On a few occasions, the Jordanians and King Hussein, in particular, got some attention. Their opinions were used to demonstrate, beyond doubt, that the Palestinians, who comprise half of the king's subjects, were supporters of the demonized Saddam Hussein. According to this guilt-by-association imagery, the Jordanians deserved the same treatment being meted out to the Iraqis. At the very least, the footage of the king and his constituents served as a further reinforcement for the remarkably unquestioning and sympathetic coverage bestowed on Israel.

Yet the full extent of the cocoon drawn around the American mind can only begin to be appreciated *by what was excluded,* day after day, about international sentiment on the buildup, the bombing, and the ground war in the Gulf. To document this requires a comprehensive review of press and broadcast coverage of scores of countries—clearly a task beyond the reach of a single article. But not beyond the facilities and capabilities of billion dollar media organizations, but markedly beyond their willingness to provide such coverage. All that can be attempted here are a couple of the most egregious omissions that had they been widely publicized might have facilitated a modest amount of public awareness of what kind of an enterprise was unfolding—at least in the minds of a significant number of others.

For example, a paid advertisement in the *New York Times,* on March 18, 1991, weeks after the war's end, by a private group of Japanese citizens made an impassioned statement against the use of military force in international disputes. From the advertisement, it can be learned what one would never have known from earlier media coverage—that the war has been widely opposed in Japan. "When the Japanese Government tried to send our already unconstitutional Self-Defense Forces to the Gulf," the ad stated, public opposition was massive. "Rallies, meetings, and demonstrations were held all over the country." No recognition of this can be found in the American media. Nor can it be said that these manifestations occurred *only* in an unimportant, Third-World country.

Spain was another center of massive popular opposition to its government's contribution, modest as it was, to the coalition fighting in the Gulf. There also, huge rallies and governmental resignations might have been expected to receive some American media attention. They didn't.

Passing references were made to the closing of Egyptian schools and universities to prevent student demonstrations against governmental policy, but these were scarcely sufficient to counterbalance the footage of President Mubarak endorsing U.S. actions. Similarly, five-second flashes of huge rallies held in North African cities against the war were completely inadequate in providing a sense of the massive opposition in that part of the world to American policy.

What was repeated endlessly for domestic consumption was that the United States was engaged in an allied effort, supported by the United Nations, that also embraced the sentiments of a good part of the world.

Unreported also were the views of Latin Americans, Asians, and Africans. The admirers, or at least supporters, of the American intervention and war were the leaders of the usual handful of European and English-speaking industrially developed economies and a clutch of other states who were paid or coerced into joining the coalition.

Most telling of all about the role of the American media has been its utter unconcern with the number of Iraqi casualties suffered from the incessant bombing and, in the waning hours of the war, from the strafing and decimation of thousands of retreating soldiers. Here again, the Pentagon point of view was callous but straightforward. General Colin Powell stated flatly, about the number of Iraqi dead from the air and ground operations, "It's really not a number I'm terribly interested in" (*New York Times,* March 23, 1991, p. A4).

But American journalism might have been expected to hold to another standard, especially since massive killing *is* a news story. Yet it never came out that way. In the one instance when it could not be overlooked because it had been reported live—the bombing of the Baghdad shelter—the networks gave special unlimited opportunities to the Pentagon and other "construction experts" to explain that the shelter was actually a communication center or that Saddam Hussein had deliberately arranged the horror to stage a propaganda coup. But for the most part, references to Iraqi casualties were notable for their absence. There were a few honorable exceptions; one in particular was the *New Yorker* magazine (March 25, 1991). It observed in the midst of the media-promoted victory euphoria that "celebrations that fail to acknowledge the catastrophe those [U.S.] troops are leaving behind are more than unseemly. They trivialize a human tragedy of almost inconceivable proportions" (p. 26).

Yet all this passed practically unremarked in TV accounts throughout the weeks, which announced almost jubilantly the "record" number of daily bombing missions—"sorties" was the preferred word—flown by American pilots.

It must be repeated that the coverage of the crisis and the war by the print press, woefully inadequate as it generally was, cannot be equated with the deplorable reporting by the TV networks and CNN. The national audience which received its understanding of what was happening in the Gulf from television was locked tightly into the government's version of events.

CNN, Cable News Network, deserves a few words of its own. Given near-total acclamation for its round-the-clock, on-site reporting, to a global audience, CNN was made into an instant legend. Is it deserving of this esteem?

Though a relatively large number of international locales and speakers were presented, CNN, with the limited exception of its one correspondent in Baghdad, differed very slightly from the routines and patterns that dominated the three national networks. Exclusion of dissident voices and general omission of material critical to the war policy were not as blatant. The extent and varied scenery of CNN programming gave an impression of comprehensiveness. It was largely an impression.

However, CNN's emergence, overnight as it were, as *the* international source of news was a striking phenomenon. The fact that a single, U.S.-owned TV channel had become the reference point for global information was no trivial development. Earlier global concern about the domination of a few Western news agencies—AP, UPI, Reuters, Agence France Presse—had been contributory to the demand for a new international information order. Yet here was an altogether new dimension of informational monopoly. After the initial euphoria over CNN's admittedly impressive technical achievements, some reflection has occurred in the international community over such excessive dependency on a single source of information. *Business Week* (March 18, 1991, p. 48) reported that the head of Japan's major network "is increasingly concerned about America's domination of global TV news. . . . He joins a growing list of international broadcasters who are attacking the Atlanta-based TV network's virtual monopoly on 24-hour international news coverage."

European public broadcasters, in fact, are organizing a "Euronews" program to relieve their "concern . . . that CNN plays too strong a role in shaping public opinion."

This amounts to a (belated) recognition of the near-total control exercised by the United States over information about the Gulf events. The "solution" being considered by the Japanese and the Europeans will not bring Africans, Asians, and Latin Americans any closer to information pluralism. The new world order in information seems not very different from what the old one was like.

What television, under the watchful direction of the White House, the Pentagon, and its own managers have produced, in the words of the *New Yorker* magazine (March 25, 1991, p. 26) is "a nation . . . suffering an extended scotomic episode," an occlusion of the visual field. "It hardly occurs to us to try to imagine what they [the Iraqis] have been living through, or will have to live through in the coming months."

The president of the United States has a different view. Praising U.S. press coverage of the Gulf events, "George Bush said that the press kept its eyes and ears open during the war" (*Los Angeles Times,* March 25, 1991, p. E1). Apparently, the American people agree. In a recently released poll, a *Los Angeles Times*–sponsored survey "discovered that two institutions enjoyed significant boosts from the war—the military and the television news organizations. Seventy-three percent of Americans felt that television reporters dug harder into the war than their print competitors" (*Los Angeles Times,* March 25, 1991, p. A9).

Such is the triumph of information and image management!

◆

CHAPTER THREE

Roots of War: The Long Road of Intervention

Hamid Mowlana

THE PERSIAN GULF WAR underlines three major developments that have characterized the relationship between the communication media and international relations and that have been in the making since World War I:

1. A trend toward media adherence to norms of the state, particularly the superpowers and the global economic and political order—thus, international media functioning as major proponents and defenders of the status quo.
2. The rise of a neo-Clausewitzian philosophy of war in which mobilization of world public opinion and manipulation of public support have shifted from the national level and those directly involved with the conflict to the global level as total propaganda becomes a prerequisite for the conduct of modern international warfare.
3. The decline of traditional democratic institutions and the merging of two discrete sources of power and influence—the media and government—into one as public communication channels gradually cease to be watchdogs and fail to play their perceived adversarial roles with officialdom.

Media as a Supporter of the Status Quo

The devastation resulting from the Persian Gulf War was described by the U.N. undersecretary general's March 1991 report as a "near-apocalyptic" event and by various U.N. missions as a "catastrophic" occurrence in which a portion of Iraq was turned into "stone-age" land and a "preindustrial" state. The media coverage of the Persian Gulf War was only a chapter in that long history of the illusory concept of "objectivity" whereby the media perceived themselves as somehow operating outside international society, eschewing all responsibilities for what took place within it. International media, whose coverage includes modern electronic imagery sent through radio, video, and television, are not meant to settle interstate disputes; rather, they are organized and utilized to reinforce the international and domestic economic and political networks of their own constituencies. In contemporary global politics this process has meant international media's continual support of the status quo, including cold war systems, new détente between the superpowers, and "old" and "new" world orders. In this meaning, mainstream global communication and media systems, including major news agencies, newspaper networks, and now worldwide television systems, facilitate the flow of information and move more within and among the international elite networks.[1] In terms of domestic constituency, the media's supreme loyalty is to patriotism, the nation-state system, and the national interest. Although the media's sphere of operation and coverage has become global, their worldviews have remained fairly parochial.

The mainstream Western media coverage of the Persian Gulf War illustrates a number of outstanding items that have been in the forefront of international relations discourse but that have been put aside by various forces in the interests of political expediency. This type of coverage has resulted in such attributions as "superficial coverage," "failure to cover," or "knowledge gap" regarding the mass media's overall performance in reporting the Persian Gulf War. But in light of historical trends in international relations during the last several decades, the media did not "fail" in reporting on the Persian Gulf War. In fact, they succeeded in their continual support of the international status quo. The media's reporting of the Persian Gulf War in support of the existing regional system was no different from that of other wars. A number of studies conducted over the last four decades, for example, showed how the U.S. and European mainstream media, especially the elite press and the major media outlets, have consistently supported their country's foreign policy decisions—at least in the initial stages when the defeat of a particular foreign policy was not yet on the horizon—without seriously challenging their basic assumptions.[2]

Until the Iraqi use of chemical warfare and poisonous gas against its own Kurdish population of Halabja in March 1988, in which thousands were killed, the international media, including the mainstream U.S. and European press and broadcasting, presented Saddam Hussein as a benevolent dictator who protected vital Western interests in the Persian Gulf by preventing the spread of the Islamic Revolution from Iran to the rest of the region. According to a U.N. report, Iraq had been using poisonous gas against the Iranian troops and civilians in the border towns since 1984. The Western media's silence during the eight-year imposed war against Iran, in which more than 1 million people were killed on both sides, was replaced by a campaign against Ayatollah Imam Ruhollah Khomeini, Iran's spiritual leader and the Western world's most detested political figure in the modern era. Iranians who were defending their country against Saddam Hussein's onslaught were pictured as brutal, uncaring, fundamentalist Shiite zealots who dispatched the country's youth to die on the Gulf War battlefields. Stated another way, patriotism was associated with secularism, and defense of one's land under Islamic tenets and ideology was termed *fundamentalist* and *fanatical.*

The Islamic Revolution in Iran and its Shiite ulama (religious scholars and leaders), which had reduced the U.S. influence in the region to a minimum, had proved themselves a far more durable institution under pressure than the Pahlavi family that represented the Western interests. Indeed, had it not been for the billions of dollars of financial support given Iraq by the Saudis, the Kuwaitis, and other conservative Persian Gulf states, and the military hardware and economic aid provided by the United States, the Soviet Union, Britain, and France, the Iranians would have been completely capable not only of overthrowing Saddam Hussein but also of marching into the streets of Baghdad. The eight-year Iran-Iraq War, however, became a "forgotten war" in the pages of the Western media until the U.S. decision to reflag Kuwaiti oil tankers in 1987 and to side with Iraq by allowing Iraq to bombard Iranian oil fields and thereby prevent oil shipments from Iran. That decision was the beginning of direct U.S. military involvement in the Persian Gulf, which was supported and publicized by the dominant media.

It must be recalled that it was Iraq, with U.S. acquiescence, that precipitated the first round of the Persian Gulf War in September 1980 by attacking Iran, an act of aggression under the U.N. Charter. And it was Iran that in response engaged in legitimate self-defense under the same charter. Saddam Hussein attacked Iran for three main reasons:

1. Witnessing the powerful campaign waged by the West and the international media against the Islamic Revolution, Hussein thought that if he could destroy the Iranian Revolution, he would have the blessing of the United States and other Western countries as well as of the conservative Arab regimes and that he would emerge as the new pan-Arab leader with considerable support from the United States and the Soviet Union. He succeeded in getting the support of these countries but failed to destroy the Islamic Revolution.

2. Given the record of his secular and brutal regime, which had campaigned against the unrest of the Shiite population in the south and the minority Sunni Kurds in the north, Hussein felt threatened by an Islamic and popular revolution. As he failed in his war objectives, he increased his repression against all forms of opposition to his regime.

3. Hussein had little access to the waters of the Persian Gulf and had various disputes with Iran regarding territories over which, by all international standards, he had no legal claim. Nevertheless, the great powers, the United Nations, and the international media were not ready to honor Iran's simple request—to denounce Saddam Hussein as an aggressor—to end the war. Reinforcement of international norms and laws was put aside simply for international political expediency. Islamic resurgence had become a threat to the interests of the superpowers, and Islamic awakening was perceived by Washington, London, Paris, and Moscow not only as a possible force of mobilization in the Third World but also as a potential political and economic alternative to the prevailing dominant ideologies.

Indeed, Iran had single-handedly pushed the Iraqi army back almost to the international border, despite all the military and financial support given to Saddam Hussein. The Iranian post of Khorramshahr had been liberated, the Faw Peninsula (a strategic and oil-rich area in the head of the Persian Gulf) was captured by the Iranian army and Revolutionary Guard, up to fifty thousand Iraqi soldiers were taken prisoner, and the Iraqi regime seemed on the verge of collapse. The media, which viewed the Iran-Iraq War as a primitive battle comparable to World War I, noted the low morale among Iraqi soldiers and acknowledged the incompetence of the Iraqi air force and army in using modern Western weaponry systems.[3]

The Iran-Iraq War ended in August 1988 with Saddam Hussein in disgrace, but two years later the same Iraqi army was publicized by the great powers and the media as one of the greatest armies in the world, capable of annihilating all its neighbors. This alleged strength justified the half-million-troop multinational presence in the region. No reporter or media personnel in the West was willing to interview Iranian soldiers and generals as to how they had been able to keep the Iraqis in check with so small a military arsenal. No interview and reporting were done with the Iranian population as to how it had resisted the two hundred Iraqi Scud missile attacks on the population centers in Tehran and the Iranian provinces during the so-called city war in 1987–1988.

War as a Total Propaganda

Two major reasons underline the great powers' attempts at and strategic needs for an all-out global propaganda to accompany the Persian Gulf War: (1) the globally integrated nature of communication technologies and the media in the previous two decades and (2) the dependence of international finance and trade on modern infrastructures of communication and media technologies. In this sense, the Persian Gulf War marked a new era in "communication dominance" and a shift from a partial to a total propaganda.

The transnationalization of telecommunications technologies, which has taken place at an accelerated pace over the last two decades, has integrated the international political and economic environment to such a degree that for any major power to successfully wage a war, it must have access to and control over global communication networks. Personal computers, satellites, facsimile, telegraphy, telephony, television, and video conferencing are all telecommunications innovations of the modern period that have made possible the advent of CNN and other global networks with far-reaching potentials that, if unrecognized and unused by the state and those supporting a war, could foster chaos by eroding the legitimacy of the multinational force.

The integrated nature of global communication technologies with international financial and banking infrastructures now necessitates nation-state rationales for the conduct of war to be extended beyond conventional national considerations to new international levels of accountability. Because of this interdependence, the conduct of war can no longer be a unilateral national decision or a self-contained isolated event. The Persian Gulf War affected not only Iraq and Kuwait but also the major corporations, nations, and laborers dependent on sources of income from oil, tourism, and other forms of trade from the Gulf region. These international constituencies had to be propagandized and persuaded that the reasons for war were serious enough to merit international support of a war effort and the sharing of costs to the integrated global system it imposed. The transnational distribution of information and communication technologies extended the costs of war beyond the military and human dimension into the global financial infrastructure.

The inseparable nature of global economic and global communication networking was illustrated by the testimony of Alan Greenspan, chair of the U.S. Federal Reserve, before a congressional committee. Greenspan learned of the start of the Persian Gulf War on the night of January 16, when, while looking at his computer screen, he saw the impact of the conflict on the U.S. economy. According to Greenspan, "You could see the effects minute by minute—in the exchange markets, in the interest rate markets, in the gold markets—all arbitraged across and around the world."[4] Greenspan was not the only witness to this integrated system of communication and finance. At another location, personnel in the AT&T Network Operations Center were watching the war on an electronic map of worldwide networks. As Robert E. Allen, chair and chief executive officer of AT&T stated, "They saw the circuits to Baghdad go dead at 7:30 P.M. New York time. Then they saw the map light up with record calling volumes to Saudi Arabia." Additionally, within five minutes of the news reports of the first Iraqi Scud missiles launched against Israel, Allen reported "we had 60,000 calling attempts over the 800 circuits we have to Israel."[5]

In the Persian Gulf War, the propaganda and communication strategy surrounding the conduct of war entered a new dimension not seen in previous conflicts. While the United States and its allies were ready to mobilize and control communications media to their advantage, producing press conferences, bulletins, in-field interviews, and home audience and citizenry participation in support of their war efforts, their further strategy called for a new total destruction of Iraq's civilian communications and power infrastructure. Of equally high priority on the allied target list were Iraq's telecommunications sector, telephone, and other utilities. AT&T's telecommunications building in Baghdad was one of the first targets of the multinational force's warplanes, as was one of Iraq's multibillion-dollar state-of-the-art telecommunications facilities, the losses of which damaged the civilian economy. In short, unlike previous conflicts, conventional confrontation in the battlefield did not come until after the propaganda and communication strategy had succeeded both domestically and internationally.

The Decline of Democratic Institutions

It can be said that war is, not the extension of dispute, but the refusal to dispute. When a particular world order, worldview, or ideological system is preserved as an ideal system without being beneficial for humankind in general, it becomes fossilized as the status quo and resists change and innovation. The Persian Gulf War was no exception. At the center of the conflict were two old and dominant orders: on the international level, a dominant capitalist economic and social system, led by the United States and a number of industrial countries, trying to preserve its own global interests under the pretense of a new world order; on the national level, a number of authoritarian rigid state systems, including the Iraqi Baath regime and the Kuwaiti and Saudi royal families, attempting to preserve their own dominance over populations subjected to brutality and a nonparticipatory way of life. These systems of dominance would not have been possible in modern times without dominant global media systems supporting and preserving the global political and economic order.

Even though the mainstream media not only reflect but also have functional relationships to international conflict, their role in conflict management is, at best, a tenuous one. The media are thus unwilling and unwitting participants in the social process as opposed to enlightened managers of or neutral third parties to it. Moreover, their participatory role varies with the circumstances in which they find themselves. This process is exacerbated by the media's refusal to view events structurally and historically. Given the consistency with which the media cover major international events, one then can speak, not so much of the "failure," but rather of the "success" of the media. The dominant international media in the Persian Gulf War succeeded in exactly what they were supposed to do; but this failure implied different roles and expectations that were functions of democratic systems and were not inherent in the nature of the media themselves.

Price Prophecy and the War

There were three major and broad reasons underlining the Persian Gulf War that were ignored by the dominant media and thus little noticed by the public. These were (1) the sales price of oil, (2) the capital flow from the Persian Gulf region, and (3) the transition of power in the region as well as the world and the U.S. drive for a new world order.

Standing aboard a ship at Sharjah in the Persian Gulf in 1903 with the Arab chiefs then in treaty with Britain, Viceroy Lord George Curzon of Britain declared that "the British Government must remain supreme in the [Persian] Gulf and any challenge would be resisted by all means."[6] Earlier in 1899 Curzon had described British interest in the Persian Gulf as "commercial, political, strategical, and telegraphic."[7] Communication networks, then in the form of telegraphic technology, were essential to the British Empire and its hegemony in the region in order to protect its crown jewel, India. With the discovery of oil in the Persian Gulf in the first decade of the twentieth century, a vital link was added to the strategic and navigation aspects of the region. In 1919, Lord Curzon, then in charge of the British Foreign Office, stated that the Allies had floated to victory on a sea of oil as World War I had brought petroleum into the world limelight for the first time as a strategic resource of great importance. British policy was reflected in Lord Curzon's long-cherished dream of a chain of vassal states stretching from the Mediterranean to the Far East. Curzon's imperialism and his worldview, Sir Harold Nicolson wrote, were "founded not so much on mystic determinism as upon a more precise, if less defensible, belief that God had specifically selected [British] upper classes as an instrument of the Divine Will."[8]

The British hegemony in the Persian Gulf was challenged in 1951 when Iran nationalized its oil industry, then in the hands of British Petroleum, and began a religio-political movement in the region that was followed by Egypt's nationalization of the Suez Canal under Gamal Abdel Nasser in 1956. The British sent a naval force to the Persian Gulf, threatened to land troops at Abadan oil refineries, and took its case to the U.N. Security Council. Unable to win the argument against Iran, London convinced Washington that Iran's popular government headed by Muhammad Mossadegh should be removed. In August 1953, a CIA-inspired and -supported coup removed Mossadegh and brought back the shah, who had fled the country when the earlier first coup attempt to topple the nationalist government had failed.

The Western media that had been hostile to Iran and negative in their treatment during the Mossadegh administration suddenly changed their perception about that country in a favorable manner. Iran joined the Central Treaty Organization (formerly the Baghdad Pact) and became what the U.S. secretary of state, John Foster Dulles, called "the keystone of the Northern Tier" defense line across the roof of the Muslim Middle East. Interestingly, two of the main U.S. actors in the 1953 CIA coup were Kermit Roosevelt, grandson of President Theodore Roosevelt, and General H. Norman Schwarzkopf, the father of the U.S. commander of the multi-national force mounted against Saddam Hussein in 1990.[9] Roosevelt, a veteran of the CIA, had for some time headed the Middle East Department of the agency. Schwarzkopf, known in the United States as the man who investigated the Lindberg kidnapping episode in 1932, was a colonel commanding the Iranian Imperial Gendarmerie, or state police, and became a troubleshooter in the Middle East for a number of U.S. administrations.

If production and distribution of oil and access to world markets dominated the politics of the Persian Gulf in the early part of this century, it was the price tag of oil exported from the fields of the Persian Gulf that determined international political and military maneuvering in the 1970s and 1980s. Increases in world oil prices meant higher revenues for oil-producing countries in the Middle East and a corresponding increase in the price of manufactured goods and in the level of inflation for the United States and the rest of the industrial West, which were accustomed to getting inexpensive oil in comparison with other raw materials in the world market. Political and military access to the Persian Gulf states, especially to such countries as Saudi Arabia and Kuwait that were able to increase their production and thus offset oil price increases, was vital for the West.

With prices of oil fluctuating from $17 or $18 to $30 a barrel between August 1990, when Iraq invaded Kuwait, and April 1991, when the war was over, one can appreciate the traditional role of Saudi Arabia and Kuwait, both U.S. allies and friends, as the swing producers whose small populations but high level of oil production could guarantee some price stability and low price levels for the West. For years, Iran and Algeria had tried to get the production of oil lowered in the Organization of Petroleum Exporting Countries (OPEC) and the price thereby increased. These demands had gone unheeded by Saudi Arabia and other Persian Gulf states and were rendered moot by the so-called oil glut that became apparent in the 1980s. President Bush made clear in August 1990 that the "new world order" he envisioned would be impossible without a secure supply of oil: "Our jobs, our way of life, our own freedom and freedom of countries around the world would all suffer if the control of the world's great oil reserves fall into the hands of Saddam Hussein."[10]

Indeed, Saddam Hussein, on the eve of invading Kuwait, was transforming his action into a debate over the distribution of wealth in the region. In 1988–1989, Iraq, with $80 billion in debts as a result of its war with Iran, watched the price of oil slide, while Kuwait and Saudi Arabia boosted output virtually at will. In February 1990, Kuwait announced its intention to exceed its quota as long as prices remained above $18 a barrel. During the summer of 1990 just before invading Kuwait, Iraq grabbed the leadership of OPEC by forcing Kuwait to cut its production in half, to one million barrels a day, and Saudi Arabia to 5.5 million a day, far below its capacity. Kuwait's promise in July 1990 to help the price of oil spurt to $22 did not satisfy Saddam Hussein, thereby forcing him to push his army into Kuwait. At the end of the war, Saudi Arabia emerged as the undisputed master of OPEC. In September 1991, the price of oil stood around $19 a barrel, with the group producing 23 million barrels a day and the Saudis raising their own production level to 8.6 million barrels of that daily total. According to Vahan Zanoyan, senior director of the Petroleum Finance Company of Washington and an OPEC affairs expert, by raising the level of production and keeping the price of oil at a low level, "the Saudis tried to erase the memory of the OPEC meeting of July, 1990, which was one in which they lost control and were no longer in charge."[11] So it was the change in oil price to $30 a barrel that brought multinational forces, led by the United States, to the Kuwaiti theater.

Controlling the Surplus Capital

One of the major reasons for waging war in the Persian Gulf, which was ignored by the general media and was not mentioned publicly by European and U.S. leaders, was the importance of the Persian Gulf states, especially Saudi Arabia and Kuwait, as major sources of global capital flow. Simply stated, the West not only needs the continuation of free flow of oil at a low price from the Persian Gulf; it also looks to this region as the major source of surplus capital for its military and financially troubled economic sectors. Since the early 1970s, the United States and Europe as well as other smaller nations have profited substantially from the Arab investment cache abroad as well as from expensive high-tech military orders and the luxurious lifestyle associated with the sheikhs and princes of the Persian Gulf region. For example, Kuwait now earns more from its overseas investment than it does from its oil exports. The flight of capital alone from such countries as Kuwait and Saudi Arabia often exceeds their gross domestic product. Government agencies from Saudi Arabia, Kuwait, and the United Arab Emirates have huge investments worth hundreds of billions of dollars. In addition, private investors from these three states alone have holdings in the United States amounting to $150 billion. The government-fund agencies of Saudi Arabia, such as the Saudi Central Bank; the Kuwait Investment Authority; and the governments of Qatar, Oman, and Bahrain all hold an estimated $200 billion in investments abroad.[12]

Testing a New World Order

Conceptualization of world, regional, and national problems is the basis for political, economic, and military mobilization. Thus, control over information flow and communications must accompany access to material and natural resources. It is only under a powerful communication and information system that one can determine the parameters of international security debates.

Until recently, the emphasis of the great powers and the media was on the centrality of the North in the international system, with the South usually being treated under the rubric of Third World development and regional conflict. Beginning with the Helsinki Agreement of 1975, a definite sense of territorial status quo was established and accepted by the superpowers, with the South as their major arena of conflict. The tone of the media in regard to the East-West relationship shifted then from conflict to cooperation. With *glasnost, perestroika,* and the eventual downfall of the regimes in Eastern Europe, a new political and economic equation was created. International conflict now moved southward.

Whereas East-West relationships are stable in that they are predictable, North-South relations are potentially volatile and remain unpredictable. Thus, one of the major reasons for the United States to lead the multinational forces into the Persian Gulf theater was precisely to have the leading role in determining the political and security arrangements in this region by protecting its old Arab allies and Israel. This meant testing the new world order concept echoed by President Bush, especially in light of the USSR's declining influence in the region and the possibility of Iran or any other state emerging as a leader of the security matter in the Persian Gulf and the Middle East as a whole.

Communication and Geopolitics of the Persian Gulf

A crucial, yet unexplored, area in the study of the Persian Gulf is the geopolitical and strategic aspects of communication and information flow in the region. Modern telecommunications, especially space-age technology, have changed traditional notions and strategies of international conflict and cooperation. It is now possible that these technologies, if desired, could form the core of an alternative security system. Historically, extensive transportation, navigation, and communication services have been the indispensable nerve system of the strategic aspects of the Persian Gulf. In recent times, with the development of modern communication/information worldwide, the region has acquired an even more vital role. In the past, the volume of commodity productions, such as oil and other minerals, was the index of the area's trade and military importance. Today, capital and information systems have been added to this list and have become the socioeconomic, military, and political infrastructures of the Persian Gulf states. This development is particularly accelerated by the growing desires of external powers to exert influence and intervene in the region's geopolitics in order to protect their worldwide interests.

Prior to the outbreak of the war, information and communication in the Persian Gulf could be observed in three distinct areas: (1) the expansion of military and security alliances accompanied by the growing hardware and software of communication technologies, (2) the expansion of international trade and services in connection with banking and international finance competing for existing and potential markets, and (3) the efforts of national governments to implement domestic developmental projects and to expand their internal infrastructure for national and regional integration.[13] These areas, which were not mutually exclusive, have characterized the region's development since World War II and especially since the early 1970s.

The geography of the Persian Gulf did not change much over the century, but the ecological dimensions of the area in the struggle for military, security, economic, and ideological dominance were altered by technological shifts in the human ability to build, destroy, transport, and communicate. The geopolitics of information ecology wrapped in modern communication technology became a crucial and decisive element in the area's international relations, thereby elevating this region to one of the most sophisticated centers of telecommunication in world politics. In the arena of economic, military, political, and cultural power, information assumed its place beside petroleum, natural gas, and strategic metals as an international resource to be bartered, boycotted, and blackmailed. Megabyte streams of digitalized data became the perceived source of power in the Persian Gulf, with far-reaching effects on economic, social, and political development. In short, the geopolitics of information was now a new dimension in the strategic balance of power in the area. As information and communications systems were perceived as alternative security shields in the Persian Gulf, more than $47 billion of telecommunications and data-gathering equipment were shipped and installed in such countries as Saudi Arabia, Kuwait, and Bahrain.

Information Technologies and International Finance

For hundreds of years the Persian Gulf has been plagued by pirates, navigators, colonial powers, and (now) nation-states that have used this important waterway to the Indian Ocean to transport, communicate, and link their financial interests and transactions. From the fifteenth century to the present, external powers such as Portugal, Holland, Britain, and the United States have established communication facilities across the Persian Gulf. The quest for valuable minerals, local alliances, trade markets, and military facilities has been carried out through the establishment of navigation facilities, telecommunications networks, and information posts.

The 1860s marked a significant change in the nature of regional communication because of the telegraphic systems established by the British to protect their colonial interests in India and the Gulf's coastal lines. The introduction of the telegraph and the construction of modern communication and navigation lines enabled economic and military news of international and regional interests to reach London and other parts of the empire. As a result, the Persian Gulf area became a significant center for international information flow.

Because of its geographical position linking the British interest in Asia to Europe and Africa, the Persian Gulf countries were among the first recipients of telegraphic lines in the world. Sir Percy Sykes gave a vivid account of the development of telegraphic communications between England and India, of which the Persian Gulf region formed a part.[14] Indeed, by the end of 1864, exactly twenty years after the invention of telegraph by Samuel F.B. Morse, the first telegraph line was constructed in some of the Gulf countries, including Iran.

The interconnection among finance, colonialism, communication, and the expansion of international news agencies is well illustrated by the adventures of a British banker, Baron Julius de Reuter, who founded the British news agency Reuters in 1851. Reuter's scheme involved organizing several companies to work the vast enterprise and obtaining an extensive concession from Nasser-u-Din, the shah of Iran, in 1872. Detailed in more than twenty articles, the concession gave Reuter the right to construct railways and street car lines, to export minerals and oil for a period of seventy years, and to manage the customs services for twenty-four years. Reuter earlier had laid down a special cable from Cork to Brookhaven, Ireland, that enabled him to circulate news of the U.S. Civil War several hours before steamers could reach Liverpool, England. Reuter's news agency was then one of the three international news agency operations (Havas of France and Wolff of Germany) that had formed a monopoly cartel for the distribution of news and information around the world. Reuter extended his vast empire to France and the United States in 1865 when the king of Hanover granted him a concession for a cable beneath the North Sea to Cux Haven and when he received a concession for a cable between France and the United States. The latter line was jointly worked out by Reuter and the Anglo-American Telegraph Company.

Today, the geopolitics of communication has made the Persian Gulf region the fifth largest and most complex center of telecommunications and digital networks in the world after the United States, the former Soviet Union, Western Europe, and the Pacific Basin (which includes Japan). What made Kuwait of high interest to the United States and the West was not its geographical position in the area but the amount of capital it exported to the United States and other industrialized countries in the West. In the 1980s, Kuwait set up two investment funds worth $40 billion each. Prior to the Persian Gulf War, Kuwait's investment in the United States and Western Europe was estimated to be $100 billion, $80 billion of which was in government holding and the remaining invested by the Kuwaiti rich and upper class. Half of Kuwait's investment portfolio was with U.S. corporations, including virtually every company on the Fortune 500 list.

With the Saudis high investment in economic, military, and strategic sectors and their close relationship with the United States in military and intelligence matters (Saudi Arabia is the sixth most important overseas market for the United States and one of the few in which the balance of trade is in favor of the United States), Saudi Arabia, Kuwait, and Bahrain alone have established enough dependencies with the West to make the information and communication infrastructure of this region, at least technologically, vulnerable to the existing policies of external powers as well as potential developments in the future. That the Persian Gulf countries have more communication networks with some power centers of the world than among themselves not only prevents them from concentrating their resources for regional economic, social, political, and cultural integration but also creates a condition of vassalage.

Communication, Integration, and National Development

The efforts of the Persian Gulf countries to implement domestic developmental projects for the purpose of national integration, political unity, and social and cultural cohesion was another major factor in the rise of communication and information as crucial elements in the region's geopolitics and strategic map. This could be seen in the development of mass communication facilities and conventional telecommunication infrastructures (such as postal service, telephone, telegraph, radio, television, and scores of other cultural industries) in relation to educational, cultural, social, and political sectors.[15]

Among the technological changes that have been sweeping through the Persian Gulf since the end of World War II, the development of communications has been the most fundamental and pervasive of all in its effects on the region's diverse societies. The early arrival of modern mass media in the Persian Gulf region was an "import" from the West, an aspect of the impact of the West upon the Middle East. Importation of mass media usually occurred on two levels: via communication technology—through the introduction of the printing press, telegraph, telephone, radio, and television; and via media content—through various forms of nationalism, ideology, news, and entertainment material. Each level stimulated growth of the other, and although communication content at times came to reflect indigenous cultures, the influence of Western technology and ideology remained unabated.

Since the demise of Western-style development in Iran and the Islamic Revolution of 1978–1979, the mass media in the region have developed a new awareness of the outside world and at the same time a great degree of Islamic self-consciousness. If the substance and strategy of the revolution in Iran were new, so, too, was the realization that in Islamic societies of the Persian Gulf such as Iran, control of modern communication media does not guarantee political control. Modern media must achieve the power and penetration of traditional channels of communication if they are to be useful as social, political, and economic tools. The distribution of receivers also increased, especially in Bahrain, Kuwait, Saudi Arabia, and Iran, even though radio ownership figures are still below the minimum defined by the United Nations Educational, Scientific, and Cultural Organization (UNESCO) (one hundred radios per one thousand inhabitants). The statistics, however, do not indicate the true extent of exposure to radio, given that group listening in homes, schools, and coffeehouses is very popular in the region.

Being on the crossroads between Europe and Asia, the Persian Gulf region receives a significant amount of international broadcasting. Stations in Europe, India, Pakistan, and the former Soviet Union can be clearly heard. The Voice of America and the British Broadcasting Corporation are among the many international sources that for years have beamed programs in Arabic, Persian, and other languages to the region. Political developments in the Persian Gulf have had considerable influence on interstate broadcasting in the area.

With the exception of Iran, most states in the region import from 40 percent to 60 percent of their television programs—most of which consist of entertainment—from the United States and Europe. There has been a good deal of criticism of these programs in the media on the grounds that they not only convey values foreign to the region's cultures but also create an alien world of commercialism and consumerism. Nevertheless, more imaginative cultural programs and documentaries, coupled with greater discrimination among audiences, have been on the increase in several countries of the region.

The indiscriminate importation of foreign and Western values through media products since World War II has had a dysfunctional and negative impact on the region's population because such imported values have undermined traditional national and religious values without providing new sources of community cohesion. As many Middle Easterners see it, such "cultural imperialism" or the "Westoxification" of the lifestyle and socialization of urban and younger peoples has set the stage for inevitable confrontation of the old ruling elites and the new generation, which clearly manifested itself in the Islamic Revolution in Iran and the continuing protests against the cultural domination of the West elsewhere in the region.

In sum, since the mid-1970s four important developments have had the most profound impact on the region's media and communication:

1. The Islamic Revolution in Iran, setting the tone for Islamization of the region's media and creating a new ecology of communication by integrating the modern mass media with the already enhanced and well-developed traditional channels of communication and organization.

2. The war and conflict in Lebanon and the Iran-Iraq War, resulting in media crises, factional politics, ideological warfare, and regional disunity.
3. Expansion of national and international telecommunications through satellites and the effect of this on economic, political, media, and military institutions.
4. The Persian Gulf War with all its political, economic, and cultural consequences.

Political and Cultural Consequences of the War

The consequences of the Persian Gulf War are culturally and politically profound. First, from the perspective of Middle Easterners, the U.S.-led intervention in the Persian Gulf was yet another chapter in the continual battling of great powers for hegemony over the Middle East in general and the Persian Gulf in particular. In this sense, U.S. actions represent a new stage of imperial power, which began with the Portuguese in the seventeenth century and was continued later by other European powers, principally Dutch, French, German, and British.

It is notable that such unusually small, underpopulated countries as Bahrain, Kuwait, Qatar, and the United Arab Emirates can be recognized internationally as states, while a population of some 20 million Kurds cannot even gain cultural autonomy. These states exist as historical anomalies that contradict the tenets of a "rational modern world." In the face of efforts for Arab unity and at least two strong and determined neighbors, Iran and Iraq, these small sheikhdoms have always stood, as one observer referred to them, as "gazelles" in a world of colonial lions.[16] The dependence of these sheikhdoms on external powers, such as Europe and the United States, has been great.

Without doubt the increasing Western military and economic clout appearing in the Persian Gulf will coincide with the West's increasing influence over the future of the region. This influential position can be compared to the 1820 British naval expedition against the Pirate Coast. In this maritime venture, the many tribal confederations, mercantile outposts, and tiny villages of the region were forced to consolidate, eventually evolving into the anomalies of today. Pirates, whether European or local, invaded the Persian Gulf for several hundred years. But with the decline of the Iranian Safavid dynasty in the eighteenth century, the Arabs gained primary control of the Gulf under the tribal dynasty of the Qawasim. This powerful entity, based at Ras al Khaimah next to the Straits of Hormuz, expanded its reign beyond the islands on the opposite side of the straits to the Iranian coast.

The Qawasim confronted only one immediate setback—the alliance of a small desert chieftain, Muhammad Saud, and the Wahhabi, a tribe of the interior desert that sought to reform and overpower most of the Arabian Peninsula. Later, after Portuguese and Dutch attempts to penetrate the land of the Qawasim, the British pushed the tribe to the borders of Bombay in hopes of securing a trade route between the Gulf and India. During Britain's conquest in the 1800s, it formed a Pax Britannica in the Persian Gulf with various sultanates and sheikhdoms. In particular, the British engaged the sultan of Oman, the most historically established of the Persian Gulf polities, in an agreement that would withstand French designs or any other foreign entry.

Meanwhile, at the other end of the Gulf, Kuwait stood as an independent sheikhdom. Kuwait maintained its autonomy because of its strong mercantile relations with the East India Company, despite the efforts of Wahhabi tribesmen to dismantle it. No more than a single, part-time political officer in London was needed to handle treaty relations with the Trucial Coast in the 1930s. Although such minimal supervision did not protect the political entities created by the British from encroachments or conflicts, it did protect them from losing their borders. In this way, the British maintained influence over the region and got involved in Arab affairs.

By World War I, the British had concluded "exclusive agreements" with all the Arab sheikhdoms ensuring that they would neither cede nor lease any of their territory without British approval, that Britain would conduct all their foreign affairs, and that Britain would in turn protect them from outside threat. Thus, the British gained a foothold in the region for both commercial and strategic reasons. After World War I and the demise of the Ottoman Empire, the acceleration of economic, political, and social change fostered even more British intervention in the Middle East.

Given the forceful combination of religion and the military strength of Saud Abdul Aziz (now Saudi Arabia), the Wahhabis finally achieved victory over a large expanse of the Arabian Peninsula, including the interior desert, Qatar, and four-fifths of Abu Dhabi. Only the British-protected coastal settlements remained untouched. Even after Kuwait became an independent state in 1961, the British intervened to thwart the probability of an Iraqi attack. A decade later, Britain completely withdrew from the Gulf. Concurrently, Bahrain, Qatar, and the newly established United Arab Emirates gained independence. This withdrawal caused some local fearful rulers, such as newly oil-rich Sheikh Zeid of Abu Dhabi, to request continued military support. This was the beginning of U.S. intervention in the affairs of these sheikhdoms.

Second, the Persian Gulf War and intervention of U.S. and European powers in support of conservative and unrepresentative regimes eroded the state legitimacy in such countries as Kuwait, Saudi Arabia, and Iraq without any basic reform and thus helped destabilize these countries for years to come. It must be recalled that President Bush, fearful of the Shiite rebellions against Saddam Hussein and the potential rise of an Islamic form of government in that country, never supported the Kurdish or Islamic uprisings in the aftermath of the war or, for that matter, any democratic election in Iraq. "The war wasn't fought about democracy in Kuwait," President Bush bluntly retorted.[17] Yet the United States ranks number one in weapon sales to the Third World and the Middle East, including Saudi Arabia.

Third, the Persian Gulf War provided for new forces to be unleashed. The protest against the royal family in Saudi Arabia, Kuwait, and other sheikhdoms; petitions submitted to the ruling elites in these countries to uphold democratic and Islamic principles of consultation and participation; and similar demands in Algeria, Egypt, Morocco, and Tunisia were only the beginning of wide protests that, if unanswered, will destabilize the political and security systems in the region. The war sharpened the cultural and historical divisions between state and community in a number of Islamic countries. A divisive force in Islamic countries of the Middle East arose out of the ascendancy of rulers who valued their state political authority more than their religious duties. The changing nature of the state during several centuries combined with the support given by imperial and colonial powers to the ruling elites resulted in the alienation and separation of the community from the state. This evolution of a political system from an Islamic state representing the *ummah*, or larger Islamic community, to a modern nation-state was a major source of crisis of legitimacy in the Middle East. Power became divided between the rulers who represented the political nation-state and its bureaucracy and the *ullama* who represented the community. From the perspective of loyalty, for many Muslims in the Middle East there existed only the community and its leaders; the state as such had no place. In short, the Gulf War crystallized the confrontation between rulers and community leaders, and it is the sharpening of the separation of the *ummah* and the state toward which the community is now gravitating.

Fourth and finally, the Persian Gulf War and recent transitions in world politics, including the replacement of East-West confrontation with cooperation, not only have sharpened the economic and political division between the North and South but have also widened the cultural gap between the predominantly Western-Christian and the overwhelmingly Islamic lands. The "new" North, with all its linguistic and historical diversities, now extends like a beltway from the Ural Mountains in the former Soviet Union to the Atlantic coast in Western Europe and the United States and to the Pacific shores in the West.

While the Persian Gulf War was a catalyst for the new Western integration processes reinforcing the ongoing cooperation and integration of the former Soviet Union and Eastern Europe into a trans-European and U.S. sphere of economic and political activities, it was equally an instrument of division and disintegration within the region in general and the Arab world in particular. Is the Group of Seven replacing the composition of the United Nations? How multipolar or unipolar is the world? Where do the Islamic world in general and the Persian Gulf states and the Middle East in particular fit into this new cultural and political ecology? What are the implications of these developments for the peoples and nations of the Middle East? Most nation-states in the Middle East arose as a result of the decline of great empires, such as the Ottoman and the British, following World War I and World War II, but the post–cold war world and the Persian Gulf War have been the story not so much of the building of nations as of the unmaking of the nation-state system.

The Persian Gulf War in a sense was a cultural testing ground between the West and the Islamic East, as has been going on for centuries. This time, however, the technological and social ecology was different. It should also be recalled that the Islamic community in general was a major world power in its own right until the demise of the Ottoman Empire in the second decade of this century. An accounting of the cultural impact of the Persian Gulf War has yet to be written. Today, as the majority of the people of the Middle East turn their vision inward, they perhaps remember what the Prophet Muhammad, on returning from battle, told his followers: "You have come back from the lesser to the great struggle." They asked, "What is the great struggle, O Messenger of God?" And he replied, "The struggle within."

Notes

1. Hamid Mowlana, *Global Information and World Communication: New Frontiers in International Relations* (White Plains, N.Y.: Longman, 1986), pp. 188–190.

2. For example, see Walter Lippmann and Charles Merz, "A Test of the News," *New Republic,* August 4, 1920, pp. 3–15; Walter Lippmann and Charles Merz, "More News from the Times," *New Republic,* August 11, 1920, pp. 1–3; Susan Welsh, "The American Press and Indochina, 1950–56," in Richard L. Merritt, ed., *Communication and International Politics* (Urbana: University of Illinois Press, 1972), pp. 207–231; Hamid Mowlana, "The Role of the Media in the U.S.-Iranian Conflict," in Andrew Arno and Wimal Dissamayake, eds., *The News Media in*

National and International Conflict, (Boulder, Colo.: Westview Press, 1984), pp. 71–99; Hamid Mowlana, "World's Best Informed Public?" *SAIS Review* 6 (Winter-Spring 1986): 177–188; Edward W. Said, *Covering Islam: How the Media and the Experts Determine How We See the Rest of the World* (New York: Pantheon Books, 1981); Abbas Malek, "New York Times' Editorial Position and the U.S. Foreign Policy: The Case of Iran," *Gazette* 42 (1988): 105–119; Abbas Malek, "Chemical Warfare in the Persian Gulf War: U.S. Response," *Iranian Journal of International Affairs* 1 (Winter 1989–1990): 441–450; Margaret A. Blanchard, *Exporting the First Amendment: The Press-Government Crusade, 1945–1952* (White Plains, N.Y.: Longman, 1986); William C. Adams, ed., *Television Coverage of International Affairs* (Norwood, N.J.: Ablex Publishing, 1982); William Adams, ed., *Television Coverage of the Middle East* (Norwood, N.J.: Ablex Publishing, 1981); Satish K. Arora and Harold Lasswell, *Political Communication: The Public Language of Political Elites in India and the United States* (New York: Holt, Rinehart and Winston, 1969); Edward S. Herman and Noam Chomsky, *The Political Economy of the Mass Media* (New York: Pantheon Books, 1988); William Preston, Jr., Edward S. Herman, and Herbert I. Schiller, *Hope and Folly: The United States and UNESCO, 1945–1985* (Minneapolis: University of Minnesota Press, 1989); George Gerbner, Hamid Mowlana, and Kaarle Nordenstreng, eds., *The Global Media Debate: Its Rise, Fall, and Renewal,* (Norwood, N.J.: Ablex Publishing, 1991).

3. George Wilson, "Iraqi Pilot in Attack Viewed as Incompetent," *Washington Post,* May 25, 1987, p. A14.

4. Quoted by Robert E. Allen in a speech delivered at the Communications Week Conference, Washington, D.C./Paris, March 7, 1991, p. 3

5. Ibid.

6. Ishtiaq Ahmad, *Anglo-Iranian Relations, 1905–1919* (New York: Asia Publishing House, 1974), p. 49.

7. Ibid., p. 43.

8. Quoted in Clarmont Skrine, *World War in Iran* (London: Constable, 1962), p. 56.

9. Kermit Roosevelt, *Counter Coup: The Struggle for Control of Iran* (New York: McGraw-Hill, 1979), pp. 147–149; Richard W. Cottom, *Nationalism in Iran,* rev. ed. (Pittsburgh: University of Pittsburgh Press, 1979), p. 228; James Bill, *The Eagle and the Lion: The Tragedy of American-Iranian Relations* (New Haven, Conn.: Yale University Press, 1988), p. 90; David Wise and Thomas B. Ross, *The Invisible Government* (New York: Bantam Books, 1964), p. 117; R. K. Ramazani, *The United States and Iran: The Pattern of Influence* (New York: Praeger, 1982), p. 8.

10. Quoted in Maggie Mahar, "Crude Prophesy," *Barron's* (February 1991): 10.

11. "Oil Output Raised by OPEC in Saudi Move to Hold Price," *New York Times,* September 26, 1991, p. D3.

12. Youssef M. Ibrahim, "Arab Investment Overseas: A Vast Empire," *New York Times,* April 30, 1991, p. D12; "Saudi Oil Minister's Family in Mobil Deal," *New York Times,* June 6, 1991, p. D1.

13. The discussion here is based on Hamid Mowlana, "Geopolitics of Communication and the Strategic Aspect of the Persian Gulf," *Iranian Journal of International Affairs* 2 (Spring 1990): 85–106.

14. See Percy Sykes, *A History of Persia,* vol. 2, (London: Macmillan, 1930), pp. 367–369. For general work on maritime geopolitics and the role of technology in nineteenth-century imperialism, see Alfred Thayer Mahan, *The Influence of Sea Power Upon History 1660–1783* (Boston: Little, Brown, 1890); Bernard Brodie, *Sea Power in the Machine Age* (Princeton, N.J.: Princeton University Press, 1941); and Daniel K. Headrick, *The Tools of Empire: Technology and European Imperialism in the Nineteenth Century* (New York: Oxford University Press, 1981).

15. For a more comprehensive account of the development of telecommunications and mass media in the region, see Hamid Mowlana, "Mass Media Systems and Communication," in Michael Adams, ed., *The Middle East* (New York: Fact on File Publications, 1988), pp. 825–839.

16. David Hirst, "Gazelles Among the Lions," *Guardian,* August 22, 1987, p. 17.

17. Thomas L. Friedman, "A Rising Sense That Iraq's Hussein Must Go," *New York Times,* July 7, 1991, p. E1.

◆

CHAPTER FOUR

The Media and the War:
What War?

Noam Chomsky

AS I UNDERSTAND THE CONCEPT "WAR," it involves two sides in combat, say, shooting at each other. That did not happen in the Gulf.

The crisis began with the Iraqi invasion of Kuwait in 1990. There was some fighting, leaving hundreds killed according to human rights groups. That hardly qualifies as a war. Rather, in terms of crimes against peace and against humanity, it falls roughly into the category of the Turkish invasion of northern Cyprus, the Israeli invasion of Lebanon in 1978, and the U.S. invasion of Panama. In these terms it falls well short of the 1982 Israeli invasion of Lebanon and cannot remotely be compared with such huge atrocities as the near-genocidal Indonesian invasion and annexation of East Timor, to mention only two cases of aggression that benefited from decisive U.S. support and are still in progress.

During the subsequent months, Iraq was responsible for terrible crimes in Kuwait, with several thousand killed and many tortured. But that is not war; rather, it is state terrorism of the kind familiar among U.S. clients.

The second phase of the conflict began with the U.S.-U.K. attack of January 15, 1991 (with the marginal participation of others). This was slaughter, not war. Tactics were carefully designed to ensure that there would be virtually no combat.

The first component was an aerial attack on the civilian infrastructure, targeting power, sewage, and water systems; that is, a form of biological warfare designed to ensure long-term suffering and death among civilians

This chapter is an excerpt of "The Media and the War: What Have We Learned?" Panel, Qualitative Studies Division of the Association for Education in Journalism and Mass Communication Conference, Boston, Massachusetts, August 8, 1991.

so that the United States would be in a good position to attain its political goals for the region. Because the casualties were victims of the United States, we will never have any real idea of the scale of these atrocities, any more than we have any serious idea of the civilian toll in the U.S. wars in Indochina. This component of the attack does not qualify as war: rather, it is state terrorism on a colossal scale.

The second component of the U.S.-U.K. attack was the slaughter of Iraqi soldiers in the desert, largely unwilling Shiite and Kurdish conscripts, it appears, hiding in holes in the sand or fleeing for their lives— a picture quite remote from the Pentagon disinformation relayed by the press about colossal fortifications, artillery powerful beyond our imagining, vast stocks of chemical and biological weapons at the ready, and so on. Pentagon and other sources give estimates in the range of one hundred thousand defenseless victims killed, about half during the air attack, half during the air-ground attack that followed. Again, this exercise does not qualify as war; rather, it is a "turkey shoot," as some U.S. forces described it, adopting the term used by U.S. troops slaughtering Filipinos at the turn of the century—one of those deeply rooted themes of the culture that surfaces as if by reflex at appropriate moments.

The goal of the attack on the civilian society has been made reasonably clear. In plain words, it was to hold the civilian population hostage to achieve a political end: to induce some military officer to overthrow Saddam Hussein and wield the "iron fist" as Hussein himself had done with U.S. support before he stepped out of line; any clone of the "beast of Baghdad" will do as long as he shows proper obedience, unlike Hussein, who violated this principle—the only one that counts, as events once again demonstrate—in August 1991. The reasoning was outlined with admirable clarity by the State Department spokesperson at the *New York Times,* chief diplomatic correspondent Thomas Friedman. If the society suffered sufficient pain, Friedman explained, Iraqi generals might topple Hussein, "and then Washington would have the best of all worlds: an iron-fisted Iraqi junta without Saddam Hussein." Thus, the technique of punishing Iraqi civilians might succeed in restoring the happy days when Saddam's "iron fist . . . held Iraq together, much to the satisfaction of the American allies Turkey and Saudi Arabia," not to speak of the boss in Washington, who had no problem with the means employed *(New York Times,* July 7, 1991).

The operation of holding a civilian population hostage while tens of thousands die from starvation and disease raises only one problem: Unreasonable, soft-hearted folk may feel some discomfort at having "sat by and watched a country starve for political reasons" (Richard Reid, *Toronto Globe & Mail,* June 17, 1991). The *Wall Street Journal* observed that Iraq's "clumsy attempt to hide nuclear-bomb-making equipment from the U.N. may be a blessing in disguise, U.S. officials say. It assures that the allies [read: United States and United Kingdom] can keep economic sanctions in place to squeeze Saddam Hussein without mounting calls to end the penalties for humanitarian reasons" *(Wall Street Journal,* July 5, 1991).

In keeping with its fabled dedication to international law and morality, the United States is naturally demanding that compensation to the victims of Iraq's crimes must have higher priority than any purchase of food that might be allowed—under U.N. control, of course. A country that commits the crime of disobeying Washington has plainly lost any claim to sovereignty. For example, proclaiming this stern doctrine with suitable majesty, Washington kept the pressure on Nicaragua to abandon its claims, as mandated by the International Court of Justice, to reparations for a decade of U.S. terror and illegal economic warfare. Nicaragua finally succumbed, a capitulation scarcely noticed by the media, mesmerized as they were by Washington's lofty rhetoric about Iraq's responsibilities to compensate its victims.

Nor could the media be troubled to report that in March 1991, Washington momentarily interrupted the orations about the sanctity of international law to contest, once again, World Court jurisdiction over U.S. crimes: in this case, Iran's request that the court order reparations for the downing of an Iranian civilian airliner in July 1988 by the U.S. warship *Vincennes,* part of the naval squadron sent by Ronald Reagan and George Bush to support Saddam Hussein's aggression. The airbus was shot down in a commercial corridor off the coast of Iran with 290 people killed— out of "a need to prove the viability of Aegis," a high-tech missile system, in the judgment of U.S. Navy commander David Carlson, who "wondered aloud in disbelief" as he monitored the events from his nearby vessel (*U.S. Naval Institute Proceedings* [September 1989]). Bush further sharpened our understanding of the sacred rule of law in April 1990 when he conferred the Legion of Merit award on the commander of the *Vincennes* (along with the officer in charge of anti-air warfare) for "exceptionally meritorious conduct in the performance of outstanding service" in the Gulf and for the "calm and professional atmosphere" under his command during the period when the airliner was shot down. "The tragedy isn't mentioned in the texts of the citations," AP reported (April 23, 1990). The media kept a dutiful silence—at home, that is. In the less disciplined Third World, the facts were reported in reviews of U.S. terrorism and "U.S. imperial policy" generally *(Third World Resurgence* [Malaysia] [Oct. 1990]).

The third phase of the conflict began immediately after the cease-fire, as Iraqi elite units, which had been largely spared by the U.S. attack, proceeded to slaughter first the Shiites of the south and then the Kurds of the north with the tacit support of the commander-in-chief, who had called on Iraqis to rebel when that suited U.S. purposes. Reporting from northern Iraq, ABC correspondent Charles Glass described how "Republican Guards, supported by regular army brigades, mercilessly shelled Kurdish-held areas with Katyusha multiple rocket launchers, helicopter gunships and heavy artillery," while journalists observing the slaughter listened to General Norman Schwarzkopf boasting to his radio audience that "we had destroyed the Republican Guard as a militarily effective force" and had eliminated the military use of helicopters (*Spectator* [London], April 13, 1991). This is not quite the stuff of which heroes are fashioned, so the story was finessed at home, though it could not be totally ignored, particularly the attack on the Kurds. The Shiites, who appear to have suffered even worse atrocities right under the gaze of Stormin' Norman, raised fewer problems, being mere Arabs. Again, this slaughter hardly qualifies as war.

The Greenpeace International Military Research Group estimates total Kuwaiti casualties at 2,000–5,000 and Iraqi civilian casualties at 5,000–15,000 during the air attack, an unknown number during the ground attack, 20,000–40,000 during the civil conflict, perhaps another 50,000 civilian deaths from April through July, and another 125,000 deaths among Shiite and Kurdish refugees.

In brief, from August 1990 through July 1991 there was little that could qualify as "war." Rather, there was a brutal Iraqi takeover of Kuwait followed by various forms of slaughter and state terrorism, the scale corresponding roughly to the means of violence in the hands of the perpetrators and to their impunity. The distinction should be observed. I will use the term *war,* but reluctantly, for the reasons indicated.

The Silence of the Media

Let us turn now to the media and the war. When the guns are firing, even if in only one direction, the media close ranks and become a cheering section for the home team. Overwhelmingly, that is what happened in the Gulf conflict.

It is more revealing to study the first and third phases of the conflict: August 1990 to mid-January 1991 and March 1991 to August 1991. In these periods, the obligation of strict obedience to state violence and power was less stringent. The coverage during these two periods of relatively greater openness had several noteworthy features. One striking feature was the treatment of the Iraqi democratic opposition, which had long struggled courageously against Saddam Hussein—in exile because no dissident could survive under the regime of George Bush's good friend.

Iraqi democrats had always opposed U.S. policy. The democratic opposition opposed Washington's pre-August 1990 policy of lavish support and aid for Saddam Hussein and his satisfying iron fist. They opposed the U.S. drive for war, evident to anyone with eyes open from late August 1990 onward. And they opposed the tacit U.S. support for Saddam Hussein and his elite military forces as they crushed the popular uprisings. Accordingly, Iraqi democrats were always given short shrift in Washington. In February 1990, efforts to gain U.S. endorsement of a call for parliamentary democracy in Iraq were rebuffed (the same was true in London). Washington continued to bar any contact with Iraqi democrats, Kurdish nationalists, and other opposition figures after breaking with Saddam Hussein in August, and that policy remained in force after the cease-fire. In mid-March, the Bush administration announced that it would continue to refuse any contact with Iraqi democratic leaders: "We felt that political meetings with them . . . would not be appropriate for our policy at this time," State Department spokesperson Richard Boucher stated on March 14 (*Mideast Mirror* [London], March 15, 1991). In the *New York Times,* Alan Cowell reported from Syria that Iraqi exiles there said that "there ha[d] been no reply" to their request for a meeting with James Baker and that the embassy's doors remain[ed] closed to them," as in Washington, London, and elsewhere (*New York Times,* April 11, 1991).

On this crucial matter, the media upheld the party line virtually without deviation. Readers of the British and German press, or the marginal alternative media here, could learn, for example, that as the January 15 deadline approached, the Iraqi Democratic Group reiterated its call for the overthrow of Saddam Hussein but also opposed "any foreign intervention in the Near East," criticizing U.S. "policies of aggression" in the Third World and its intention to control Middle East oil and rejecting U.N. resolutions "that had as their goal the starvation of our people." The groups statement called for the withdrawal of U.S.-U.K. troops, withdrawal of Iraqi troops from Kuwait, self-determination for the Kuwaiti people, "a peaceful settlement of the Kuwait problem, democracy for Iraq, and autonomy for Iraq-Kurdistan." A similar stand was taken by the Tehran-based Supreme Assembly of the Islamic Revolution in Iraq (in a communiqué from Beirut); the Iraqi Communist Party; Mas'ud Barzani, the leader of the Kurdistan Democratic Party; and other prominent opponents of the Iraqi regime, many of whom had suffered bitterly from Hussein's atrocities. Opposition leaders called for reliance on sanctions and diplomacy. "All the opposition parties [were] agreed in calling for an immediate withdrawal of Iraqi forces from Kuwait," British journalist Edward Mortimer reported, "but most [were] very unhappy about the military onslaught by the US-led coalition" and preferred economic and political sanctions. They also condemned the murderous bombing

(Gruppe Irakischer Demokraten, "For a Peaceful Settlement," *Frank-furter Rundschau,* January 14, 1991; *Manchester Guardian Weekly,* February 3, 1991; *Financial Times,* January 21, 1991).

The silence in the United States was deafening and instructive. Throughout, Iraqi democrats were in essential agreement with the mainstream of the U.S. peace movement and indeed with most of the world. But all these sectors were opposed to the stance of the U.S. government and were therefore not fit subjects for the media, which had quite different responsibilities.

Peace or Violence

A second striking feature of media coverage in the period from August 1990 to the January 15 onset of hostilities had to do with what was, uncontroversially, the basic question: Shall the allied nations pursue peaceful means in accord with international and domestic law, or shall they resort to violence? The former path was strongly supported by most of the world, including Iraqi democrats. It was also supported by the U.S. population up to the last moment. The possibility of a negotiated diplomatic settlement, however, was rejected at once by Washington. From the outset, the president made it clear and explicit that negotiations were excluded. The options were reduced to total Iraqi capitulation to U.S. demands or war. The media approached unanimity in their unquestioned support for this stand. When the president thundered that there would be no negotiations, a hundred editorials and news columns lauded him for "going the last mile for peace" in "extraordinary efforts at diplomacy."

There was debate over the secondary issue of continued reliance on sanctions. That was an acceptable topic. Who could know, after all, whether sanctions would ultimately succeed? On matters of speculation and guesswork, one could be sure that authority would prevail, so the issue would be safely joined. But it was next to unimaginable that a deeply conformist intellectual culture might address the serious and important questions: Should the United States seek a peaceful diplomatic settlement? Had sanctions *already* worked?

Had discussion of the central topics been tolerated, it would have become apparent that, quite possibly, the sanctions had indeed already worked, perhaps by mid-August. At least, that seems a reasonable explanation for the series of Iraqi proposals confirmed or released by U.S. officials. The apparent effectiveness of the sanctions was not very surprising. They broke new ground in two crucial respects. First, they were of unprecedented severity; even in the case of far more grave crimes than these, there had been no sanctions of a comparable sort. Second, these sanctions were observed by the usual sanctions-busters (the United States, the United Kingdom, and France). In both respects, the sanctions were quite unlike those imposed on South Africa, for example, though a qualification is necessary: The United States does scrupulously observe the embargoes and sanctions it regularly imposes in its illegal economic warfare against criminals that disobey Washington orders. Again, none of these topics could possibly enter into mainstream discussion, though— or, more accurately, because—they were crucial for understanding what was taking place.

Were the Iraqi proposals serious? Was there a realistic possibility for a negotiated settlement? We cannot be sure, of course; diplomatic options can be tested only by pursuing them. But one conclusion stands out clearly: Washington feared that the possibilities were realistic and there-fore moved rapidly to undercut them, unwilling to face the risk of a peaceful settlement. The media went along in subordination to power.

On August 9, the United States received a back-channel offer from Iraq to withdraw from Kuwait in return for settlement of some border issues. It appears that there were two issues: Iraqi access to the Gulf, which would have meant some form of control (perhaps lease) of two uninha-bited mudflats assigned by Britain to Kuwait in the imperial settlement to keep Iraq landlocked; and Iraqi control over the Rumalah oil field, 95 percent within Iraq, extending about two miles into Kuwait over an unsettled border. The proposal was considered by the National Security Council on August 10 and rejected as "already moving against policy," according to the retired army officer who arranged the meeting. Former CIA Director Richard Helms attempted to carry the initiative further, but with no success. Further efforts by high Iraqi officials and U.S. interlo-cutors elicited no response. "There was nothing in this [peace initiative] that interested the U.S. government," according to Helms. A congressional summary, with an input from intelligence, concluded that a diplomatic solution might have been possible at that time.

These facts were revealed by investigative reporter Robert Parry in the *Nation* (April 15, 1991). There is good reason to believe that they were known to the press at once. On August 22, *New York Times* diplomatic correspondent Thomas Friedman had outlined the administration posi-tion on diplomacy: The "diplomatic track" must be blocked, he wrote, or negotiations might "defuse the crisis" at the cost of "a few token gains" for Iraq, perhaps "a Kuwaiti island or minor border adjustments." A week later, Knut Royce revealed in *Newsday* that a proposal in just those terms had been offered by Iraq but had been dismissed by the administration (and suppressed by the *New York Times,* as it quietly conceded). The proposal, regarded as "serious" and "negotiable" by a State Department Mideast expert, called for Iraqi withdrawal from Kuwait in the terms just outlined. The prominent report in *Newsday* compelled the *New York Times* and a few other papers to make a few marginal and dismissive comments, but the story quickly disappeared from the record and was scarcely known to the public.

The last-known prewar Iraqi offer was released by U.S. officials on January 2 and was again reported by Knut Royce in *Newsday* (January 2, 1991). In this offer, all border issues were dropped, to be settled by later negotiations. (Those obsessed with mere fact may recall that U.N. Resolution 660, the first and basic resolution after Iraq's aggression, demanded that Iraq withdraw from Kuwait and that Kuwait and Iraq simultaneously negotiate their border dispute. The second demand, inconsistent with Washington's goals, disappeared at once from history.) The Iraqi withdrawal proposal called for "agreement on the Palestinian problem and on the banning of all weapons of mass destruction in the region," Royce reported. U.S. officials described the offer as "interesting" because it mentioned no border issues, taking it to "signal Iraqi interest in a negotiated settlement." A State Department Mideast expert described it as a "serious prenegotiation position." Washington "immediately dismissed the proposal," Royce continued. The story received virtually no attention elsewhere and no mention at all in the *New York Times,* though a *Times* report of an interview with Yasser Arafat the next day indicated that a mere statement by the National Security Council of an intention to deal with the "linked" issues might have sufficed for complete Iraqi withdrawal from Kuwait. Again, the United States was taking no chances; it quashed the threat of peace at once, while the media played the appropriate supportive role.

The significance of the media suppression of the diplomatic option was made dramatically clear by polls taken just at that time. On January 11, the *Washington Post* published a national poll revealing that two-thirds of the population favored a conference on the Arab-Israeli conflict if that would lead to Iraqi withdrawal from Kuwait. The question was framed to minimize a positive response, stressing that the Bush administration opposed the idea. It is likely that those who nevertheless gave a positive response believed that they were virtually alone in that stance. Few, if any, would have found any advocacy of their position in the media or the political system. And it is safe to assume that none of the respondents knew that a week earlier Iraq had made such a proposal, which was regarded as serious and negotiable by U.S. government Mideast specialists, was supported by the Iraqi democratic opposition, and was flatly rejected by Washington. Had the media permitted the crucial facts to be known to the public, and had they been willing to tolerate discussion of the basic issues, the percentage favoring a peaceful settlement would have been far higher, probably overwhelming. In short, had minimal standards of journalism been observed, it is doubtful that the administration would have been able to pursue its unwavering commitment to undermining the pursuit of peaceful means and establishing the preferred rule of force.

The issue could hardly be more clear or more significant. A decision to go to war is always a grave matter, particularly so with the means of violence and destruction now available, and even more so when those means are largely monopolized by the side that has historically been committed to extreme measures of violence and that faces no deterrent. We understand very well how the decision is supposed to be made in a democratic society. The chief executive is to present his case for going to war. The media are to make the relevant facts publicly available and provide a forum for debate and discussion of the basic issues. The population then expresses its agreement or dissent, directly or indirectly through its elected representatives.

None of this happened. The president offered no reason for going to war—no reason, that is, that could not be demolished in a moment by a literate teenager. President Bush did indeed give one argument, repeated in a litany by his acolytes from August onward. The argument was summarized in the words of his response to the rejected Iraqi offer of January 2: "There can be no reward for aggression. Nor will there be any negotiation. Principle cannot be compromised."

It is highly instructive that instead of collapsing in ridicule, the media, and the educated classes generally, treated these pronouncements with sober approval and mock seriousness, at least in the United States and United Kingdom. Again, one would have to go to the alternative press or the Third World to find the reaction of any civilized and rational person. True, principles cannot be compromised. But given that the United States has historically been a major perpetrator and supporter of aggression, notably during the period when George Bush was part of the decisionmaking apparatus, opposition to aggression is no principle held by Washington. Hence, the argument offered against negotiations had precisely zero force.

A further pertinent observation was also beyond the pale: No one argues that the proper response to aggression is the quick resort to violence; no one has proposed the bombing of Jakarta, Damascus, Ankara, Tel Aviv, Cape Town, or Washington, to pick a few recent examples of aggression that match or in several cases vastly exceed Hussein's crimes in his invasion of Kuwait. The rhetoric is particularly absurd when it is produced by the sole head of state to stand condemned by the World Court for the "unlawful use of force," the man who inaugurated the post–cold war era by invading Panama, and the man who lent his support to the murderous Israeli assault on Lebanon in 1982 and to Israel's continuing rejection of U.N. Security Council Resolution 425 (March *1978*) calling for its immediate withdrawal from Lebanon. This is the official who took over the CIA just in time to take part in the U.S.-backed Indonesian invasion of East Timor and then lent his talents to Ronald Reagan's war against the church and other deviants in Central America, leaving another several hundred thousand corpses. This is the man who pursued "quiet diplomacy" and "constructive engagement" with South Africa as it held Namibia for twenty years after its occupation was condemned by the World Court and the U.N. Security Council, while some 1.5 million people in neighboring countries were killed during the Reagan-Bush years alone in the course of South African aggression and terror. Again, such truisms are foreign to the U.S. media, which solemnly reported the president's words, admiring his uncompromising stand against international violence and "the stark and vivid definition of principle . . . baked into him during his years at Andover and Yale, that honor and duty compels you to punch the bully in the face" (*New York Times,* March 2, 1991)—after you have been assured that he is securely bound and beaten to a pulp. The fraud could hardly be more disgraceful.

The conclusion is clear and stark: No reason was given for going to war, and the media suppressed this fact with virtual unanimity, just as they successfully barred politically incorrect fact and opinion on every crucial issue. This is the very hallmark of a totalitarian culture, a phenomenon that is particularly remarkable in a society that is, perhaps, the most free in the world. We do ourselves no favors by failing to acknowledge these facts.

The U.N. Coverage

Media treatment of the United Nations was no less remarkable. Commentators marveled at the amazing change at the United Nations, which was acting as it was originally intended to do for virtually the first time in history and thus offering a bold peacekeeping response for the post–Cold War world. The standard explanation was that with the U.S. victory in the cold war, Soviet obstructionism and the "shrill, anti-Western rhetoric" of the Third World no longer rendered the United Nations ineffective. Again, these welcome thoughts were proclaimed in hundreds of news reports, editorials, journal articles, and so on.

There is a very simple test of the truth of these grand propositions. We simply ask, "Who has been blocking the peacekeeping function of the United Nations, say, in the twenty years since George Bush achieved national prominence as U.N. ambassador?" The answer to the question is, again, politically incorrect and therefore inexpressible in respectable journalism: The United States is far in the lead throughout this period in vetoing Security Council resolutions and voting against General Assembly resolutions (often alone or with one or two client states) on aggression, observance of international law, terrorism, human rights violations, disarmament, and so on. Britain is second. Between them, the two righteous warriors of the Gulf account for about 80 percent of Security Council vetoes since 1970. France is a distant third, and the former USSR is fourth. One will have to turn to the alternative media to discover even an inkling of these crucial facts, which reveal that the wondrous sea change at the United Nations merely reflected the fact that for once the United States and its British lieutenant happened to oppose an act of aggression because it was not in the perceived interest of dominant domestic forces.

Also suppressed in the newfound acclaim for the United Nations was that the United States and its British ally had again succeeded in subverting it, as they have so often done before. Under extreme U.S. pressures, the Security Council was compelled to wash its hands of the Gulf crisis, radically violating the U.N. Charter by leaving individual states free to respond to Iraq's aggression as they chose. The charter explicitly precludes the resort to force before the Security Council determines that peaceful means have failed. No such determination was made because they clearly had not failed, in fact had scarcely even been tried. And the charter further assigns responsibility for any exercise of force to the council, not to George Bush. Further U.S. pressures prevented the council from responding to the call of member states for meetings, as stipulated by council rules that the United States had vigorously upheld when they served its interests. That Washington has little use for diplomatic means or institutions of world order, unless they can be used as instruments of its own power, has been dramatically illustrated in Southeast Asia, the Middle East, Central America, and elsewhere. About all these matters, one will learn next to nothing from news reports or commentary in the media or in the mainstream journals of opinion. Without pursuing the matter any further, we reach a conclusion of no small significance to those who care about democratic values and intellectual integrity: The media, along with the educated classes generally, contributed mightily to driving the country toward a war that was, predictably, an utter catastrophe.

And so it was recognized to be by Iraqi democrats. Well after the hostilities ended, the *Wall Street Journal,* to its credit, broke ranks and offered a little space to London-based banker Ahmad Chalabi, one of the leaders of the Iraqi democratic opposition. He described the outcome of the the war as "the worst of all possible worlds" for the Iraqi people, whose tragedy was "awesome" (*Wall Street Journal,* April 8, 1991). From the perspective of Iraqi democrats, remote from that of Washington and New York, restoration of the iron fist would not be "the best of all worlds."

The media did, in fact, face a certain problem as the Bush administration lent its support to Hussein's crushing of the internal opposition. The task was the usual one: to portray Washington's stance, no matter how atrocious, in a favorable light. That was not easy, particularly after months of praise for George Bush's magnificent show of august principle and supreme courage in facing down the reincarnation of Attila the Hun, who was poised to take over the world. But the transition was quick, smooth, and successful. True, few can approach the U.S. devotion to highest principles, but U.S. moral purity is tempered with an understanding of the need for "pragmatism" and "stability," useful concepts that translate as "doing what we chose."

In a typical example of the genre, *New York Times* Middle East correspondent Alan Cowell attributed the failure of the rebels to the fact that "very few people outside Iraq wanted them to win." Note that the concept "people" was used here in the standard Orwellian sense, meaning "people who counted." Many featherless bipeds wanted them to win, but "serious people" did not. The "allied campaign against President Hussein brought the United States and its Arab coalition partners to a strikingly unanimous view," Cowell continued. "Whatever the sins of the Iraqi leader, he offered the West and the region a better hope for his country's stability than did those who have suffered his repression" (*New York Times,* April 11, 1991).

Cowell's version was the standard one, and, as was also standard, it passed without analysis of his rendition of the facts. To begin with, who were these "Arab coalition partners"? Answer: Six were family dictatorships established by the Anglo-U.S. imperial settlement to serve as what Lord George Curzon called an "Arab facade" to manage Gulf oil riches in the interests of the United States and its British client. The seventh was Syria's Hafiz al-Assad, a minority-based tyrant and murderer indistinguishable from Saddam Hussein. The last of the coalition partners, Egypt, was the only one that could be called "a country."

Pursuing minimal journalistic standards, then, we turn to the semi-official press in Egypt to verify Cowell's report, datelined Damascus, April 10, 1991, of the "strikingly unanimous view." The day before, Deputy Editor Salaheddin Hafez of Egypt's leading daily, *Al-Ahram,* commented on Saddam Hussein's demolition of the rebels "under the umbrella of the Western alliance's forces." U.S. support for Hussein proved what Egypt had been saying all along, Hafez wrote. U.S. rhetoric about "the savage beast, Saddam Hussein," was merely a cover for the true goals: to cut Iraq down to size and establish U.S. hegemony in the region. The West turned out to be in total agreement with the beast on the need to "block any progress and abort all hopes, however dim, for freedom or equality and for progress towards democracy," working in "collusion with Saddam himself" if necessary (*Al-Ahram,* April 9, 1991). Speaking abroad at the same time, Ahmad Chalabi made essentially the same point, attributing U.S. support for Saddam Hussein's repression to its traditional policy of "supporting dictatorships to maintain stability" (*Mideast Mirror,* April 10, 1991).

It is true that there was some regional support for the U.S. stance apart from that of the friendly club of Arab tyrants. Turkish President Turgut Ozal doubtless nodded his head in agreement. He had in fact made use of the opportunity offered by the Gulf War to step up his brutal attacks on his own Kurdish population, confident that the U.S. media would judiciously refrain from reporting the bombings of Kurdish villages and the hundreds of thousands of refugees in flight trying to survive the cold winter in the mountains without aid or provisions.

The U.S. stance also received support in Israel, where many commentators (including leading doves) agreed with retiring Chief of Staff Dan Shomron that it was preferable for Saddam Hussein to remain in power in Iraq (Ron Ben-Yishai, interview with Shomron, *Ha'aretz,* March 29, 1991; Shalom Yerushalmi, "We Are All with Saddam," *Kol Ha'ir,* April 4, 1991). Suppression of the Kurds was a welcome development, one influential commentator explained, because of "the latent ambition of Iran and Syria to exploit the Kurds and create a territorial, military, contiguity between Teheran and Damascus—a contiguity which embodies danger for Israel" (Moshe Zak, senior editor of *Ma'ariv, Jerusalem Post,* April 4, 1991). But all this was unhelpful and was therefore suppressed.

A final task was to portray the outcome as a grand victory, not "the worst of all possible worlds." The task was eased by the effective suppression of the apparent opportunities for a peaceful negotiated settlement beginning in mid-August. But even with that journalistic achievement, it was no simple matter to chant the praises of our leader as we surveyed the scene of two countries devastated, hundreds of thousands of corpses, an ecological catastrophe, and the "beast of Baghdad" firmly in power thanks to the tacit support of the Bush-Baker-Schwarzkopf team.

Even this onerous task was accomplished. In its editorial on the anniversary of the August invasion, *New York Times* editors dismissed the qualms of "the doubters," concluding that Bush had acted wisely. He "avoided the quagmire and preserved his two triumphs: the extraordinary cooperation among coalition members and the revived self-confidence of Americans," who "greeted the Feb. 28 cease-fire with relief and pride—relief at miraculously few U.S. casualties and pride in the brilliant performance of the allied forces" (*New York Times,* August 2, 1991). Surely these triumphs far outweighed the "awesome tragedies" in the region.

PART TWO

◆

Many Nations, One Image

◆

CHAPTER FIVE

The New World *Odour:*
The Indian Experience

P. Sainath

THE DECORATIVE ANNOUNCEMENT in the lobby of the five star hotel was inviting. It read, "Live coverage of Gulf War via satellite at Bolan Bar." CNN had arrived in India.

The Hotel Park Sheraton, Adyar, Madras City, was not alone. The Chola Sheraton, another elite hotel in the same city, exhorted people to "watch latest video on Gulf War on Channel 2 of your CCTV." But the Park Sheraton had been quicker off the mark in marketing the war as a customer service.

The day the war broke out, the hotel had a television set in its lobby. Noticing the crowds swarming around the set, the management quickly disconnected it and shifted it to the bar. People could still watch Baghdad burn, but they had to buy a drink while doing it.

In the capital city of New Delhi, five-star hotels receiving CNN organized special viewing sessions for journalists, who then wrote about the marvels of technology, particularly those evidenced by CNN. The idea caught on. "Gulf War Live! Our TVRO system brings the Gulf War into your living room in colour on TV," began an advertisement in the *Indian Express* daily newspaper during the first week of the war.

One or two publications even hired rooms in these expensive elite hotels so as to get a "constant update" on the war via CNN. In Bombay, the commercial heart of India, several rich individuals also hired rooms in the Oberoi Hotel, inviting their friends to join them in "viewing sessions" that caught the war "live." This notion of live coverage held sway despite virtually every frame of the footage carrying a "cleared by military censor" note. Ironically, the very hotels that experienced a spurt in occupancy for these reasons during the first days of the war were adversely affected in the next few weeks as the war smashed Indian tourism (several Western nations, including the United States, advised their citizens to stay away), bringing occupancy in some five-star hotels down to 25 percent in a season when it should normally have been three times that figure, if not more.

Regional Effects of the War

It was a very real war for the people of this subcontinent—one that threw up a tremendous challenge for the region's media. Hundreds of thousands of jobs were lost. More than 1 million families suffered a devastating loss of income. India, a poor country, was compelled to organize the biggest and most expensive civilian airlift in history to get tens of thousands of its stranded citizens out of the Iraq-Jordan border area.

Sri Lanka, dependent on tea export for its foreign exchange, found its economy in a shambles when sanctions saw an end to its Iraqi market— that country being one of its largest customers. Bangladesh was rocked by a wave of strikes (including a nationwide general strike) protesting the deployment of some five thousand Bangla troops on the coalition side in the Gulf and the loss of thousands of Bangladeshi jobs in that region. These developments, in fact, further stirred up the already building sentiment against General Hussain Mohammed Ershad, the U.S.-backed dictator then ruling Bangladesh.

In Pakistan (eleven thousand troops on the side of the anti-Iraq coalition in the Gulf), hundreds of thousands of people marched in the streets demanding a recall of the troops and denouncing the war. So severe was the antiwar sentiment that even the Pakistani chief of army staff, General Mirza Aslam Beg, criticized the massive bombardment of Baghdad, terming it "another Karbala" (*Times of India,* January 31, 1991, p. 10). The government did not dare to discipline the army chief, who went on to publicly state that "peace alternatives had not been fully explored" when the bombing began. These were particularly significant remarks given that few military establishments across the world have benefited from U.S. aid to the extent that the Pakistani military has.

In India, in just the southern state of Kerala alone (a small state by Indian standards but with almost twice the population of Australia), money orders from the Gulf bringing precious foreign exchange used to account for 25 percent of "internal production." Gulf money also led to a boom in construction and therefore to tens of thousands of jobs. Remittances from the Gulf enabled Keralites to spend much more on health, food, and education. All this was shattered by the Gulf crisis and war.

Even more striking, the Indian union (i.e., central) government experienced its first major crisis, which played some part in its final downfall shortly after. At the time, the Janata Dal(S) party had a minority government headed by Prime Minister Chandra Shekhar that was totally dependent on the outside support of the Congress Party. The Chandra Shekhar government was caught refueling Gulf-bound U.S. warplanes on the sly (*Times of India,* January 28, 1991). So great was public anger over this act, which undermined India's nonaligned credentials, that the government found itself totally isolated on the issue. It also marked the first occasion when the Congress Party, on whose sufferance Chandra Shekhar's minority regime ruled the country, lashed out at the government, with Rajiv Gandhi condemning the refueling in strong terms. Soon, the cleavage deepened over other issues, and the government fell.

In August 1991, Subramaniam Swamy, a member of parliament known for his pro-U.S. views (more importantly, he was union minister for law and commerce in the administration that undertook the refueling) explained that the refueling was done because it "facilitated the one billion dollars loan that India had received from the International Monetary Fund earlier this year" (*Indian Express,* August 16, 1991).

It was thus a very real war for the countries of this subcontinent. In itself, the war was clearly a major disaster and dilemma. But there was another problem for journalists here: They were not allowed to cover it.

Effects on Indian Media

No Indian journalist (or journalist from any neighboring country) was encouraged to even apply for Saudi visas. Those journalists already in the Gulf region found themselves stuck under heavy censorship. Some in Baghdad were served quit orders. Two Indian journalists on board an Indian ship taking food and medicines to Indians in Iraq were taken off the ship (despite having been cleared by the External Affairs Ministry) at Khor Fakkan in the United Arab Emirates, and sent home. It remains unclear on whose order or under whose pressure they were removed. Incidentally, the ship on which they were sailing was also boarded by U.S. Navy personnel from a U.S. warship checking to see if India was breaking sanctions. During this same period, the United States and the United Kingdom were paying hundreds of thousands of dollars to Saddam Hussein to hire his Boeing aircraft to ferry Western hostages out of Baghdad—but that was not seen as a violation of sanctions! The irony, however, escaped the Indian media. Not a single editorial made this point.

Throughout the crisis and war in the Gulf, the Indian media, particularly the press, were trapped by a series of dilemmas from which they did not emerge with credit. Some sections of the media did try, and some tried much more than others; but objective reasons, structural factors, geopolitical realities, and subjective failures contributed to a performance that overall was very poor. Although the media did not fully go along with the pro-Western elite that marveled at CNN, it could do little to present a more sober view of the war once it began.

The day the war broke, the *Times of India,* the country's most powerful daily newspaper, carried a two-column editorial, spanning the full height of the front page, that denounced the war. Titled "Pax Americana," the editorial, while making no excuses for Saddam Hussein, criticized the United States for pushing the world to a needless war that could have been averted had Washington been serious about a peaceful settlement.

Several other newspapers, including the *Hindustan Times,* the *Economic Times,* and the *Independent,* agreed with this. Their editorials made that clear—which led to the first dilemma. The news pages of the very issues carrying these antiwar editorials were suffused with prowar news reports that came exclusively from Western news agencies/syndicated services. This pattern had already been evident in the months preceding the war. Once the conflict began in military terms, the divergence between editorial page and news page was sometimes dramatic.

The dominance of the major Western agencies (AP, Reuters, UPI, and Agence France Presse) is very real in the press of the subcontinent, not just in India. AP and Reuters alone account for one out of every three column centimeters of foreign news published in major Indian newspapers. Magazines such as *Time* and *Newsweek* enjoy a high circulation in India, and the *Economist* and the *International Herald Tribune* are widely quoted (several articles from which are reproduced every day).

In addition to direct flows from the agencies, and reproduction from Western magazines and journals, there was (and remains) the problem of plagiarism and emulation of these news sources and their views in the developing world press. Thus, it is difficult to quantify how extensively the Western viewpoint was put across in the Indian media during this period.

So a situation arose and persisted in which antiwar editorials were drowned in a torrent of prowar news reports! This was so much the case that when some journalists analyzed the output of the Indian media during this period, they found themselves analyzing the Western media.

The second dilemma was the problem of "shared values"—several Indian editors, despite their opposition to the specific conflict in the Gulf, had spent a lifetime looking at the world through Western eyes. As a result, they had difficulty tackling what even they acknowledged was a problem. (One reflection of this "borrowed brains" syndrome was apparent in editors talking about problems in the "Middle East"—for those in India the area ought to be called "West Asia".)

State-controlled television actually did slightly better than the print media. It introduced an element of debate, brought out the point that there were Arab perspectives beyond those of Riyadh, and even raised important questions about the implications of the war for the Third World and the nonaligned movement.

Admittedly, everybody's task was difficult. Indian reporters were stuck in places such as Nicosia, Amman, and Dubai trying to cover the war from there. Indian publications circulating in the Gulf states were subject to censorship. Pieces raising questions about Palestinian rights were routinely snipped out by censors in the Gulf states such as Dubai, and some Indian publications (from November 1990 onward) were restricted by the Gulf authorities, their entry not being permitted.

The journalist for the *Times of India* based in Nicosia, G. H. Jansen, actually did a fine job under the circumstances, but his reports, though far more analytical than those emanating from Western sources, were lost in the sea of the latter's verbiage. The *Times of India*'s Washington correspondent, however, exemplified the borrowed brains syndrome at its most dramatic.

Several journalists India were concerned about what was happening in the press. This concern was reflected in more than a dozen meetings organized by journalists' unions across the country to examine Gulf War coverage. I attended several of these meetings, and the dilemma over the nature of the material coming in was reflected at every one of them. Desk people came in for criticism. They in turn asked what they could do. Assistant editors and others at middle-senior levels offered to carry alternative material if it could be obtained, which did occur in a limited way. Newspapers such as the *Independent* carried detailed analyses examining the historicity of the U.S. claims about war. The *Times of India* gave a good deal of space to journalists' meetings criticizing biased war coverage.

On television, India's one international affairs program, "The World This Week," found itself imprisoned by its footage—all of it from Western sources. Many of the journalists working on the program were clearly against the war, but their footage was not. They even tried to get around this dilemma by creatively interspersing war footage with clips from Vietnam and antiwar poems by Pablo Neruda, but the larger problem of the source of material could not be resolved.

One of the first conclusions that journalists analyzing the war coverage arrived at was that though the United States may have gone to war on January 16–17, 1991, the Western media went to war on August 2, 1990. From that day on, every development in the Gulf was viewed through the prism of war—no framework for a peaceful settlement was ever allowed serious consideration (beyond a very limited point in some exceptional journals).

The concerns expressed by these Indian journalists included:

- The romanticizing of the technologies of death ("precision bomb-ing," "surgical strike," "smart bombs"), which was highly dehuman-izing and desensitizing
- The lack of context to the war, the sense that its entire framework was just the "instant history" of the previous week (Indian publica-tions had noted Saddam Hussein's use of chemical weapons against Iran for five years when Western, primarily U.S., media were playing that down)
- The vicious demonization of Arabs and Muslims in general and Iraqis in particular
- The double standards involved in the use of sanctions or the fact that twelve resolutions on Iraq were followed by a war, whereas hundreds of resolutions on apartheid or the Arab territories occupied illegally by Israel produced nothing

Most journalists were revolted by the racism running right through the coverage.

References on CNN to Baghdad looking lit up like "a Christmas tree" or reminding someone of the "Fourth of July" raised questions as to whether such expressions would ever have been permitted if the capital burning had been, not Baghdad, but Washington, London, or Paris. This revulsion also found reflection in a few articles and editorials.

At about this point, the U.S. and British embassies got into the act (in Commonwealth countries, the British Mission is called the high commis-sion instead of the embassy). P. J. Fowler, the deputy high commissioner of the British High Commission in New Delhi, wrote an angry, aggressive letter to Praful Bidwai, a senior assistant editor of the *Times of India,* blasting him for being critical of the Western coalition's objectives and methods. So aggressive was the tone of the letter that the matter came up for discussion in the Indian parliament on February 27, 1991, where there was a very sharp reaction to what was seen as blackmail of the journalist (*Times of India,* February 28, 1991).

Meanwhile, the U.S. Embassy let it be known that it was maintaining a file of clippings hostile to the United States on the subject. The first hint of this action came in a report by Barbara Crossette of the *New York Times,* who also quoted an unnamed source that said provincial Urdu-language newspapers in Pakistan were beneficiaries of "Iraqi money being lavished on propaganda" (*International Herald Tribune,* February 2–3, 1991, p. 5).

It was Crossette who in this piece first dropped the hint (or warning?) that the "Pakistani and Indian press has given prominence to stories that prove to be cases of disinformation. . . . The U.S. Information Service has a collection of such stories." That the largest quantities of disinformation were from Western sources—indeed, that almost the entire *output* on the war, up to 80–85 percent, was from Western sources—did not deter Crossette from making this fantastic claim.

In case anyone had missed point, U.S. diplomats in Delhi hinted not too subtly to Indian editors that these trespasses would be remembered when journalists were applying for visas to the United States. Although one or two publications softened their stance (also because of an opportunistic desire to be on the winning side), this attitude did not deter journalists from joining hands with trade unions and other associations to organize relief supplies for those hurt by the war (*Blitz Weekly,* March 18, 1991, p. 28).

Very interestingly, while the pro-Western elite was undoubtedly influenced by the propaganda permeating the news pages, public mood remained firmly antiwar. Several U.S. libraries/centers throughout India closed down during this period, even though India had no record of attacks on U.S. embassies (the one exception being an attack on a U.S. Mission in Bombay by an ultra-right-wing group in the early 1980s). In Calcutta, dock workers struck work and refused to pick up gunnysacks bound for U.S. Army service in Saudi Arabia.

At the international children's competition (painting, short story, and cartoon) in New Delhi in February (*Times of India,* February 17, 1991), the Iraqi representative received the loudest applause—though that reflected no support or sympathy for Saddam Hussein. In a historical sense, this was inevitable. Indians are not about to march on the streets on the issue of the Ethiopian famine or the Brazilian debt. But a colonial war situation mobilizes them. South Africa and Palestine are powerful, emotive issues. Indians can identify with those situations. They have been ruled for 250 years by the very powers backing St. George as he took on the dragon.

Thus, news reports about a war against a villainous dictator (even if relatively unknown to most Indians) cut little ice with an Indian public that had seen tens of thousands dead in three wars launched against them by U.S.-backed dictators. One such war in 1971 saw the birth of the nation Bangladesh.

But the Indian media did not live up to this historical legacy. Even some of the antiwar arguments were based on traditional Western premises that led to a dead end. In fact, the Indian media failed to use the one potent source available to them: thousands of highly trained and experienced nurses and technicians returning from Iraq. The nurses were in a position to give accurate accounts of the devastation and damage done to civilian areas and hospitals. But because the lower-middle-class nurses had little interaction with the elitist press (except, perhaps, in Kerala), this information never surfaced.

In sum, the Indian media failed to cover the Gulf War adequately—even in light of the limitations over which they had no control. The Western media, however, did not fail. They actually succeeded beyond belief in their objectives. They drummed up support for their war, they packaged it as a just war, and they succeeded in dehumanizing and depersonalizing Third World peoples in general and Iraqis in particular. ("It's almost like you flipped on the light in the kitchen late at night and the cockroaches start scurrying, and we're killing them," said a U.S. Air Force commander after a bombing raid [*International Herald Tribune,* February 1, 1991, p. 1]. Ironically, the Indian media, in reproducing most of the very material that made the Western media successful, ensured their own failure.

◆

CHAPTER SIX

The State, the Malaysian Press, and the War in West Asia

Zaharom Nain

THROUGHOUT THE RELATIVELY short span of what John Pilger (1991, 8) rightly termed the "one-sided bloodfest" in the Gulf, Malaysia was quite detached physically from the fighting. Nonetheless, there was virtually saturation coverage of the war in the Malaysian media during this period, providing Malaysians with a sense of immediacy and involving them, albeit indirectly, with the war. Not unexpectedly for Malaysia, as perhaps for many other Third World nation-states, coverage of the war was almost exclusively derived from the major Western news agencies and the daily CNN and NBC news reports that were received "live" from the United States.

Hence, whatever understanding the Malaysian public might have had of the war was invariably based almost totally on these reports. It is the framing of this understanding that this chapter investigates—not only the framing by the Western agencies from which the reports originated, but also the reframing of these reports by the mainstream Malaysian media organizations.

Malaysia's Official Stand on the War

With regard to the situation in West Asia, the Malaysian government has been consistent in its condemnation of Israel and Israeli aggression. At the same time, it has been a staunch supporter of the PLO and an ally of Saudi Arabia and similarly "moderate" Arab nations. The administration's relationship with more radical Muslim states—"those especially eager to exercise their independence from the United States and the West, like

Libya, Syria and Iran" (Mutalib 1990, 131)—is more cautious, however. The administration is cautious because Malaysia has a cordial relationship with the West and because the government wishes to placate those domestic sensitivities that could lead to political instability.[1]

When Iraq invaded Kuwait, the Malaysian government took a firm stand against the invasion. It solidly supported U.N. Security Council Resolution 660, which condemned the invasion and demanded the withdrawal of Iraq from Kuwait. But the Malaysian government's decision to support Resolution 678, which effectively sanctioned the war against Iraq, was a controversial one that met with some local opposition. The opposition generally came from two fronts. The *humanitarian* argument against the decision was that Malaysia, being a nonaligned nation, should not have supported Resolution 678 and instead should have continued to work toward the resolution of the crisis though diplomatic and peaceful means. The *ethno-religious* argument was that by supporting Resolution 678, Malaysia, a predominantly Muslim country, had sanctioned attacks on a Muslim country by non-Muslim armies.[2]

Midway through the conflict, the Malaysian government's stand appeared to waver. In response to local criticisms and a feeling of unease, especially among the local Muslim population, Prime Minister Mohamad Mahathir stated that his administration was asking for a review of "the implementation of the resolution which called for the liberation of Kuwait." Ironically, having earlier supported Resolution 678, he now argued that "any conflict should be resolved though negotiations and not by going to war." Almost displaying total ignorance of the colonial past of the region and the region's strategic importance, Mahathir went on to say that "outsiders, who were absent from the area previously, have now entered the area as a result of the invasion of Kuwait" (*Star,* February 2, 1991).

And when the war was coming to an end, when the coalition forces were clearly headed for victory, the Mahathir administration backslided, falling back on its initial stand. As Khay Khoo Jin (1991, 132) succinctly put it, "There was more than a hint of opportunism in Malaysia's changing pronouncements once the war started. Initially, the government expressed concern over the terms of the Security Council resolution and called for this to be looked into. However, as the U.S.-led forces headed towards a military victory, the government reverted to its old stand."

Where the Malaysian press stood during all these developments is what this chapter seeks to reveal by examining war coverage by four mass-circulation newspapers. But let me first provide some background on the relationship between the Malaysian media and the state.

The State and the Malaysian Media

So long as the press is conscious of itself being a potential threat to democracy and conscientiously limits the exercise of its rights, it should be allowed to function without government interference. But when the press obviously abuses its rights by unnecessarily agitating the people, then democratic governments should have a right to control it.

—(Mahathir 1981, 19)

Since the early 1980s, the relationship between the state and the mainstream Malaysian media has been cordial and complementary. Throughout this period, during which Prime Minister Mahathir has been in office, greater controls on and greater expansion of the mass media have helped legitimize the present social order.[3] These developments helped, though not with complete success, in maintaining hegemony during a period when the process of change created dissatisfaction, turbulence, and conflict.[4] Indeed, there have been two distinctive trends in the development of the mainstream Malaysian media, particularly the press and broadcasting.

First, legalistic controls on the mass media industries have been intensified.[5] The official rhetoric accompanying this tightening of controls, as personified by statements made by Mahathir, has stressed a greater need for the preservation of order and for political stability. As Mahathir (1985) himself has emphasized, "For a society precariously balanced on a razor's edge where one false or even true word can lead to calamity, it is criminal irresponsibility to allow for that one word to be uttered."

Second, the mass media have undergone increasing commercialization; more publications have emerged, and more printing permits have been issued. In 1981, when Mahathir first took office, there were 56 local newspapers, magazines, and journals in circulation (*Information Malaysia* 1980–1981, 304–309). By 1985, despite the introduction of the Printing Presses Publications Act in late 1984, there were 102 local newspapers, magazine, and journals in circulation throughout the country (*Information Malaysia* 1985, 335–344)

As for broadcasting, a supposedly alternative commercial television station, TV3, was set up in June 1984. Before it was formed, there was the general expectation "that a commercial television station will provide newer, better quality and better choice of programmes" (*Malaysian Business,* June 1, 1984, p. 23). After it was established, an air of misplaced optimism prevailed—a misguided belief that the commercialization of broadcasting would simply lead to the production of a greater variety of media artifacts. More than that, the increasing commercialization of the media created an illusion of greater freedom.

But the reality is quite different. Increasing commercialization has in fact resulted in greater state intervention and domination in the mass media industries. Direct political party ownership of the mainstream mass media has increased tremendously, with the ruling Barisan Nasional (BN) coalition having virtually a stranglehold on media ownership.[6]

The Ethno-Religious Dimension

Malaysia is a multiethnic, multireligious country with three major ethnic groups (Malays, Chinese, and Indians) and numerous other ethnic minorities (including Kadazans, Ibans, Bajaus, and Meruts), particularly in the East Malaysian states of Sabah and Sarawak. According to the 1980 census, out of a total population of 13.07 million, 6.9 million Malaysians are Muslims. The rest are made up of Buddhists, Hindus, Sikhs, Christians, followers of traditional Chinese religions such as Taoism, and a smattering of others.[7] Since Malaysia's political independence from Great Britain in 1957, Islam has been the official state religion.

Given Malaysia's multiethnic nature, its history since independence has been dominated by ethnic-based parties and ethnic politics. The three major political parties that form the basis of the BN coalition government, for instance, are stringently ethnic based.[8] Indeed, it would not be an exaggeration to suggest that ethnic preoccupations color Malaysian society and culture as a whole.

Media Coverage of the Conflict

I selected four mass-circulation newspapers—two English-language national newspapers, the *Star* and the *New Straits Times* (NST), and two Malay-language national newspapers, the *Utusan Malaysia* (UM) and the *Berita Harian* (BH)—to investigate media coverage of the Gulf War.

According to mid-1987 figures, the *Star* and the *New Straits Times* are the most popular English-language dailies in Malaysia, with daily circulation figures of 148,000 and 168,900 copies, respectively. The *Berita Harian* and the *Utusan Malaysia* are the two most popular Malay dailies, with daily circulation figures of 213,600 and 239,800 copies, respectively.

Both the *New Straits Times* and the *Berita Harian* are published by the New Straits Times Press, which in turn is owned by Renong, the investment arm of the United Malays National Organization (UMNO Baru).[9] The *Star,* a daily tabloid, is published by Star Publications, which in turn is owned by Hua Ren Holdings, a holding company of another political party, the Malaysian Chinse Association (Gomez 1991, 96). The

TABLE 6.1
News Items About the War, by Type

Newspaper	Report	Feature	Columnist/ Commentary	Editorial	Letter	Total
NST	326	10	2	10	11	359
Star	388	4	3	0	8	403
UM	281	13	13	5	7	319
BH	348	14	8	7	5	382
Total	1,343	41	26	22	31	1,463

Utusan Malaysia is published by Utusan Melayu. Here, too, the newspaper's links with the ruling coalition are obvious. Three of its seven directors are members of UMNO Baru—one is an ex-cabinet minister, another is a former member of parliament, and the third was once Mahathir's press secretary. The latter is also a director of TV3, which is also owned by Renong.[10]

The sample period of this investigation is from January 17, 1991, to February 28, 1991. This period was chosen because it consists of coverage of the war from the day the first U.S.-led allied attacks on Iraq were initially reported to the day Kuwait was deemed liberated.

A total of 1,463 news items about the war were examined. The breakdown of these items are provided in Table 6.1. These items are by no means exhaustive because items of less than two column inches were disregarded. Not surprisingly, the majority of the items, especially the news reports, were of foreign origin, all coming from the wire services. Indeed, 1,343 (91.8 percent) were news reports, and 85.7 percent of these were of foreign origin (see Table 6.2).

TABLE 6.2
Local and Foreign Reports and Features About the War

Newspaper	Reports			Features		
	Local	Foreign	Total	Local	Foreign	Total
NST	51	275	326	1	9	10
	(15.64%)	(84.36%)	(100%)	(10.00%)	(90.00%)	(100%)
Star	58	330	388	2	2	4
	(14.95%)	(85.05%)	(100%)	(50.00%)	(50.00%)	(100%)
UM	32	249	281	8	5	13
	(11.39%)	(88.61%)	(100%)	(61.54%)	(38.46%)	(100%)
BH	51	297	348	11	3	14
	(14.66%)	(85.34%)	(100%)	(78.57%)	(21.43%)	(100%)
Total	192	1,151	1,343	22	19	41
	(14.30%)	(85.70%)	(100%)	(53.66%)	(46.34%)	(100%)

Because my aim was to look at local representation of events, for the English-language newspapers I decided to place greater emphasis on the words and phrases used in the headlines of the foreign reports because the original main body of the text would not likely be changed. I employed a different strategy for the Malay-language newspapers. Here, even though most of the news reports were also from the wire services, there was greater potential for re-presentation during the process of translation. Hence, I paid equal attention to the headlines and the main text.

The findings that follow do not pretend to constitute an exhaustive, quantitative survey of Malaysian press reports of the war. At best, they are an interpretative, initial fact-finding mission that attempts to identify some trends in the coverage of the war by the Malaysian mainstream press. These trends may be tentatively linked to two important elements in the Malaysian social structure: media relations with the state and Malaysia's ethno-religious makeup.

The English-Language Press

Overall, the majority of the items were from the wire services/agencies. But only nineteen of these were features. There was a conspicuous absence, for example, of features published by the *Guardian* (England) from the pages of the *Star* and the *NST.* After all, for a long time prior to the conflict, both the *Star* and *NST* regularly ran *Guardian* features. Yet during a period when the *Guardian* was publishing features critically examining the war, none were to be seen on the pages of these two newspapers. In addition, out of a grand total of 214 local reports and features, only 22 were features. And of these, only 3 appeared in the English-language dailies, 1 in the *NST* and 2 in the *Star.* These omissions raise serious questions about the willingness or ability of the English-language press to analyze the Gulf conflict in some depth.

Indeed, there was a tendency in these newspapers to indulge in "straight" reporting, to merely quote statements given by Mahathir and other members of the administration in toto. And when there was any opinion given by those who had differing thoughts about the war, including parliamentary opposition parties, these were relegated to the inside pages. On January 21, for example, when the parliamentary opposition parties released a statement condemning the war and criticizing the government, the *NST* carried a small item on it on page three. Headlined "Joint Opposition Pleas to Stop the War," the report was virtually buried under a bigger report headlined "Tourists May Come Here Because of War." This report contained the gist of a statement made by the culture, arts, and tourism minister.

In a January 19 local report headlined "Dewan Debates PAS [Pan Islamic Party] Motion on Gulf Crisis," the *NST* outlined the proposals tabled by the Islamic opposition party, PAS, in parliament. Immediately below that in a report headlined "Abu Hassan Raps PAS for Being Hypocritical," the paper reproduced the foreign minister's rebuttal of PAS's proposals without providing any assessment of his comments or a counter from PAS. The editorial of the same day, headlined "No Change in Issues and Principles," reiterated the government's stand. The editorial stressed that, "Malaysia should not waver from its stand even if the Israeli government decides to unleash its forces in retaliation. . . . There has been time for Iraq to consider the opinions of the international community and to withdraw to avoid a war. . . . This war has nothing to do with Islam or a battle against American imperialism." The editorial, not surprisingly, blatantly upheld the government's stand, and the last sentence was a clear dismissal of the motion presented by PAS in parliament.

Editorials are often assumed to reflect a newspaper's stand or policy regarding an issue or event. (The *Star* does not carry any editorials.) The ten editorials produced by the *NST* during the period were extremely instructive. None of them questioned, let alone criticized, the stand taken by the Malaysian government or the United Nations. Indeed, the paper's first two editorials following the outbreak of the war, headlined "The World Is Waiting" (January 17) and "Thunder and Lightning in the Gulf" (January 18), were full of sympathy for the United Nations ("The U.N. Chief played his part. . . . He did his utmost. . . . It was not his fault"). The editorials also chastised the Iraqis ("The point is past for reasoning and talking"), marginalized advocates of sanctions ("Their appeals drowned in an overwhelming acceptance that it has just become a question of whether a war must be fought"), and supported war ("The waiting is killing everyone . . . and all hopes for peace. . . . Many people are just dying for relief from the tension").

In early February, however, when the Malaysian government's stand was wavering, both newspapers began playing a different tune. On February 3, having run a front-page report on Mahathir's statement with the boldfaced headline "PM: Don't Take Sides," the *Star* ran numerous reports on its inside pages with headlines such as "Saddam a Hero: Supporters," "U.S. Underestimated Saddam: General," "Iraq Plays Guessing Game with Allies," and "Holy Sites Destroyed and Many Civilians Killed—Iraq." These headlines, at least, indicated that a softer line was being adopted toward the Iraqis.

And so it also was with the *NST*. On February 7, the paper ran a report headlined "UN Mandate 'Perverted by Allies'" in which the Tunisian foreign minister was quoted as saying, "There is no new international order. What we are seeing here is the old order we knew too well, the colonialist order which speaks through the barrel of a gun." Hence, just as the Malaysian government's stand was modified, so, too, was there a tendency for both the *Star* and *NST* to become more critical of the United States, cautiously supportive of the Iraqis, but nevertheless, still right there behind the government and the good old United Nations.

Overall, the *Star* was more ambivalent in its stand throughout the conflict, supporting the Malaysian government more by implication (by providing a ready platform for all statements made by the government, by not critically assessing them, and by marginalizing oppositional viewpoints, which were safely relegated to the "letters" page). The *NST* was vitriolic in its support of the government's stand and that of the United Nations. After all, Malaysia was then a member of the Security Council and had supported Resolution 678. Reading the *NST* editorials was akin to reading the government's statements. Both papers appeared to be aware, as perhaps was the government, to borrow from S. Hall (1982, 67), that "in order for one meaning to be produced regularly, it had to win a kind of credibility, legitimacy or taken-for-grantedness for itself . . . [which] . . . involved marginalising, down-grading or de-legitimizing alternative constructions."

The Malay-Language Press

Right from the start of the war, the tone adopted by the *Berita Harian* and the *Utusan Malaysia* was markedly different from that of the English-language newspapers. The anti-U.S. stand, only taken later and even then in a qualified manner, by the *Star* and the *NST* was clearly put forth by both *BH* and *UM* right at the start of the war. And whereas the *Star* and the *NST* clearly did not ethnicize the conflict or play up issues of religion, the *BH* and the *UM* had no such qualms.

On January 17, the day the news of the war first hit Malaysian news stands, on page four of the *BH* the headline read "Baghdad Pantang Menyerah Kalah" (Baghdad Will Not Surrender). The text was accompanied by a photograph of Saddam Hussein kneeling in prayer. The *UM* had the headline "Bahang Api Neraka Menunggu—Saddam (The Fires of Hell Await—Saddam) emblazoned on its front page. The headline was from a statement made by Saddam. It did not take much to read in "the fires of hell" a religious connotation—that is, that the fires of hell awaited the infidels (the U.S.-led coalition in this case).

The next day, Israel was linked directly to the conflict. In a front-page report headlined "Israel Siap Berperang" (Israel Gets Ready for War), the *BH* reported the preparations being undertaken by Israelis to face missile attacks. The *UM* feature on page eight the same day, headlined "Apakah Akan Terjadi Selepas Perang?" (What Will Happen After the

War?), linked the conflict to the increasing might of the Israelis, the corresponding loss of power of the Arab nations, and the Western interference in West Asia.

The focus on religion and the emphasis on Israel were persistent dominant themes in both newspapers' accounts of the war. Photographs of religious signification—the icon of Saddam at prayer, in particular—regularly accompanied news items. This religious imagery was also verbally present. The page one lead article in the *UM* on January 28 was headlined "Lautan Api Bakar Musuh?" (River of Fire Engulfs the Enemy?), thereby linking the oil spills to imagery of the river of death in hell that God uses to torture infidels.

On February 4, the *UM* front-page headline boldly read, "Bush Tewas" (Bush Loses) because, according to the subheading, Saddam was not defeated in three days, as predicted by Bush. On the same day, the *BH* argued that the Gulf was being used by the United States as a weapons testing ground ("Teluk Jadi Sasaran Amerika Uji senjata").

To briefly sum up, there was a marked difference in terms of style and content between the representation provided by the Malay-language newspapers and that of the *Star* and the *NST*. Religious issues were greatly played up by both Malay-language newspapers right from the start. For instance, even after the prime minister and a senior religious official had urged Malaysians not to view the war as a jihad, the *BH* carried a feature on February 14 headlined "Dimensi Agama Dalam Krisis Teluk" (The Religious Dimension in the Gulf Crisis). The feature argued that the presence of U.S. and other forces in the Gulf provided them with an easy opportunity to further split up Muslims and the Muslim world. Predominantly anti-U.S. photographs and cartoons were utilized more freely and purposefully in the *UM* and the *BH* than they were in the *NST* and the *Star*.

Overall, there was also a noticeable difference, albeit a stylistic one, between the *BH* and the *UM* presentations. The *UM,* which is akin to the popular tabloids in the West, thrives on sensationalism, especially in its presentation of potentially controversial news. The *BH,* coming as it does from the same stable as the sedate and officious *NST* and perhaps being more closely aligned to the Mahathir administration, is less prone to sensationalism, particularly when the controversy directly invokes the credibility of the government, as with the Gulf conflict.

Indeed, the prominent feature of the overall coverage by both these newspapers, as with the *Star* and the *NST,* was the total absence of criticism or questioning of the government stand and the role of the United Nations. Any possible linkage between local vested interests and the government's willingness to accede to U.S. requests was never considered, let alone assessed, by any of these newspapers.

Conclusion

What is evident from this investigation is that the Malaysian mainstream press, preoccupied as they were with toeing the official line or providing an ethno-religious angle to the conflict, lost a valuable opportunity to educate the Malaysian public about the Gulf War.[11] The Malaysian press failed to provide the public with sufficient knowledge with which to more fully comprehend the conflict and its implications for Malaysia and for a new world order.

Notes

1. Given Malaysia's delicate ethnic situation and the phenomenon of Islamic resurgence, the government fears that the revolutionary fervor, sparked off by "radical" Iran especially, could spread to Malaysia and pose a threat to its secular institutions. See Chandra (1987) and Mutalib (1990).

2. On January 18, an opposition Islamic party motion condemning the military incursions into Iraq was debated in the Malaysian parliament. The humanitarian argument was put across most convincingly by the Malaysian social reform movement Aliran. See Jin (1991).

3. Mahathir came to power in 1981 and has held office since. He heads the ruling Barisan Nasional coalition, which consists of the United Malays National Organisation, the Malaysian Chinese Association, the Malaysian Indian Congress, the Parti (Gerakan Rakyat Malaysia Gerakan), the United Sabah National Organisation, the Parti Bersatu Rakyat Jelata Sabah, the Parti Pesaka Bumiputera Bersatu Sabah, the Parti Bansa Dayak Sarawak, the Sarawak United People's Party, and the Sarawak National Party (SNAP).

4. The events are too numerous and complex to relate in great detail here. A brief mention of the more important ones will have to suffice.

Numerous financial scandals have momentarily rocked the Mahathir regime. These—including the United Malayan Banking Corporation deal involving the minister of finance and the Maminco tin fiasco—all came to light in the mid-1980s. See Aliran (1988, 191–354) and Hui (1987) for some critical comments.

The most highlighted financial scandal was the Bumiputra Malaysia Finance loans scandal, which came to light in 1983 and has yet to be resolved. Conservative estimates put the overall financial loss at M $2 billion. Despite numerous calls for an independent royal commission of enquiry to investigate the scandal, the Mahathir regime appointed only a committee of enquiry with limited powers.

Since early 1987, the ruling component party, the United Malays National Organisation, had been openly split into two blocks or factions—initially called "Team A" and "Team B." The bitterly contested UMNO party elections of April 1987 reinforced this split. Almost immediately after narrowly winning the party's presidential post, Mahathir purged his cabinet and other influential political posts of members identified with Team B. These struggles culminated in UMNO being declared an illegal party by the Malaysian High Court on February 4, 1988, which paved the way for Mahathir to form a "new" party, UMNO Baru.

There have also been numerous clashes between the executive and the judiciary.

5. Since Mahathir came into office at least three acts—the Official Secrets Act of 1972, the Internal Security Act of 1960, and the Printing Presses and Publications Act of 1984—have either been introduced or brought into play to control the media industries and their personnel.

Under the Printing Presses and Publications Act, all local publications must carry a license—renewable yearly at the discretion of the home minister—before they can be published.

In 1986, after the *Asian Wall Street Journal* had exposed the billion-dollar Bumiputra Malaysia Finance scandal, the Mahathir regime, utilizing the Printing Presses and Publications Act, suspended publication of the *Journal* for three months and ordered the expulsion of its correspondents. Such decisions are in the hands of the home minister, who happens to be Mahathir. In December 1987, this act was amended and six new sections were introduced, further strengthening the power of the home minister. Under Article 9, subsection 13B of the amended act, the home minister is now at liberty to reject, revoke, and/or suspend publishing licenses and permits as and when he deems fit. His decisions cannot be questioned in any court.

During the 1987 crackdown (Operation Lallang) on political dissidents, members of religious bodies, and social interest groups, three national newspapers—the English-language *Star,* the Chinese-language *Sin Chew Jit Poh,* and the Malay-language *Watan*—were suspended indefinitely, their licenses revoked under the Printing Presses and Publications Act. They were allowed to resume publication in March 1988, after apparently agreeing to certain terms and editorial restrictions imposed by the Home Ministry.

6. The BN coalition government directly controls the national broadcasting organization, which is essentially a department in the Information Ministry. UMNO has controlling interests in the only other national television station, TV3, the New Straits Times Group (which publishes English national dailies such as the *New Straits Times* and the *Malay Mail,* the Malay daily *Berita Harian,* and their Sunday editions via its investment arm, Renong Holdings). See Gomez (1990).

The second largest component party in the BN coalition, the Malaysian Chinese Association, via its investment arms Hua Ren Holdings and MultiPurpose Holdings Berhad, has controlling interests over Star Publications, which publishes, among other things, the *Star.* See Pang (1990, 98–100). Indeed, the president of the party, Ling Liong Sik, has openly declared that his party owns Star Publications (*New Straits Times,* December 5, 1989).

The *New Straits Times* and the *Star* are the only nationally distributed mass-circulation English dailies. They have regional offices and a well-oiled nationwide distribution network.

7. See *Population and Housing Census of Malaysia 1980: Report of the Population Census,* vol. 2 (Kuala Lumpur: Department of Statistics, 1983).

8. The three major parties are the United Malays National Organization, the Malaysian Chinese Association, and the Malaysian Indian Congress. Their names reveal their blatantly ethnic composition.

9. See Gomez (1990, 1991).

10. Tan Sri Abdul Samad Idris is a former Minister of Culture, Youth, and Sport. Dato' Abdullah Ahmad is a former member of parliament who lost his seat in the last election, running on a Barisan Nasional ticket. Mohammed Noor Yusof @ M. Noor Azam was Mahathir's press secretary. See *Utusan Melayu Annual Report* (1990).

11. Any future work of this nature should also look at the vernacular press, including Malaysian Chinese, Arabic, and Tamil newspapers. Local television representations of the war should also be analyzed because there were variations in the way English and the Malay news programs on Malaysian television presented the conflict.

References

Newspapers

Berita Harian
Berita Minggo
Mingguan Malaysia
New Straits Times
New Sunday Times
Star
Sunday Star
Utusan Malaysia

Other Sources

Abas, Tun Salleh, with K. Das. 1989. *May Day for Justice.* Kuala Lumpur: Magnus Books.

Aliran. 1988. *Issues of the Mahathir Years.* Penang: ALIRAN.

Anuar, Mustafa K. 1990. "The Malaysian 1990 General Elections: The Role of the BN Media." *Journal of Malaysian Studies* 8, no. 2 (December): 82–102.

Beng, Tan Chee. 1991. "Resorting to Ethnic Games (Again)." *Aliran Monthly,* 11, no. 1: 20–24.

Brennan, M. 1985. "Class, Politics and Race in Modern Malaysia." In R. Higgott and R. Robison, eds., *Southeast Asia: Essays in the Political Economy of Structural Change,* 93–127. London: Routledge and Kegan Paul.

Chandra, Muzaffar. 1987. *Islamic Resurgence in Malaysia.* Petaling Jaya: Fajar Bakti.

―――. 1988. "The 1988 Constitutional Amendments." In Committee Against Repression in the Pacific and Asia, ed., *Tangled Web.* New South Wales: Haymarket.

Gomez, E. T. 1990. *Politics in Business: UMNO's Corporate Investments.* Kuala Lumpur: Forum.

―――. 1991. *Money & Politics in the Barisan Nasional.* Kuala Lumpur: Forum.

Hall, S. 1982. "The Rediscovery of 'Ideology': Return of the Repressed in Media Studies." In M. Gurevitch et al., *Culture, Society and the Media,* 56–90. London: Methuen.

Hui, Lim Mah. 1980. "Ethnic and Class Relations in Malaysia." *Journal of Contemporary Asia* 10 nos. 1–2: 130–153.

Information Malaysia. 1980–1981. Kuala Lumpur: Berita.

———. 1985. Kuala Lumpur: Berita.

Jessop, B. 1982. *The Capitalist State.* London: Martin Robertson.

Jin, Khoo Khay (ed.), 1991. *Whose War? What Peace? Reflections on the Gulf Conflict.* Kuala Lumpur: Aliran, Forum, and Gerak Damai.

Jomo, K. S. 1988. *A Question of Class.* New York: Monthly Review Press.

———. 1990. Growth and Structural Change in the Malaysian Economy. Hampshire: Macmillan.

Lawyers Committee for Human Rights. 1990. *Malaysia: Assault on the Judiciary,* New York: LCHR.

Mahathir, Mohamad. 1981. "Freedom of the Press—Fact and Fallacy." *New Straits Times,* July 9, pp. 14, 19.

———. 1983. "New Government Policies." In K. S. Jomo, ed., *The Sun Also Sets: Lessons in Looking East.* Kuala Lumpur: Insan.

———. 1985. Keynote Address at the World Press Convention, Kuala Lumpur, September 18.

Malaysia. 1976. *Third Malaysia Plan.* Kuala Lumpur.

Malaysian Business, June 1, 1984.

Morais, J. V. 1982. *Mahathir: Riwayat Gagah Berani.* Kuala Lumpur: Arenabuku.

Mutalib, Hussin. 1990. *Islam and Ethnicity in Malay Politics.* Singapore: Oxford University Press.

Pathmanathan, M., and D. Lazarus (eds.). 1984. *Winds of Change: The Mahathir Impact on Malaysia's Foreign Policy.* Kuala Lumpur: University of Malaya Press.

Pilger, John. 1991. "A One-Sided Bloodfest." *New Statesman and Society,* March 8, pp. 8–9.

Population and Housing Census of Malaysia 1980: Report of the Population Census. 1983. Vol. 2. Kuala Lumpur: Department of Statistics.

Raju, S. K. S. et al. 1984. "Treating the Indo-Pakistan Conflict: The Role of Indian Newspapers and Magazines." In A. Arno and W. Dissanayake, eds. *The News Media in National and International Conflict,* pp. 101–132. Boulder, Colo.: Westview Press.

Siang, Lim Kit. 1987. *The $62 Billion North-South Highway Scandal.* Petaling Jaya: Democratic Action Party.

Soong, Kua Kia (ed.). 1987. *Defining Malaysian Culture.* Petaling Jaya: K. Das Ink.

Utusan Melayu Annual Report. 1990. Malaysia.

Yin, Hua Wu. 1983. *Class and Communalism in Malaysia.* London: Zed Books.

Yue, Pang Hin. 1990. "How the Press Covers Trade Unions: A Content Analysis of Coverage of the Malaysian Trade Union Congress by the *New Straits Times* and the *Star.*" Undergraduate diss., Penang: Universiti Sains Malaysia.

A SENSE OF *KENBEI* IN JAPAN: More than six months after the Persian Gulf War, the *New York Times* (October 16, 1991, p. A-14) reported a growing sense of *kenbei,* "dislike of the United States," in Japan. (*Kenbei* is a new word.) "For Japanese, these feelings were sharply focused by the negative reaction in that country to the seeming eagerness of the United States to go to war in the Persian Gulf. Criticism of Japan's role in the Gulf appear to have brought these emotions out into the open, resulting in some criticism of the United States that is unusually harsh and direct by Japanese standards." This report is illustrated by the following two commentaries.

JAPANESE POSITION IN THE WAR AND REGIONAL ISSUES
Masanori Naito

Every day, the war in the Persian Gulf strays further from the stated objective of U.N. Security Council resolutions, liberating Kuwait, and closer to an Anglo-American overthrow of the government of Iraq. From the eyes of Muslims in the Middle East and those as far away as Southeast Asia and Africa, this state of affairs is increasingly viewed as an attack by the United States on the Islamic world.

While there is criticism of the aggression of President Saddam Hussein of Iraq here in Turkey, there are also more than a few pained expressions on the faces of the Turkish people, who watch as America attacks their Muslim brothers in Iraq. There is a movement afoot among the non-oil-producing Arab members of the multinational forces aligned against Iraq to break from the coalition, depending on how Israel reacts in the conflict.

It is of paramount importance to recognize that this is the context in which Japan is about to launch its program to support the multinational contingent in the gulf, a policy based on a naive and one-dimensional concept of right and wrong. Saddam Hussein has been maligned for demolishing the regional status quo, but who was it that created the nations of the Middle East? Who built the applecart that Saddam upset? Around the time of World War I, the British and French were carving up the former Ottoman Empire between themselves, making plans to control the region, an

(continues)

(*continued*)

effort which eventually yielded the modern Middle Eastern states. It is true that they are sovereign nations, but it is also a fact that the territory of each was in effect established by the mere drawing of lines on early twentieth-century maps.

In order to extend its own national interests, Great Britain settled Jews in Palestine and was their patron. Following World War II it has been the United States which has offered continuing support to Israel. The "established order" has left plenty of wounds festering throughout the Middle East. Now the Gulf crisis has sent the pus gushing forth.

Unfortunately, British, French, and U.S. successes in both world wars have left these countries with the worldview of the victor. Having defeated fascism in World War II, they have forgotten to reflect on their own colonial domination during World War I. Thus, strident assertions of "justice" by the United States and the United Kingdom are taken with a grain of salt by people not only in the Middle East but elsewhere in the Third World.

Saddam Hussein's linkage of the Gulf crisis to the Palestinian problem is certainly nothing more than a subterfuge, however, and does little to move people who live with scars of the past. If the conflict becomes drawn out, the Palestinian wound will not be the only one in the area to open. In the vicinity of northern Iraq, there is the question of independence for the Kurds, while Muslim voices within the Soviet Union cry out for their own freedom from Moscow. Saudi Arabia risks losing the trust of the Islamic world by virtue of its facile reliance on the United States to protect its wealth. We must be aware that in respect to these movements and developments, justice as reiterated by the United States and the United Kingdom is a meaningless concept.

Discourse in Japan seems to be that we are highly dependent on oil from the Middle East, and if we want to stay lubricated and maintain order in that vital area, we had better put up or shut up. I simply cannot fathom how that line of logic can bear positively on Japan's long-term relations in the region or indeed with the entire Muslim community. From the outset of the Gulf crisis, arguments from both ruling and opposition parties have centered on assistance to the Middle East, all the while leaving out the Middle Eastern point of view.

(*continues*)

(*continued*)

Similarly, in contemplating the dispatch of Self-Defense Force aircraft to the region, Japan is concerned with the influence its own past aggression has had on its Asian neighbors. Yet it remains oblivious to past experiences in the Middle East. Japan has no history of subjugation in the area. However, it is on the verge of entering, hand in hand with Europe and the United States, a path toward dominating the Middle East.

The enormous sum of money the Japanese government is preparing to contribute for essentially military purposes represents a consciousness of world affairs in which maintaining the status quo is the goal. I can only conclude that if this is what we consider to be Japan's contribution, we have not thought about it rationally enough.

This piece was originally published in *Asahi Evening News,* February 28, 1991.

JAPANESE MEDIA AND THE WAR

Interview with Tetsuo Kogawa, social critic and media activist from Tokyo, conducted in February 1991 in the New York offices of the Gulf Crisis TV Project, with producers from that project.

Just after the Gulf War had begun, I received a package in Japan. It was the first four programs of the Gulf Crisis TV Project.[1] As I watched the video I was astonished at the contents because almost all of our Gulf War coverage was television images from the major U.S. networks—ABC, CBS, NBC, and CNN. Japanese TV has contracts with these news sources and regularly uses footage from the U.S. As the Gulf War continued, this situation became so extreme that Japanese television news was almost entirely U.S. mass media images simultaneously translated into Japanese. Japanese television *became* American television.

The Japanese people were told by U.S. media that 90 percent of the U.S. population supported the war. We had no opportunity to evaluate this position. I, myself, however, could not be satisfied with this report as I have many friends in the United States who told me of the movement against the U.S. policies and the criti-

(*continues*)

(*continued*)

cism of the media coverage, although I had no documentation of that reality. When I received these tapes I was delighted, and I circulated them to many persons in the antiwar movement. The scale was small, but it was the beginning of political activity. Officially the Japanese government had decided to send $9 billion to the United Nations to support the war. Many were against this, but I must confess that they did not have much support in terms of major political organizing. In recent years in Japan progressive political activities have been at a low point.

I circulated over thirty copies of the Gulf Crisis videos to key persons in various organizations and friends of mine in many locations throughout Japan. All of those who received the tape were very interested in the video, and they either personally or with their organizations duplicated it and circulated it to other groups and individuals. So that one package of video made a loose network.

Each person and each organization that received the video began to connect with each other. The act of duplication, transcription, and translation became a means of organizing: After they received the tape, groups made copies and sent them to new groups. Many collaborated in making the transcriptions and translations and sending copies to those who received the video next.

Ludger Balant: Did you approach any of the mass media in Japan?

Kogawa: I tried to get the major broadcasting stations to use it. I have several friends who work in Japanese television and asked them to use sections on their news. They proposed it for broadcast but were refused. None of the stations would touch it because Japanese mass media is very tightly controlled and we have neither public access channels nor educational stations.

However, I suddenly recalled that in Poland in the 1980s Solidarity used video and cassette tapes to promote their movement. At that time they couldn't use broadcast channels, but they used the fact that most meeting places for political activities have video or audio cassette players. Each meeting place used tapes to circulate political ideas and opinions. That became my model.

Indu Krishnan: What has been the opposition to war in Japan?

(*continues*)

(*continued*)

Kogawa: The situation against the war in Japan is different because we experienced Hiroshima and Nagasaki. In spite of this, Japan contributed $9 billion to the United Nations for the Gulf War. When the war started, the government promoted the opinion that we must assist the war effort because every Western country supported the war. According to the Japanese constitution, we cannot be involved in any kind of military activities. The Japanese government has stated that the money will not be used for warfare but for reconstruction of the damaged areas. But there is no accounting of this, no proof. How does one differentiate which dollar pays for what? In addition to money, Japan sent many technicians, physicians, medicines. Japan also sent ships for carrying material between the Middle East and the Philippines. The United States used this money and this material assistance for warfare. If we were to abide by the constitution, we could not allow any of these activities.

The Japanese were reluctant to be isolated in the international economic community. We have felt isolated in the past—Japan-bashing is strong in many countries. Corporate leaders are very vulnerable to that situation and are looking for ways to become more integrated. However, there is not a complete consensus. In Japan there has been much disagreement with the government policy. Several groups have sued the government for going against the constitution. That action was very important not only because of the suit itself, but because through the activities of preparing the suit, new networks have been formed.

Ludger Balant: Did the Japanese send any soldiers to the Gulf?

Kogawa: Because of the constitutional restrictions, we could not send our soldiers. Congress discussed this question at great length. Eventually, although the Socialists and other small parties appealed to maintain the constitution, the Liberal Democratic Party won the right to send airplanes to the Gulf. However, the constitution was still in effect, and they couldn't send soldiers. But they found a trick. According to the regulations, they could send the VIPs out of the border in airplanes. So they used their airplanes to bring refugees from the Gulf and described them as VIPs, as "special guests." The reasoning was that they were on a "peacekeeping" activity.

(*continues*)

(*continued*)

Indu Krishnan: Were there large demonstrations against the war in Japan?

Kogawa: The largest was around three thousand in Tokyo, with others in Osaka and Nagasaki. Although there were not massive numbers, this period did see the development of many smaller (spontaneous in a sense) demonstrations of one hundred to two hundred people in many locations without central control.

Indu Krishnan: What has been the influence of the Japanese experience with the atomic bombs? Does this have an effect on the way people feel about the war and the bombing of civilian populations?

Kogawa: In Japan, in spite of the atomic bomb, Japanese people do not have prejudice against the United States. There are a lot of interpretations of this. One is that participation in World War II was forced by orders from Hirohito. Military forces before the war belonged to the emperor's family, which is somewhat independent, so that every soldier went to battle on the personal orders of Hirohito. After the war people felt that now they were free and in general did not harbor personal antagonism against the United States. In Japan a culture of revenge is not strong—not personal revenge. If revenge exists, it is as family or organizational revenge but not personal revenge. The atomic bomb did not invoke individual revenge feelings against the U.S. This has been criticized by radial sociologists as a kind of amnesia. Even though we have had the experience of the atomic bomb, we quickly forgot. Our history was useless to us; we could not utilize this experience.

On the popular level there is a great deal of confusion about the United States. The U.S. media portray Japanese as industrial invaders. Japan is very sensitive about that sort of portrayal. Ever since World War II, the tie between the United States and Japan has been strong. They promoted each other, and Japan experienced great economic and social development. The people of Hiroshima, of course, feel differently, but without a feeling of revenge. It is psychologically very complicated. We cannot say that the people in Hiroshima are especially active in criticizing this war. It is not true. With the Gulf War, the activity against the war was mostly supported by the intellectuals. It was in a sense an isolated group. However, most of the people over the age of forty have some

(*continues*)

(*continued*)

memory of bombing. So they have a basic feeling: "No more war."
Even major TV will give you "person-on-the-street" interviews
that express that view. These expressions are not that effective,
they have no exact direction, they are just feelings. Generally
speaking, the Japanese people *do* have some vague resistance
against war.

Indu Krishnan: Could you summarize how Bush's new world
order will affect the Third World?

Kogawa: A very complicated question.

The accepted data is that 90 percent of oil in Japan comes from
the Middle East. However, I think that this dependency is changing. Last year Japan negotiated a new contract with the Soviet
Union for developing oil wells in Sakhalin. Japanese companies
also have plans to develop the oil in China. Already Indonesia and
Japan have close connections. There are possibilities that Japan
can change the dependency on oil to other places. The important
point about the Gulf War, however, is the relationship between the
U.S. and Japan. This time around Japan is no longer the "Far East."
The U.S. and Japan are almost indistinguishable—Japan has become one of the states of the United States. The Japanese government could not resist the demands of the United States.

Indu Krishnan: Some here feel that the Gulf War was engi-
neered to change the balance of power. How will their participation affect the Japanese people?

Kogawa: It is, first of all, an economic problem: $9 billion trans-
lates into ¥10,000 for each citizen. This results in an instant tax
increase, a rise in the price of oil, and difficulties for the automo-
bile industry, which has already been hit hard by a declining U.S.
market.

The ecological consequences will be great. When Japan invests
in developments in Indonesia and Sakhalin, where there are
thought to be oil deposits, there will be extensive destruction of
what until now have been relatively undisturbed primitive areas.
These will be destroyed as the oil industry is developed.

The impact of the war is to push the world to retain the oil-
oriented system. Even before the war, the United States was reluctant to stress efficient energy and cleaner sources—solar energy,

(*continues*)

(*continued*)

for example. Due to the success of the war for the United States will still promote the use of oil. . . . There are also changes in the media worldwide. The information systems of most countries, including Japan, are becoming more integrated into international capital.

NOTE

1. The Gulf Crisis TV Project was a series of ten video programs, produced by Paper Tiger Television and distributed via satellite by the Deep Dish Network, that were made before and during the Gulf War and used extensively by activists in many locations throughout the United States, Canada, and other countries. Compiled from activist footage from over two hundred producers and video organizations, these tapes show the widespread opposition to the war. Two of the programs are also specifically about media distortions of the U.S. "consensus" and criticism of the one-sided war reportage. These tapes are available from Paper Tiger Television, 339 Lafayette Street, New York, New York, 10012.

◆

CHAPTER SEVEN

The War Close to Home: The Turkish Media

Haluk Sahin

DESPITE TURKEY'S PROXIMITY to the combat zone, the Gulf War was a satellite television war for that country, as it was for countries on the other side of the globe. This meant, of course, that the people of Turkey viewed the conflict primarily from an Anglo-U.S. angle. Clearly, in this first major international conflict of the post–cold war era, the U.S. media achieved "air supremacy" much earlier than the allied air forces did. As military jargon implies, this achievement was more than "superiority"—there was no real competition.

From a communication research viewpoint, one of the curious discoveries of the most intense phase of the conflict was the decline in newspaper circulations. It had been widely predicted in journalistic circles that the highly publicized war, like other "earthshaking" events in the past, would give chronically stagnant newspaper circulations a much-needed boost. On the contrary, circulations dropped significantly, especially during the first week of the air campaign.

It was obvious that this was not due to a lack of interest; people talked about little else. But they, like media patriots everywhere, "satisfied" their curiosity with television, which in this instance meant the U.S. satellite station, CNN. Watching a war "live" on a foreign station was a unique experience. The commercial satellite channel *Magic Box,* which broadcasts from Germany in Turkish to bypass the state monopoly of broadcasting in Turkey, showed via CNN the first bombs falling on Baghdad and remained hooked to it. The public network, Turkish Radio and Television (TRT), surrendered after three days of autarky and began transmitting CNN pictures with simultaneous translation.

Newspapers discovered that there was no way they could catch up. The perceived gap between the time of an event and its printed report gained abyssal proportions. The first "live" war dealt to newspapers another blow. They, too, became adjuncts to television coverage by providing behind-the-scenes information about the coverage rather than about the war itself. After a few days, information fatigue set in. The people who stayed up to watch the air raids on CNN were left with no appetite for additional information in other media. The morning's newspapers looked as stale as yesterday's newspapers.

The infatuation with CNN was rather brief, however. Just as people quickly tire of video games, many viewers soon got tired of the repetitive, mechanical, clean, and strictly managed visual coverage of the war. The U.S. preoccupation with the Israeli scene was a surprise for most viewers who were not familiar with this aspect of U.S. news values. After a few weeks, newspapers fought back with domestic politics and local repercussions of the war. The public television network, which is controlled by the government, also found itself in the embarrassing position of crudely censoring a CNN report on U.S. planes taking off from the Incirlik airbase in the southern part of Turkey on bombing missions in Iraq. Magic Box ran the story without interference, thus bringing the official double standard into plain view. TRT decided that "national security" could not be entrusted even to allied TV stations. It cut off the CNN connection and opted for localized coverage.

In Turkey, TRT news presents the official version of the day's events as seen from Ankara, the political capital, while newspapers offer the oppositional and sensationalistic version as viewed from Istanbul, the commercial and cultural capital. The overlap between the two is usually very small. In other words, the people of Turkey are presented with two different, highly unrelated agendas. The war, of course, imposed itself on both agendas, although differences in approach continued. TRT was compelled to watch out for official state policies while covering the conflict. President Turgut Ozal, who favored an "active" Turkish policy against Saddam Hussein and remained in close touch with President George Bush (their numerous telephone conversations were routinely reported as one of the lead items on TRT), emerged as its leading commentator.

The printed press, however, assumed a critical stance about Turkey's active involvement in the war and especially about the possibility of opening a "second front." With few exceptions, most influential columnists urged caution. There was wide-ranging debate about the war in the newspapers; it stretched from lunatic-fringe leftists, who urged Turkey to support Saddam, to extreme religious rightists, who called for a holy war.

Public opinion polls indicated that the cautious, anti-adventurist line advocated by much of the press was shared by a majority of the people. While there was no real sympathy for Saddam, there was even less eagerness for an active role in the war. Compared to the United States and United Kingdom, there was much less unanimity and considerably greater meaningful debate about the war in the Turkish media. This was probably a reflection of the Turkish political arena, where the war remained a matter for discussion and debate rather than for crushing consensus.

For pictures from the front, the Turkish media relied by and large on the Western news agencies and television services. The Turkish reporters who went to cover the war found themselves in a disadvantageous position compared to their U.S. and British colleagues. The dependence on Western news agencies and television services was accepted by Turkish reporters, with few complaints, as a fact of life. This changed, however, in the aftermath of the war when the same "foreign" reporters came to Turkey to cover "the plight of the Kurds" camping along the Turkish border. Their reports were discovered to suffer from extreme doses of anti-Turkish bias and blatant sensationalism. There was sharp reaction from various quarters, including the media. The news values of the predominant Western sources, such as the BBC, Visnews, and U.S. networks, came under critical questioning. At least in this respect, the Gulf War as seen through Western lenses may have been an eye opener.

◆
───────────────   ───────────────

CHAPTER EIGHT

The Iranian Press and the Persian Gulf War: The Impact of Western News Agencies

Kazem Motamed-Nejad, Naiim Badii,
and Mehdi Mohsenian-Rad

FOR MOST IRANIANS who spent eight years struggling with Iraq after its attack on Iran in September 1980, the events that followed ten years later elicited both joy and anxiety. The joy was that a threatening neighbor, with a more than one-thousand-kilometer border in the west, had involved itself in yet another devastating war that could lead to its military destruction and defeat. The anxiety was that a new regional balance of power was probably emerging out of the U.S. leadership in that war.

The Iran-Iraq War has been considered "an obviously unfair, unnecessary and pointless war."[1] And yet all the great powers that took up arms against Iraq in defense of Kuwait not only did not try to stop Iraq from attacking Iran, but also did all they could to help Saddam Hussein not lose the war against Iran.[2] This great-power response led Iranians to feel that they were the victims of an "imposed" war.

For Iranians, particularly Tehran journalists, the seven-month Persian Gulf War presented a special case because of Iran's previous war with Iraq, Iran's geopolitical situation in the region, the Islamic Revolution and its impact on other Islamic countries, and Iran's lone neutrality in the region during the Persian Gulf War. Given Iran's unique situation, this chapter looks at how the two major Tehran dailies, *Ettelaat* and *Kayhan,* covered the Persian Gulf crisis and the subsequent war. Issues of these two papers were content analyzed for the first two weeks of the Iraqi aggression on Kuwait and then for the entire period of the multinational operations in the region.

TABLE 8.1
ETTELAAT AND *KAYHAN* Reporting of the Gulf Crisis and War

Type of Reporting	First Time Period	Second Time Period
Straight news		
%	79.31	84.50
Number[a]	23.00	109.00
Commentary		
%	10.34	3.10
Number	3.00	4.00
News analysis		
%	10.34	3.10
Number	3.00	4.00
Other		
%	0.00	9.30
Number	0.00	12.00

[a]All numbers represent major stories. Minor stories are omitted.

The Persian Gulf War has been labeled the first "communication war" because the news media, particularly television, were on the scene every moment.[3] For the first time in the history of humankind, a major conflict was followed every minute all over the globe electronically. The war was also a "media war." Journalists saw themselves as involved in the war, even when their participation was indirect. As a result of overt military censorship by allied forces, a distorted picture of the war's reality was given to the people around the world.[4]

As Table 8.1 shows, straight news stories accounted for a large portion of items published by both papers during the periods under investigation. During the first time period, nearly 80 percent of the stories were hard news, whereas while during the second time period, nearly 85 percent were purely hard news. Whereas commentary and news analysis accounted for 10 percent of the stories published by both papers during the first time period, such activity almost disappeared during the second time period.

In reporting the war, the two newspapers were heavily dependent on various sources. The two Iranian news agencies—Islamic Republic News Agency (IRNA) and Central News Unit (CNU)—were mentioned as sources of one-fifth of the stories during the first time period, and they were used as source of one-third of the stories during the second time period. Note, however, that most of the stories carried by IRNA and CNU wires were translations of major international news agency wires. Thus, it is misleading to assume that these two domestic news agencies had correspondents at the war zones.

During the second time period, both papers sent correspondents to Iraq. Their stories, along with reports by the newspapers' correspondents in southwestern and western Iran concerning the war refugees in border towns, accounted for nearly one-fifth of the stories for the first time period and almost one-sixth of the stories for the second time period.

Most of the stories reported in the two Tehran papers during the first time period were anti-Iraq and anti–Saddam Hussein, making up 41.8 percent of the total. In these stories, Iraq's aggressive acts were condemned. Anti-U.S., anti–allied forces, and anti–George Bush stories accounted for only 23.52 percent of the stories during the first time period. During the second time period, anti-U.S. and anti–allied forces stories accounted for nearly half of those reported by both Tehran papers. Stories containing anti-Iraq and anti-Saddam sentiments made up about one-fifth of the total stories.[5]

None of the stories during the first time period mentioned the existence of any form of censorship in the war reports by Western sources. During the second time period, about 8 percent of the stories made reference to Western censorship. Although most of the information about the war was obtained from military spokespeople at the war zones, and it was clear that this material was passed through military censors, it was received and reported as if it were objective.

Just as wire services were told by military censors and other guidelines to ignore the human catastrophes produced by the war, Tehran papers apparently did the same. The Tehran gatekeepers reported the war unconsciously through the eyes of Western correspondents. Likewise, when military policy and propaganda were against Iraq and its leader, the Tehran papers' reportage took on the same tone.

Nevertheless, despite the Iran-U.S. conflict in the postrevolutionary era, the first period's few stories against the United States, allied forces, and President Bush could have been a result of the postponement of the military showdown between the two countries.

During the second time period, there were twice as many stories against the United States and the allied forces. Stories against Iraq and particularly against President Saddam Hussein decreased during the second period. This conflict in the direction of the stories could be attributed to the improvement of the two countries' political relations, the withdrawal of Iraqi forces from Iranian territories, trips to and via Tehran by high Iraqi political officials, and the news selection behavior of the Tehran papers' gatekeepers.

The shift toward underestimating Iraq's military capabilities during both time periods could be attributed to the Tehran papers' acknowledgement of the U.S. intervention in the conflict as well as to the effects of the war propaganda. During the first time period, Iraq's military capabilities were of less concern. During the second period, as a result of military deployment of U.S. and allied forces as well U.S. and Western propaganda, the Tehran papers were more pessimistic toward Iraq's military capabilities, as were the mass media in the other parts of the globe. Underestimating U.S. military capabilities during the second time period was a result of the peculiar relation between Iran and the United States in Iran's postrevolutionary era.

During the first time period, there were few references to the human disasters for Kuwait because limited confrontation between Kuwait and Iraq had occurred. During the second time period, when heavy and continual air attacks were being waged against Iraq, there were also few stories in the two Tehran papers with this focus.

As for international processes of propaganda and disinformation in Persian Gulf War reporting, it can be said that the major objective of the war, was to strengthen the military, economic, and political power of the West—that is, war, oil, and power."[6] The decision by the Islamic Republic of Iran Broadcasting to show a small barrel of oil on the right corner of the screen with the inscription: "Oil War" during its entire war reporting period recognized this objective.

In Iran, as in other Third World countries, vulnerability toward international communication dominance is considerable. Journalistic education and training is weak, worthy specialized reporters, columnists, and commentators are in short supply; and most journalists are not knowledgeable about important world issues and domestic needs. These weaknesses conflict to some extent with the objectives of the Islamic Revolution, which calls for a challenging of all kinds of dependencies, especially cultural dependency.

The undesirable experience of the Persian Gulf War reporting demonstrated how essential it is for the Third World to struggle for change of great-power dominance over international news and communication.

As a result of postrevolutionary internal reorganizations and the effects of the Iran-Iraq War, among other reasons, the Iranian press had a limited opportunity to train the qualified professional journalists needed to counteract this dominance. (In the very last weeks of the war, the two major Tehran dailies did dispatch a few correspondents to Iraq, but their reports were of negligible significance as compared with the flood of news received from the international news agencies.) Thus, during the Persian Gulf War, people in Iran, as well as the people around the world, were not only poorly informed about the "why" of the war but were also misinformed and manipulated by correspondents and news agencies that reported only what the military wanted known.

Notes

1. Habib Chini, "Regional Cooperation: Only Positive Result of the Oil War," *Iran Export & Imports,*" no. 12 (May 1991): 90.

2. Ibid.

3. "Guerre du Golfe: Appel de journalistes," *L'Envers des Medias,* no. 2 (February 22, 1991): 7.

4. Ibid.

5. The reported data were a 20 percent random sample of the two time periods. No statistical tests were used in this preliminary report. The data were presented in a series of crossbreaks. As the sample showed, in both time periods the two papers published eighty-four brief stories on the crisis and war, twenty-nine in the first time period and fifty-five in the second. Analysis of the brief stories was omitted. Content-coding reliability was 0.96 on the average for all variables.

6. Nathalie Magnan, "Comescope contre television: Video-resistance a l'heure des satellites," *Le Monde Diplomatique* (May 1991): 15.

WESTERN MEDIA: GUILTY UNTIL PROVED INNOCENT
Khawla Mattar

Arab public opinion was one of the most important casualties of the Gulf War. From the beginning of the crisis until the outbreak of the war, the British public was not informed by the media about the Arab reaction, with the exception of Jordan. Demonstrations in the Jordanian capital were given enough coverage because the British media took the side of the British government in its continuing attack on the Jordanian king and his country. King Hussein, an old ally of the West, was a big disappointment to the Western leaders when he sided with Iraq. Reporters in Amman insisted on saying, in each and every dispatch they sent, that the majority of the Jordanian population was made up of Palestinians. They were implying that Palestinians were the only ones against the war and were thus siding with the Iraqi dictator.

At the same time that demonstrations were taking place in Amman, other Arab capitals were being stormed by thousands of angry people who were not happy to see another Arab country being destroyed by the West. There were demonstrations in Sudan, Libya, Algeria, Tunisia, Mauritania, Yemen, Morocco, and even Egypt, which had sided with the United States and its Allies. British and U.S. media either ignored or had brief news items about the unrest in Cairo where many were shot and killed and others were arrested. In other Arab countries with high amount of repression, individuals talked privately about their anger at the West.

Even in Saudi Arabia and other Gulf states, people were not happy with the Western presence and with the use of one Arab country to attack another. Contrary to the picture that the media tried to present (the people in this region were behind their leaders), Robert Fisk and a few other reporters gave a different version of the region. Fisk talked to many Saudis who told him that they were not in favor of the bombardment of Iraqi cities. Others told the *Independent on Sunday* correspondent John Bulloch that they did not like Saddam Hussein but that they favored him over George Bush and company. A Saudi businessman told Fisk that he was very upset with the U.S. presence in his country.[1]

The U.S. administration was able to acquire support for the war from most nations around the globe, with the exception of a few

(*continues*)

(*continued*)

Arab and Third World countries. Some countries with economic difficulties were bribed; others were promised a piece of land here or a backing there, at least for awhile. The Gulf countries, which have always been dependent on Washington, were ready to sign the letters sent to them by President Bush to authorize the Western military presence in their region. They even attempted to acquire an Islamic base of support for the deployment of non-Muslim armies that included females in a country where women are not even allowed to drive cars or travel without a *mahram* (male companion).

Other Arab countries that joined the U.S. coalition, such as Egypt, were promised a reduction of their debts or at least of interest on them. Syria was given billions of dollars as a bribe to send its forces to the Saudi desert. The Saudis and Kuwaitis were ready with their checkbooks to pay the bill of the new world order that was introduced with substantial help from the media.

NOTE

1. "The Calm Before Desert Storm," *Independent on Sunday,* January 20, 1991.

CHAPTER NINE

War Reporting: Collateral Damage in the European Theater

Farrel Corcoran

WHEN RONALD REAGAN pulled the U.S. plug on UNESCO in 1985 by withdrawing from the organization (and was followed by Margaret Thatcher pulling the British plug), his action was in massive protest against the sustained campaign by the nonaligned nations for a new world order that would rectify the ills of neocolonialism. When George Bush unfolded his vision of a new world order five years later following the 1989 revolutions in Eastern Europe, the shibboleth remained an empty signifier for many months. Nevertheless, it was clearly going to reflect a global alignment that would be North, rather than South, centered. With Iraq's invasion of Kuwait in August 1990, Bush's appropriation of the term *new world order* began to take on some real substance. By the end of the Gulf War seven months later, it could be said that never in recorded history had one view of how the world should be ordered received such near universal acceptance, at least in the First and Second Worlds.

This chapter sets out to explore the role of the mediated war in the Gulf as a symbolic construct within the general ideological process of building a hegemonic structure of thought and feeling around "modernity." I argue that just as previous wars in this century, such as the two world wars and the Vietnam War, have had well-documented cultural effects in destroying old ways of life and creating new ones, so is the Gulf War of 1991 now exerting a cultural impact, the outlines of which we are only beginning to discern. Just as the Gulf War has introduced new patterns of power and possibilities for politics, it has introduced new categories of thought and feeling.

Within its esthetic of realism and its code of objectivity, television seemed to be giving us the unmediated verisimilitude of the camera, but outside the frame of the picture were a number of pressures shaping what we saw. The first comprised the governmental and military news managers, on both the U.S. and the Iraqi sides, attempting to control what audiences in the different parts of the world thought about the conflict. The second pressure was the accepted flow of television into which war news must fit, news as show business, entertainment, and commercial product. We sit down for a night in front of the war ("Did you watch the war last night?"), and the gatekeeping system ensures that our night's entertainment will not be subjected to the shock of recognition of the human horror of what we are actually witnessing. Emotional responses in such conditions have yet to be fully explored. The third was the battle among television networks in multichannel areas, which had more to do with commercial competition than with getting the best news available. For many television systems worldwide, there was little scope for repackaging visual material coming from the Gulf, and therefore there was a great tendency to depend on the U.S. television view of events. The fourth pressure was the fact that much of what emerged from the region through television was not news at all but constant activity that produced a presence with no depth. The emphasis on live reports and on-the-spot coverage and the magnetic gravitation of the medium toward compelling images and dramatic events (nightly news centering on Scud and Patriot missiles streaking across a dark sky) reproduced an endless presence that annulled history.

Cable News Network

The most significant role in the televising of the war was played by CNN, which established its credentials very early by being the first network to "cover" the start of the war on January 16, with all the force of instant reaction, excitement, and danger. ("It looks like a million fireflies, like sparklers on the Fourth of July." "I've never been there, but this feels like the center of hell!" "Holy cow! That was a huge outburst.") We are told that George Bush learned of the start of the war from CNN, even before he was informed by the Pentagon. He was reported on the first night to be watching the nation go to war, almost exactly following his script, as he sat in a little study off the Oval Office clicking his TV remote control between ABC and CNN and calmly remarking, "Just the way it was scheduled." It was reported that the start of the war was simultaneously watched by George Bush, Saddam Hussein, Mikhail Gorbachev, John Major, and the emir of Kuwait, thus making CNN "an intercom service for world leaders" with its instant transmission of every unedited move on each side. The sense of timeliness and of being there central to the CNN style had already been established by its reporting from Tiananmen Square and Berlin in 1989.

It is now estimated that CNN is available in one hundred countries either directly or indirectly through conventional channels. It reaches 20 million household in the United States and has an audience of 7 million in Europe. Any thorough history of the Gulf War must take into account the enormous role played by CNN not only in its direct transmissions from the battle site but also in its ability to control the agenda for many other press outlets in print and broadcast journalism. Television's fascination with the minutiae of war, which creates a depthless, ahistorical presence is itself a powerful form of censorship and turns journalism into moral persuasion of the public that the war is fought by decent people for honorable objectives. Alexander Cockburn concluded that in such television coverage "the reporters—actors in fact—have mostly as little relationship to reality as the Greek chorus in Agamemnon debating among themselves what Clytemnestra is up to ("is that a noise I hear?") as she hacks the king to death" (*Nation,* February 19, 1991, p. 181).

Demonizing

If war reportage has the essential function of moral persuasion, a key part of its rhetoric in the case of the Gulf War was the demonizing of Saddam Hussein. A case in point was the charge against Iraq that 312 premature Kuwaiti babies were torn from incubators that were then shipped to Baghdad. This was the single most publicized atrocity, the most vivid evocation of Iraqi vileness. It was included in Amnesty International's report on the region and was publicly reported to the U.S. congressional Human Rights Caucus by a fifteen-year-old Kuwaiti girl. The story was seized upon by the Kuwaiti government in exile and was frequently alluded to in speeches by George Bush. Investigative journalism in January, however, disputed the story on the basis of the evidence of Kuwaiti doctors and nurses then in exile, including a Red Crescent doctor who reported the original story. Aziz Abu-Hamad, a Saudi consultant researching Iraqi atrocities for Middle East Watch, said no credible eyewitness or testimony was available to sustain charges of the mass murder of babies, though some newborns did die in hospitals because of shortages of medication and, in one or two cases, respirators (Alexander Cockburn, *Nation,* February 4, 1991, pp. 114–115).

The Amnesty International report was taken as authoritative in this instance, but other Amnesty reports on human rights violations in the region in 1990 were ignored. It would surely have been good journalistic practice to set side by side with the atrocities of Saddam Hussein Amnesty reports of torture by the U.S. allies: Kuwait, Turkey, Egypt, Saudi Arabia (atrocities against hundreds of thousands of Yemenis expelled in 1990), and Syria (electric shock, beatings with metal cables, water immersion). The human rights record of Saudi Arabia in particular was strictly off limits, despite the platoons of reporters and camera crews in the area. Of special interest to U.S. journalists might have been the case of Abdel Rahman Munif, whose portrayal of Americans in his book *Cities of Salt* resulted not only in banning of the book but also in his being stripped of his citizenship.

Smart Weapons

If the function of war reportage is to persuade the citizenry that war is being fought by decent people for honorable objectives, then in the Gulf news became saturation advertising for "smart weapons," which kept the scales of morality heavily weighted in favor of the United States and its allies. The predominance of retired military officers on both U.S. and British television kept a news emphasis on the smart weapons and on how they would be used in advance of the ground offensive. Consideration of possible scenarios to end the war without more human bloodshed was thus crowded out. No questions were asked about the effect and placement of B-52 carpet bombings. No questions were asked about what an Iraqi "military asset" was until mid-February, when it became clear that the civilian infrastructure of Iraq was under full-scale bombardment: water and irrigation systems, pumping stations, roads, bridges, bus terminals, telephone exchanges, and so on. The term *collateral damage* began to surface with greater frequency amid all the military jargon, but there was little scrutiny of what it meant. The fascination with high-tech weaponry was producing its own collateral damage on television viewers, the flavor of which can be sensed in the following:

> "We *hate* the war," a young mother, veteran of countless progressive, political and cultural battles of the last decade, said after a few days of watching techno-combat over Iraq. "But we are *into* the planes." She and her husband had marched against U.S. aid to El Salvador and for women's reproductive rights. Now settled in front of their TV, they admired with delicious excitement, the wheeling and diving of F117As, A-6Es and FA-18s, the matchless tornadoes, Apaches, and Wild Weasels, the lumbering deadly B52s. "We don't think of them as weapons," the woman said, suddenly apologetic, "they are like new cars." (Editorial, *Nation,* February 11, 1991, p. 147)

Former U.S. Attorney General Ramsey Clark visited Iraq during the bombing campaign and reported in detail on the extent of "collateral" damage to the civilian infrastructure. Included in his report was the declaration that the air assault deliberately targeting the civilian population of Iraq constituted a war crime (*Nation,* March 11, 1991, p. 309). Later he suggested that General Norman Schwarzkopf should be tried for war crimes. This report was largely ignored by the mainstream media, as was the U.N. Mission report that Iraq had been sent back to a preindustrial age. Later visitors to the country (for example, Erika Munk, *Nation,* May 6, 1991, p. 583) documented the likely long-term effects of the bombing campaign on the civilian population, in particular the breakdown of the water and sewage system. Its effects will show up slowly, especially in children in the form of cholera and typhoid epidemics. As in other human disasters involving disease and famine in other parts of the globe, the fear is that the long-term effects of this high-tech, low-gore, heavily censored war will not be telegenic and will therefore remain invisible even when the U.S. networks feel that the pressure to be patriotic above all other responsibilities has eased.

Economic Motives

What was *not* reported by the mainstream media during the Gulf War also merits attention. Among these invisible aspects were (1) the links between the Iran-Iraq War and the Gulf War and (2) the economic motives underlying the latter war. As Pierre Salinger (1991) pointed out, on the day after the Iran-Iraq cease-fire, Kuwait increased its oil output in violation of an OPEC agreement and increased extraction from the disputed border wells of Rumalah. These moves marked the beginning of the countdown to the Gulf crisis of 1990–1991.

The Kuwaiti move had the effect of beginning the process that would drive down the price of oil. Iraq, it is claimed, lost $1 billion per year for every $1 drop in the price per barrel at a time when Saddam Hussein was under pressure to return money lent by Kuwait and other oil states. Salinger wondered if the Kuwaitis, feeling sure of U.S. support after consultation with the CIA in November 1989, deliberately provoked Iraq by overproducing oil, driving down the price, drawing oil from a field located across a disputed border, and refusing to lease the Bubiyan Islands (unused by Kuwait but strategically important to Iraq). And in the period between November 1989 and August 1990, U.S. signals were confusing. Diplomatic cordiality and encouragement were followed by hostile Voice of America broadcasts.

Historical Amnesia

The historical amnesia brought about by high levels of uniformity across the dominant media resulted in the closing down of cognitive space within which to compare the Gulf War with similar recent events. Throughout the period of the Gulf crisis, for instance, it should have been normal to see discussion of parallels with other invasions across sovereign borders.

In 1983, the United States invaded Grenada, overthrew the government of Maurice Bishop, and ruled the country under a state of emergency for twelve months. In 1989, the United States invaded Panama, overthrew the government of Manuel Noriega, and established a new government the same day at Fort Clayton, a U.S. military base. In 1979, France invaded the Central African Empire and overthrew Emperor Bokassa. In each of these cases, there were no repercussions from the United Nations. In the past few decades, Israel occupied the West Bank and Gaza, Indonesia invaded East Timor, and Turkey invaded Cyprus. All three were condemned by the United Nations, but they repeatedly ignored U.N. resolutions and continued to receive massive military aid from the United States.

Two other invasions show clear parallels before the invasion (a neighboring country suffering from government-controlled terror, famine, and genocide, with no internal opposition and only a token force of exiles outside) but no parallels after. In 1978–1979, when Tanzania invaded neighboring Uganda to overthrow the government of Idi Amin, initially there were token speeches in international bodies about violation of international law. But then international help was quickly provided, including peacekeeping forces that allowed a new government to take shape in Uganda. At about the same time, Vietnam invaded neighboring Kampuchea to overthrow the government of Pol Pot. But in this case, the consequence was the total political and economic isolation of both countries right up to the present day (even after the withdrawal of the Vietnamese army) and the installation in 1990 of the renegade Pol Pot as Cambodian representative at the United Nations.

This selective treatment by the superpowers and the United Nations of these invasions was not a theme in mainstream press coverage of the Gulf War. Nor were thoughtful juxtapositions when different Arab groups were criticized for supporting Iraq. The treatment of Palestinians was a case in point. The image of Palestinians cheering at the spectacle of Israelis sitting in sealed rooms wearing gas masks as Scud-warning sirens wailed outside seemed pernicious and vile without a comparison of the suffering endured by Palestinians throughout the *Intifada:* nine hundred Palestinians dead, eighty-eight from gassing; dozens of accounts of torture at the hands of Israeli police; 1,726 homes destroyed, many by bulldozing, in acts of reprisal by the Israeli military (Palestine Human Rights Information Center, *Nation,* February 18, 1991, p. 1988).

The closing in of ideological space left no room to query some of George Bush's interpretations of history. The most important of these was of what happened in Vietnam, often implied in comments such as his assertion in his address to the nation on the night of January 16 that this time U.S. forces would not fight "with one hand tied behind their backs." Once again, it was the alternative, rather than the mainstream, press that reminded its readership that U.S. forces had in fact killed almost 2 million people in Vietnam. It was the alternative press that allowed readers to wonder what the damage might have been if U.S. forces had had both hands loose.

The European Theater

One interpretation of what happened in the Gulf was that the United States became the direct inheritor of the British Empire in the Middle East, moving from ruling by a series of unsavory proxies (including Saddam Hussein until August 2, 1990) to being physically present and directly engaged. This posed a particular problem for the Left in its inability to replace the shattered Soviet model with a radical project of its own. To judge by the reaction of Neil Kinnock, Felipe Gonzales, and François Mitterrand, there was little semblance of such an alternative in Europe during the Gulf War. Any attempt by a left-wing party to move into the political mainstream clashed with the notion that opposing the Gulf War meant again becoming "odd party out" caught on the wrong side of the line.

All these developments had significance for the rapidly evolving integration of the European Community. In 1993 the single market will be achieved, to be followed by a joint monetary policy and a common European central bank. By the year 2000 it is likely that an enlarged EC will include Sweden, Norway, Finland, Austria, and Switzerland and will be experiencing migration pressure on its Eastern frontier. A search for a common foreign and defense policy is already under way, and the mainstream press coverage of the Gulf War was not shy about making linkages between the Middle East crisis and the future of Europe.

The implication of much of the Gulf War reportage was that a stronger Europe must be pro-U.S., not an alternative to the United States in the global balance of power. This was suggested in the continual references to Germany's "slowness to support," "lukewarm response," and "checkbook diplomacy." Germany hesitated (and demonstrated more forcefully against the war than any other European country) because it was "traumatized by its past."

France, too, was seen as hesitating, especially until the resignation from the cabinet on January 29, 1991, of Jean Pierre Chevenement, who warned that the logic of war risked moving France even further from U.N. aims. This was a thinly veiled reference to France's reluctance to endorse the U.S. idea of going beyond "liberating" Kuwait to smashing the Iraqi military-industrial complex. Chevenement's resignation certainly destroyed the myth of the stubborn French resisting the U.S. imperial drive in the Gulf because the French government could no longer pretend once war started that its 13,000 troops would limit their action only to Kuwait and regard Iraq itself as out of bounds.

A Peripheral View

What can be learned about these vast global ideological realignments by looking at the Celtic periphery of the European Community? The Irish press has always been characterized by a fairly high level of dependence on the international wholesalers of news (see Bell 1987). In the case of television particularly, this situation was reinforced during the Gulf War. Because British satellite and terrestrial channels are available over much of Ireland, the two local advertising-supported public-service channels, RTE 1 and Network 2, found themselves in a certain state of competition in the provision of up-to-date coverage of the Middle East. As with many other television stations worldwide, the role of CNN by relay was very significant. As RTE's head of news, Joe Mulholland, noted, the decision to relay CNN's coverage on the first day of the war was "not only the right decision but was the only decision we could make" (*Irish Times Weekend,* January 26, 1991, p. 1). In a situation in which the government had decided to put a ceiling on RTE's income in order to divert advertising revenue to nascent commercial channels, RTE managers were under more than usual pressure to ensure that they would not lose audiences to other networks. After the initial stages of the war, RTE dropped the continuous CNN relay but returned to it when "there were dramatic developments."

The print press was less dependent on and aligned with the perspective of the international news wholesalers. The *Irish Times* made good use of its own roving reporter in the Middle East and of the services of such independent commentators as Robert Fisk. According to Alexander Cockburn, the *Sunday Tribune* was the only major Western newspaper that took a clear moral position against the war. Its January 28, 1991, editorial argued with vigor and detail that the Gulf War did not fit the criteria laid down in Catholic theology for a "just war." The March 3, 1991, editorial was a very strong condemnation of the U.S. slaughter of the Iraqi conscripts attempting to leave Kuwait and an even stronger condemnation of the Irish government for congratulating the United States on its victory. The *Tribune* editorial demanded:

What kind of international order is it that permits the infliction of weapons of vast destruction on an entire country, including its civilian population; what kind of international order is it that proceeds headlong towards war without conscientiously exploring all other options; what kind of international order is it that permits the gratuitous prolongation of a war of such destructiveness *after* the central objectives of the war have been attained? . . . Above all, this war has exhibited a contempt for human beings or at least human beings of a particular ilk. The contempt was shown in the conduct of the war but it is also shown in the fawning congratulations being offered to those who have achieved such a great "success" at such a horrific price.

Neutrality

If it is true that national history conditions moral postures, then it is true that the postcolonial situation in which Ireland finds itself ensured that its media would remain at least pluralistic in their attitudes to the war. Political parties on the Right, including the government coalition, supported the war; those on the Left were in opposition. The Catholic archbishop of Armagh condemned the war, while many of his colleagues in the U.S. Catholic hierarchy agreed with such Protestant leaders as Archbishop Robert Runcie that the war was just. Ireland therefore found itself in a mix of information about and attitudes toward the Gulf crisis. And in the new space opened up in public discourse for thinking about the Gulf crisis, particularly the European response to it, the question of Ireland's traditional policy of neutrality surfaced again. While left-wing parties pointed out the dangers to neutrality posed by the Gulf War, right-wing parties focused on the need to shoulder a share of democracy's defense burden.

The scattered elements of this debate acquired a concrete focus when the United Nations requested that U.S. aircraft en route to the Gulf be serviced at Shannon Airport. A refusal of facilities—that is, an alignment with socialist thinking in Ireland—would have led to a revolt by the right wing parties in parliament and within the government coalition itself. The major coalition partner decided discretion was the better part of valor (perhaps remembering the outcry in Britain nine years previously when the Irish government adopted an independent stance during the Falklands crisis) and granted the U.N. request. The example of Austria was cited in agreeing, despite neutrality, to allow German arms shipments through Irish territory en route to the Gulf. The opposition in Parliament argued that granting refueling and landing facilities to war planes meant that Ireland was "participating" in the war and that this required full parliamentary assent. The government insisted, however, that Ireland was still acting as a neutral country, though having to abide by the obligations of EC and U.N. membership.

Many commentators saw this policy as following a line between contradictory positions and giving the impression that Irish foreign policy was facing different directions at once. The situation was complicated by fact that Ireland had substantial economic interests (mainly in the food sector) in Iraq and that many of its citizens were trapped for a long period in Kuwait as Iraqi hostages. The impression of an inconsistent foreign policy was reinforced when Ireland was singled from the other EC countries by the Iraqi foreign minister, Tariq Aziz, as having a "balanced" attitude toward the takeover of Kuwait.

There was a strong awareness in the country of two opposing factors. First, 70 percent of the Irish public was shown in polls to be supporting neutrality, and second, it was important to monitor the U.S. awareness of who stood with the United States in the crisis. For example, when asked if the United States felt "grateful" for the permission it received to use facilities at Shannon, a U.S. Embassy spokesman said, "We sent thousands of people to implement the U.N. resolutions and some did not come back. Ireland did not discriminate against the relatively few U.S. planes that transited through Shannon; they paid the same landing charges as other aircraft. How grateful do you think we should be?"

The debate on Irish neutrality in the wake of the Gulf War has now broadened out into the context of EC moves toward a common foreign and defense policy. On the one hand, the Labour Party at its annual conference in April was reminded by its leader that Ireland should retain its determination to stand apart from military conflict and to offer itself in its traditional role as peacemaker and healer of the sick and wounded.

> We will be told that it's an untenable position because it will condemn us to a passive role in the development of a new Europe. That is a totally dishonest argument. Small countries committed to peace always have a role to play and we should play it with pride and belief in ourselves. And to those people who are daily suggesting that we should be part of some European military operation let us say one thing, and one thing only: the day we abandon our military neutrality is the day that we discover that we are seen as just another puppet. (Dick Spring, *Irish Times,* April 8, 1991, p. 4)

On the other hand, the junior partners in government have been arguing that Ireland can no longer remain part of Europe and still avoid military commitments. They have even gone so far as to criticize their cabinet colleague in foreign affairs who refused to attend a ministerial meeting of the Western European Union defense body in Paris as an observer when a joint European military response to the Gulf was being discussed. And in a yet wider context, both Austria and Sweden are seeking accession to the European Community (despite their previous position that their neutrality would have to keep them out) and have openly acknowledged that their foreign policies will not have to be radically redefined with the end of the cold war.

In any case, Ireland's position on neutrality will have to be reexamined as a result of pressures within the EC, but there is no doubt that this reexamination has been hastened and redefined by the Gulf War and its link with the idea of a new world order. Some Irish politicians, such as John Cushnahan, even join enthusiastically in the British and U.S. game of EC-bashing: "The E.C. emerged with little credit from the Gulf War. . . . Its total impotence underlines the imperative need for a foreign policy and defence role for the Community if it wants to make an independent and major contribution to shaping a New World Order" (*Irish Times,* April 19, 1991, p. 5).

Conclusions

The sheer scale and intensity of Gulf War reporting (as distinct from the scale and intensity of the military onslaught itself) have dramatized the problem of global news uniformity in a new way. Indeed, they have raised questions about some elements of EC culture and information policy that would encourage the notion of European news uniformity, as in the recent suggestion from the commission that Europe needs its own answer to CNN. This problem can be seen at its starkest in a small country at the edge of Europe that is nevertheless one of the twelve autonomous states making up the EC and is currently feeling relentless pressure from its partners to abandon its traditional policy of neutrality. An analysis of the impact of mediated war on Ireland and its relations with the rest of the world may hold lessons for other countries with similar levels of economic development and similar configurations of information dependence, perhaps in Eastern and Central Europe.

Ireland is part of the Anglophone world, but because of cultural and historical factors, Ireland is not (yet?) fully aligned ideologically with its dominant tendencies. This is especially true in the area of foreign policy, as witnessed in the neutral stance Ireland adopted during World War II and the Falklands crisis. Media dependency—which in this case extended beyond the foreign-owned wire services in print and broadcast journalism to include satellite-delivered television—is the structure through which representations of Anglo-U.S. intentions in the Gulf and the conduct of the war itself were constructed. Access to such foreign television services as Sky News, NBC News, and CNN, all of which have already been heavily criticized for offering ideologically closed, tightly constructed war coverage, helped to suppress the tragic human reverberations of the killing of up to a quarter million people in six weeks. This has meant that an Anglo-U.S. geopolitical worldview has made substantial inroads into the Irish press system in general, both directly and indirectly through influence on the news agenda of indigenous media institutions. Although far from being hegemonic in a part of the Anglophone world that has its own traditions of independent comment on world affairs, this influence has had a significant impact on the political system, if not on the popular consciousness. In particular, it has quickened the country's participation in a European foreign policy debate that seems to be evolving out of frustration at not being able to mount an EC presence in the Gulf.

Not only is there an ideological correlation between the success of the technology of war and the moral superiority of the cultures that produced it; there is also a linking of scientific and cultural modernity with morality and freedom. In Ireland, and in other countries that used to call themselves nonaligned, an ideological link is being forged between the new world order and modernity. As David Lloyd put it, the unqualified military success of the U.S.-dominated coalition means "the triumph of a global narrative which allows for only one version of human history, the gradual incorporation of all nations by a Western notion of development or modernity" (Lloyd 1991, 4). This incorporation of a Western notion of modernity may ultimately be an important part of the collateral cultural damage caused by the Gulf War.

References

Bell, D., ed. 1987. *Is the Irish Press Independent?* Dublin: Media Association of Ireland.

Lloyd, D. 1991. "The Gulf War and the New World Order." *Irish Reporter* 2 (2nd quarter).

Salinger, P., and E. Laurent. 1991. *Secret Dossier: The Hidden Agenda Behind the Gulf War.* London: Penguin.

CHAPTER TEN

Ruling by Pooling

Stig A. Nohrstedt

IT IS WORTH ANALYZING the news coverage of the Gulf War from a historical perspective. In particular, the experiences from, and the interpretations of, the Vietnam War are important if one is to understand what was and was not reported from the conflict in the Persian Gulf.

Just as the Germans did regarding their surrender in World War I, leading U.S. military circles developed a dagger-thrust (*Dolchstoss*) myth to explain and in fact deny the U.S. defeat on the battlefield of the Vietnam War. But whereas the Nazis blamed cowardly officers for Germany's defeat, U.S. military leaders blamed the media. According to this view, the television coverage of the Vietnam War caused the home front to withdraw its support for U.S. forces and eventually made the president and Congress change their minds. The truth, however, is that the more critical media coverage came after, not before, the military defeat.

The myth of the Vietnam War had a great impact on relations between military forces and the media in the conflicts after Vietnam. Starting with the Falklands War, and followed by the Grenada and the Panama operations, a completely new policy for dealing with journalists was established by Western defense departments and armed forces. This was again revealed at the beginning of the air battle between the allied forces and Iraq, when in a televised speech just a few hours after the first attacks President George Bush said that the operation would "not be a new Vietnam" and that this time U.S. forces would not have to fight with one arm tied behind their backs. This was a clear declaration of unrestricted support for the forces and a promise that the home front would not be allowed to waver. This declaration also suggested the conditions for the news media in the Gulf War.

Whereas during the Vietnam War journalists were free to move about and were consequently able to demonstrate the falsity of some of the information delivered at the "five o'clock follies" (the press conferences), in the Falklands War only thirty journalists from the whole international community, apart from the Argentineans, were allowed to cover the war on the battlefield. They were all transported there by the British Royal Navy on the condition that they had signed a contract accepting complete military censorship (Knightley 1982; Glasgow University Media Group 1985; Morrison and Tumber 1988).

The news coverage of the Falklands War was thereby controlled and managed according to the requirements of propaganda and military aims. After the war, some leading representatives of the media and the military forces met to reach some sort of compromise, if possible, between security needs and the right to information. The problem with this "solution" was that it only considered what the rights of the journalists and the military were and completely neglected the citizens' right to information.

The experiences from the reporting of the Falklands War, particularly the experience of the media policy applied by the British forces, probably inspired the U.S. Defense Department to develop a new and harder strategy for relations with the media during military conflicts. So in Grenada no television photographers were allowed to cover the invasion (Morrison and Tumber 1988, 346). In the case of the Panama operation, hardly any visual sign of the approximately two thousand dead was in evidence in the media.

In sum, it seems that U.S. as well as U.K. military authorities have developed considerable suspicion toward the media and consequently have devised a strategy of restrictions, especially for television, in crisis situations. According to David E. Morrison and Howard Tumber (1988, 350), this broad symbolic offensive is intended to give a new meaning to the foundations of democracy.

There were in principle four different restrictions on journalists in the Gulf War. The most debated was censorship of reports. Nevertheless, censorship was hardly the most essential restriction on the media in this conflict. The media image of the war was ruled by restrictions on journalists' freedom to visit front areas, troops, damaged buildings, and so on without military escorts.

First, many, if not most, of the world's media could not to send their journalists to the area of conflict because neither Iraq nor Saudi Arabia gave them visas. (Although the restrictions in the former country were even more severe, I concentrate here on the conditions in the latter.) Most affected were the media outside the alliance because media from the participating countries were given priority. For example, no Swedish prestige newspaper had its visa applications accepted.

Second, of those journalists allowed to get into Saudi Arabia, only a small number had the opportunity to visit the front and the troops because the limited places offered in the so-called pools were reserved for journalists from the countries actively involved in the war. Not all the journalists from the participant countries were included in the pool groups; a total of 800 journalists had to share 133 pool seats.

Third, the pool journalists for their part were escorted by troops during the two or three weeks they spent visiting the military units, and their reports were censored either through what they were allowed to see or through controls before dispatch. These journalists were also obliged to distribute a report at the press centers in Riyadh and Dhahran for common use by the press corps assembled there.

Fourth, journalists who did not accommodate themselves to the rules stated by the central command were threatened with losing their accreditations. In some cases, this threat was implemented, at least for short periods (hours or a couple of days). Journalists were also threatened with deportation.

The official reasons for those rules were natural and hardly questionable. The intention behind the restrictions was to avoid sensitive information, the disclosure of which might endanger the security of the coalition and get into the hands of the enemy. So information about the size of military units, movements and destinations, arms, and so on was not to be revealed. Another purpose behind the rules was to stop pictures of wounded or killed soldiers from reaching their relatives through media channels. The essential point here, however, is that every crisis situation involves critical judgments about the balance between the democratic right of information and security interests. And as has been documented by John Fisk on several occasions, restrictions on the media were used for purely propagandistic purposes (*Independent,* February 6, 1991). If truth is the first casualty in war, then this is certainly a problem for democracy.

The Swedish Journalists in Saudi Arabia

To what extent was the coverage of the Persian Gulf War by the Swedish journalists different from that in the dominant Western media? The prestige papers in Sweden did not get their visa applications to Saudi Arabia accepted. Only two evening papers, *Aftonbladet* and *Expressen;* the national news agency, TT; the Swedish Broadcasting Company's news program, "Ekot"; and two television news program, "Aktuellt" and "Rapport," were admitted. The first to arrive were Stefan Borg of *Aftonbladet* and Peter Kadhammar of *Expressen,* who from different directions landed in Saudi Arabia on January 23. The other Swedish journalists arrived in mid-February. In all, six journalists with photographers from Sweden were allowed to cover the war from Saudi Arabia. The other reporters were Henrik Samuelsson of "Aktuellt," Mats Remdahl of "Ekot," Ingmari Froman of "Rapport," and Stefan Hjertén of TT.[1]

From the very beginning of their visit to Saudi Arabia, the Swedish journalists realized that they would not be offered seats in the regular pool groups. A few of them participated on one or two occasions in quasi-pool arrangements such as the daily fuel-aircraft trip over Saudi Arabia. But four of them chose to move to the front line between Saudi Arabia and Kuwait, where they could move freely along the border and visit the Arab and Egyptian military units stationed there. All four noted with a certain amount of satisfaction that it was more of an advantage than a disadvantage that they were not allowed to join the pools because they wound up giving another image of the conflict than the polished picture of the clinical war.

That the Swedish correspondents were shut out from the pools probably influenced their ethical judgments. And it is interesting to notice how the pool privileges were carefully watched over by the pool journalists. Robert Fisk from the *Independent* mentioned how he was accused of disturbing the work of the colleagues in the pool when he revealed that information from the press officers concerning the battle of Ra's al Khafji was not correct (*Independent,* February 6, 1991). A similar story was told by Ingmari Froman. After a Scud attack, she and her photographer tried to take a camera position on the roof of the Hyatt Regency, where the press center in Riyadh was established. But all the space on the roof had been divided among the pool media, and the Swedish team as well as others excluded from the pools was denied access.

Not many of the Swedish correspondents cared to follow the press conferences arranged by the central command. Most of them visited a few briefings more out of curiosity than professional interest. Their editorial home offices had access to the information through CNN and Sky News so they saw no reason to cover these briefings.

One journalist did describe the press conferences as a quiz show arranged by the military in which the press corps asked questions they did not expect to be answered and the press officers more or less eloquently avoided answering. The most frequent answer was that the war was continuing as planned, which was not very useful from a journalistic point of view. Mats Remdahl thought it was remarkable to watch how the U.S. journalists took part in the show how and how they walked around the press center dressed in combat fatigues thinking they were covering the war.

Froman spoke of what she regarded as complacency on the part of the U.S. journalists:

I was very much surprised by the reactions from the American journalists. I have seen them in action on other occasions, you know. I know how tough, hard, and without sentimentality they are in their work. But that, I must say, was tremendously absent here in Riyadh; quite a lot of the journalists followed the military's tune and . . . put questions about "we" and "us," "our troops" . . . and adopted all the military jargon, which I think is below the dignity of a journalist. And I think that mainly the American journalists, who have had a key position here, gave in surprisingly.

It seems plausible that Robert Fisk and other independent journalists who first managed to reach the border area between Saudi Arabia and Kuwait opened the way for others, such as the Swedish correspondent who arrived on the scene a week later. All four Swedes chose Hafar al Batin as a temporary base during their stay at the front. Stefan Borg had earlier tried to reach the front along the coast road from Dhahran to Kuwait City but was stopped by the military. Several had had the same experience. But an attempt to follow another road in the northwest direction proved successful, and the outposts were no problem. In spite of the warning from the central command, there was considerable slack in the controlling of the vehicles. According to Borg, the trick was to drive on and wave to the soldiers at the checkpoints. Peter Kadhammar reported that when he and others occasionally asked whether they had permission to be in the area, they said yes, and although the soldiers knew this was not true, they did not bother the journalists. Remdahl was astonished by the unlimited freedom they had to move around; it was possible to take a taxi in Hafar al Batin and drive to the front line.

One of the reasons this area was particularly accessible was evidently that the military units there were from Egypt, Kuwait, Saudi Arabia, and Syria. Contrary to the forces from the Western countries in the alliance, these units did not care much about implementing the central command's rules with regard to contact with the media. The journalists admitted that they particularly avoided the U.S. units.

The four Swedish correspondents who made their way to the front stayed there during the week before the ground offensive, which started February 24. When the central command realized that journalists were staying in the area, a new declaration was published.

Media Guidelines

It has been noticed that some members of the media are traveling to restricted and military areas without escorts. This could present a danger to themselves and to the lives of the troops by attracting attention to their location.

Media Guidelines for Travel in the Kingdom Are as Follows:
1. If you are not sure of restricted areas, please check with the Saudi Military Information Bureau prior to your departure.
2. Non-pool and unescorted civilian media personnel are instructed to remain outside a 100-kilometer radius from Al-Khafji and surrounding areas.
3. Hafr al-Batin and surrounding areas are strictly off limits to all members of the media unless accompanied by escorts or given written permission.

The last lines of the bulletin contained a clear threat: "Failure to abide by these regulations will result in a withdrawal of press accreditation and possible deportation" (Borg 1991). According to Samuelsson, to underline that the threat was serious, immediately after the ground offensive had been initiated a Saudi officer showed the press corps in Dhahram twenty-two withdrawn accreditations of journalists who had tried to reach Kuwait via Khafji on their own.

In short, the Swedish front reporters congratulated themselves for being more or less forced to find their own ways of covering the Gulf War. Is there any cause for such congratulation besides their having reported the role of the Muslim battle units more than the dominant Western news media did?

The Mystery of Saddam's Defense Line

When the ground offensive started, the four Swedish journalists in the Hafar al Batin area followed it behind the units placed in that part of the front. Because these units were not engaged in the first thrust on February 24, the first hours were remarkably calm, as witnessed by Remdahl, who visited the Saudi Arabian, Egyptian, and Syrian units. In the nine o'clock news that morning, he reported no activity and not even a single soldier to be seen at the camps: "It seemed like they were sleeping in spite of the fact that the ground offensive had started."

Later in the afternoon, these units crossed the border into Kuwait. The Swedish and other journalists followed in their hired vehicles, which were marked with allied forces' plates. From this forward position they could closely cover the advance over the Iraqi defense lines of sand walls, oil-filled ditches, and minefields as well as the entry into Kuwait City. All four Swedish correspondents expressed the same astonishment at the nature of the so-called defense line.

Borg told me that he was "tremendously surprised" when he saw for himself what this defense line was in reality, after having read "horror stories about these enormous fortifications, burning oil ditches, etc." The ditches were no hindrance whatsoever after the allied air forces had made the oil burn out through napalm bombing. They ditches were only two meters wide and one meter deep and were easy to fill up. The Iraqi troops had only light equipment, hardly any bulletproof jackets, no heavy weapons, one or two antiaircraft guns, a few machine guns, and no tanks.

Remdahl expressed similar reactions. The Iraqi front-line units were pure "cannon fodder." They had only small arms, and there were even boy soldiers and handicapped "soldiers" among them. The captured Iraqi soldiers said that they had not been fired at. Remdahl assumed that the U.S. military command had all this information and already knew that this front line would be a very easy one to crack.

Kadhammer described the defense line as of World War I vintage. "It was so strange." Like Borg, Kadhammer also referred to what had been written about the defense line earlier—"these dreadful defense fortifications one had read about"—and how miserable they turned out to be in reality. He confirmed Borg's and Remdahl's reports that the most forward Iraqi lines had not been attacked by the allied forces before the ground offensive and that the fire had been concentrated on the back lines and supply lines.

Samuelsson found it "surprising" how badly equipped the Iraqi front-line units were but what astonishingly good shape the soldiers were in, considering the extensive air attacks that had been launched before the ground war. He mentioned that of a group of seven prisoners of war with one Kalashnikov each, only three of the rifles could be fired.

Three conclusions can be drawn from these interviews. First, the most forward Iraqi units had not been bombarded by the allied forces before the ground offensive. Second, the air attacks had been concentrated on units stationed further north in Kuwait and Iraq. Third, the central command had full knowledge of the status of the most forward Iraqi units and were well aware that the latter would not constitute any hindrance to the ground offensive. These conclusions raise the question of how the picture of Saddam's defense line, as spread by the media before the ground war, should be explained. It is plausible that the exaggerated image was an intentional public relations strategy applied by the central command. There certainly seems to have been a general tendency to describe Iraq and Saddam Hussein as a terrible and formidable opponent. The purposes of this characterization were probably to legitimize the massive assaults for the general public, to prepare public opinion for possible losses in the coming ground war by stressing a worst-case scenario (Regester 1989), and to make a coming victory the more glorious.

Unanimous sources confirmed that Iraqi forces left Kuwait City on the evening of February 25. The city was taken over by the Kuwaiti resistance and the U.S. marines. These events were not covered by the media for practical and technical reasons. But to give the press corps the opportunity to make the most out of the story and to gain the propaganda profits of the war, military authorities arranged continual flights from Dhahran and Riyadh to Kuwait City beginning on February 27.

On that day, the Kuwaiti units (which various sources described as comprising civilians in uniforms) within the allied forces made their triumphant entrance into the city. And the media were filled with films of enthusiastic Kuwaitis greeting their liberators and of stories about Iraqi terror and cruelty. But not all news reports followed these well-prepared tracks. The correspondents from *Aktuellt* found out that the *Arab News* (Saudi Arabia) report that a quarter million Kuwaitis had died of cholera and plague during the occupation was grotesquely exaggerated. Visits to the largest two of the five hospitals in Kuwait City showed that the first hospital had taken care of thirty patients and the other of forty patients.

Also worthy of consideration is the "Rapport" team's coverage of what happened on the "killing fields" of Kuwait—the massacre of probably thousands of Iraqis heading north from Kuwait City on the road toward Basra. The Swedish journalists went there March 3, a few days after the slaughter. The road was a mess of burned-out wrecks of cars and lorries that had been attacked while fleeing by the allied planes. According to Froman:

Then we were taken to this macabre highway, the escape way toward Basra, and saw this incredible vehicle cemetery. . . . Horrible, it was like doomsday or an apocalypse. . . . When we arrived they had, you know, shuffled away most of the bodies and buried them in mass graves in the desert. . . . But . . . by the sight of clouds of flies around the cars and an enormously pungent, disgusting stench one understood that there were still bodies left there. And in one place I saw a civilian car overturned, and there I saw, partly hidden under a blanket, a soldier with his legs cut off. . . . People came there then and lifted the blanket in order to see. I made my story on the victors coming there for inspection because for one thing there were a lot of Kuwaiti families who were there to look and who pulled the blanket away to see the swollen corpse and people who had their photos taken there beside the twisted, burned-out cars. Helicopter after helicopter arrived there with American Marine Corps who were there to look for war souvenirs. . . . It was presented to us as if it was soldiers on the retreat who were intercepted by allied aircraft just a couple of dozen miles northwest of Kuwait City. And they had taken everything, said the Saudi officers to us, to escape with—ambulances, private cars, grocers' vans, and all those cars were there, police cars as well. And then I said, "But how can you know that they were soldiers?" It could in fact have been civilians also, and it could have been Iraqis, civil Iraqis who have lived in Kuwait; it may also have been Kuwaiti hostages. And they only shrugged their shoulders. That is the kind of question you probably never will have any answer to. . . . They were caught like rats in a trap those Iraqis who had been put to rout. It was simply a bloodbath. They were just slaughtered. The whole time I was there I had the impression that this was the last kick by the already victorious superior at the defeated lying on the ground.

Ingmari Froman contended that she had written a rather sharp report about the victors' conduct of a postbattle inspection. But she was breathless when she heard that the editors at home had cut out the part where she took up the matter of the identities of the dead bodies.

The media of the allied countries took a completely dominating position with regard to the news flow from the Gulf War. Both in Iraq and Saudi Arabia it was mainly journalists from the U.S. media who had admittance and therefore unique access to the war scene. The big U.S. media, such as CNN, could thus send their teams to the area at an early stage and establish a position as a central source of information. The pool system strengthened their position because they had a monopoly on the more spectacular news material.

At the same time as the media policy of the allied states favored their own media, it achieved coverage within a framework dictated by military and propagandistic aims. There is no indication that sensitive information that could have threatened allied military operations was spread by the journalists. There is, however, considerable evidence that the news reporting followed the goal of encouraging the home front to support "our troops out there." Human suffering during the war was conspicuous for its absence in the news, there was no body count as in Vietnam, and the image of a clinical, computerized war, which glorified the technological superiority of the alliance, penetrated all media. There was also a substantial symbiosis between the media and the military authorities with regard to perspectives, partiality, and values. Dressed in combat uniforms the journalists fought in the very same war on the very same side and for the very same aims as the soldiers, who were responsible for the journalists' security and whose activities the journalists were assumed to be watching.

The final question to be asked is to what extent the coverage of the Gulf War by the Swedish journalists was different from that in the dominant Western media. When Kuwait City was opened for the press corps, all six Swedish correspondents were there, as were most of the correspondents in Saudi Arabia, and they probably transmitted reports that were similar to those of the others concerning Iraqi cruelties and Kuwaiti euphoria and gratitude. There are certainly some differences; but, for instance, the exposure of the role of the Arab units could hardly have contradicted the propaganda aims behind the pool system and the other restrictions. On the contrary, this exposure probably promoted allied propaganda aims because the regional support of the alliance was thereby more strongly emphasized and the otherwise insignificant Kuwaiti forces were lifted to the forefront.

Note

1. Information about these journalists' experiences was gained from telephone interviews with all six journalists. Borg was interviewed on March 20, 1991; Kadhammar, March 19, 1991; Samuelsson, March 19, 1991; Remdahl, March 27, 1991; Forman, March 18, 1991; and Hjertén, March 14, 1991.

References

Borg, S. "Media Guidelines." *Guardian,* Kopia till handahållen, March 4, 1991.

Fisk, R. "Free to Report What We're Told." *Independent,* February 6, 1991.

Glasgow University Media Group. 1985. *War and Peace News.* Glasgow: Open University Books.

Knightley, P. "The Falklands: How Britannia Ruled the News." *Columbia Journalism Review* 21, no. 3 (1982).

Morrison, D. E., and H. Tumber. 1988. *Journalists at War: The Dynamics of News Reporting During the Falklands Conflict.* London: Sage.

Regester, M. 1989. *Crisis Management.* Stockholm: Svenska Dagbladet.

CHAPTER ELEVEN

◆

Innovations of Moral Policy

Heikki Luostarinen

THIS CHAPTER DISCUSSES the new methods used in restricting and controlling the international media during the Gulf War from the perspective of Finland. In the U.N. Security Council, Finland voted for the right to use military power to oust Iraq from Kuwait. During the war, the Finnish media were highly dependent on Western news agencies and CNN. Only one Finnish journalist was accredited to Saudi Arabia.

The First Appearance

The air raid at the Gulf began on Thursday morning January 17, 1991. Agence France Presse announced four hours after the first attack that the allied forces had "almost totally" wiped out the Iraqi air forces and the Iraqi elite troops in Basra. All day long the news agencies reported that in the first wave of bombings eighteen thousand tons of explosives were dropped, which made it "the heaviest bombing in history." As many as twenty-five hundred planes were said to have taken part in the first strike.

The war was evidently running smoothly but hardly as well as was claimed. Finnish military expert Pekka Visuri (1991) estimated later that probably no more than three hundred planes took part and that they had no technological facilities to carry even two thousand tons of explosives. The exaggeration was thus about tenfold.

It seems likely that a premeditated information policy was put to use to convince oil markets, the world stock exchanges, Israel, and Western opinion of the success of the attack. The tactic worked because on January 18 the Finnish nationwide newspaper *Uusi Suomi* was reporting, "Oil prices underwent the greatest drop in history on Thursday. . . . As the markets opened in Europe, the first news of the Allied's successful attacks had spread to the world and this calmed the traders. . . . The stock exchanges everywhere responded to the Gulf War with substantial rises in prices."

In the international energy and commodity markets and stock exchanges, disturbances are created and spread fast, but their remedy may be slow and expensive. The allied forces, led by the United States, took the initiative and made sure that the "unofficial" reports dispatched at the early hours of the war were good enough and reassuring.

This happened in Finland, too. Gallup polls made just before and after the beginning of the air war showed that the acceptance of the war grew in forty-eight hours from 34 percent to 55 percent. The image of the war was getting better. The public was confident that the Western forces were able to beat Iraq very quickly and without any significant losses. The war, as it was presented in the media, was a more tempting perspective than the sanctions (Suhonen 1991).

Cultural Differences

According to many commentators, the coverage of the Gulf War reflected and reinforced growing Western racism, a belief in the technological and moral superiority of the Western societies, and their assumption of the right to control the world's strategic energy and raw material resources (see, e.g., Johnson 1991; Kaidy 1991). Various racist and ethnocentrist reactions can indeed be discerned both in the media and in the speeches of individual politicians. I do not believe, however, that racism was a conscious political aim of Western governments because in the long run this attitude would have been unreasonable. For instance, in France the ethnic and religious minorities are so large that waging a war under racist emblems would necessarily have led to internal conflicts and problems in the war's moral policy. Indeed, French media got special instructions during the war not to insult France's Islamic citizens or its North African business associates (Jaumain 1991).

Just before the war, the issue of racism in Finland was more acute than it had ever been in this very isolated country. About two thousand asylum seekers came from Somalia via the Soviet Union and caused a fierce public debate and some aggressive, racist reactions. The Finnish government, nervous because of the Gulf crisis and the turmoil in the Soviet Union, declared that Finland was ready to cancel its membership in the U.N. Refugee Convention. After the war, the Finnish government announced plans to cut back its development aid budget by about 30 percent.

The Gulf War encouraged the Finnish government to be more selfish toward the Third World. Otherwise, the ethnic aspect of the war was not important in Finland because there are no noteworthy ethnic minorities in this country, the population of which is perhaps the most homogene-ous in Europe.

Operational Advantages

The superiority of Western allied forces in the Gulf War depended on technological and strategic advantages and troop skills. It was important, for example, that Western forces were capable of crippling the enemy's intelligence so that even if Iraq did have efficient weaponry, it could not be used reasonably. Iraq also had no alternative but to depend on international media for information about Western troop maneuvers.

U.S. information officers attempted to prove their reliability in many ways. One government official told the *Washington Post* on January 19, 1991, "We really don't get engaged in disinformation" (Ray 1991). But later it was revealed that the U.S. Army had misled reporters on many occasions. The most important operational bluff occurred at the outset of the land battle. The United States wanted Iraq to believe that the focus of the offensive in Kuwait would be in the south and that it would be backed up by the landing navy. Hints implying this were dropped to the newspapers, and reporters waiting for the landing on the ships were served exceptionally well by army intelligence officers.

Iraq's own intelligence was apparently so confused after the air raid that its most important sources of information were the Western media. These were showing landing drills and various operational alternatives for the occupation of Kuwait. It is difficult to estimate, however, the extent to which Iraq relied on this picture.

The reports of the destruction caused by Iraqi troops in Kuwait had elements of disinformation, the objects of which were political rather than military. Kuwait's government in exile and the United States carried out a classic propaganda trick in which the media were fed with news about atrocities and brutalities. At least two advertising and public relations agencies were also taking part in the campaign. One Finnish correspondent reported from Kuwait on April 6, 1991:

> Andrew Whitley, the head of the international human rights organization the Middle East Watch, who investigates the violations of human rights in Kuwait, told us that the most famous of the "atrocities" performed by Iraqis in Kuwait was the claim that 312 infants were taken out [of] incubators with the result that the babies died. . . . The president of the United States, George Bush, appealed to this fact on six separate occasions in one month when persuading American opinion. . . . The fact of the matter is that no babies were taken out of incubators and that they were not stolen to Iraq, Whitley said. (Saksa 1991)

The effects of U.S. propaganda and disinformation could be seen in the Finnish press. Osmo A. Wiio (1991), a professor and an influential right-wing columnist, wrote that U.S. military leaders "can hide some information but not give deliberate disinformation." According to Wiio, the United States is an open democracy in which lies are quickly unearthed.

This childish confidence was quite common in the yellow press and in smaller newspapers. But most journalists shared a more cynical attitude: They emphasized in their stories that both sides of the conflict were using propaganda and censorship and that facts could not be checked. They told rumors but did not forget to mention the possibility of disinformation.

Clean War

Phillip Knightley, author of *The First Casualty* (1975), which deals with the history of war news, has described the special characteristics of the Gulf War (1991):

> Ever since the British invented military censorship in 1856 (to crush criticism of the way it was running the Crimean War) wartime news management has had two main purposes: to deny information and comfort to the enemy and to create and maintain public support. In the Gulf War the new element has been an effort to change public perception of the nature of war itself, to convince us that new technology has removed a lot of war's horrors.

Michael Getler (1991), the *Washington Post's* foreign editor, concluded that the Gulf War was a case of "the most thorough and sophisticated" control of reporters in the present day, the totality of which clearly surpassed that of the World War II, Korea, or Vietnam. Geoff Meade (1991) gave one example of the totality of control: When one British TV crew was trying to contact London from the desert, it was picked up by allied troops; the crew's calls had been traced by an airborne AWACS plane. Three different methods of controlling the media were applied during the war: feeding, competing, and restricting.

Feeding

The group responsible for the U.S. Department of Defense information at the Gulf comprised a varied collection of professionals. One was Michael Sherman, who had been director of the navy's public relations office in Los Angeles—the people who brought the world *Top Gun*. Sherman himself had been a consultant to Paramount Studios, and his past work included *Hunt for Red October* and *Flight of the Intruder* (Schmeisser 1991).

Film-making talent can be observed in the film material the U.S. Army produced for reporters' use. These imaginary views were repeated on television screens. Even though many journalists were well aware that this material was selective, they had little alternative but to use it.

Both the commercial and public channels of Finnish television were dependent on the material transmitted by the international agencies. All the skillfully filmed shots from attacking aircraft or from missile warheads were shown on Finnish television. But the journalists had the time and the desire to edit and comment on the material; they did not depend on the interpretations and impressions offered by the U.S. Army. Sometimes Finnish television even ridiculed the U.S. propaganda—an anti-U.S. attitude was not uncommon among these journalists.

Competing

Probably the most frequently repeated story about the covering of the Gulf concerned British journalist Robert Fisk, of the *Independent,* who met a U.S. television reporter in the Saudi Arabian border town of Ra's al Khafji. Fisk was on his own. The television reporter was a member of the military pool, and he declared, "You asshole. . . . You're not allowed here. Get out" (Schanberg 1991).

The official purpose of the pools at the Gulf was to protect journalists at the front and at the same time prevent any disturbances caused to soldiers by reporters. The pools were supposed to have helped and served journalists. The problem was that only about one-tenth of the representatives of the media accredited to Saudi Arabia got to be in the pools.

Journalists had no alterative but to fight over the army's favors because working outside the pools was very difficult, even impossible. The quarrel between Robert Fisk and the U.S. television reporter reflected how the pool was used as a method of censorship; if someone broke the rules, the whole pool was punished. Thus, journalists wound up controlling one another.

The Finnish press was handled by Saudi Arabian and U.S. officials as journalists from other small countries or from the Third World were: Very few visas were given because the presence of these journalists was not crucial for the Western military effort. But in a paradoxical way this freed the Finnish press to do better journalism. In the absence of its own news dispatches, the press produced and used more background material, and Finnish journalists were not fighting over the U.S. Army's favors because only one correspondent was there!

But the Finnish military soon realized what a golden opportunity the war created for public relations activities. In 1990, the Finnish government unilaterally cancelled some military limitations of the 1947 Paris Peace Treaty. The Finnish army bought more than sixty new fighter planes and dreamed of new weapon systems.

Because the press needed military experts, the army ordered several senior officers to work on demand as commentators. Nevertheless, the role of military experts was not as prominent in Finland as it seemed to be in the United States. For instance, representatives of the Finnish peace movement were interviewed quite often, and it was more a rule than an exception to use experts who questioned the morality and goals of Western warfare in a critical way.

Restricting

Journalists' access and interviews at the front required the permission and the presence of the military. For a temporary loss of credentials it was enough, as in the case of Chris Hedges of the *New York Times,* to interview Saudi shopkeepers fifty miles from the Kuwaiti border (Schanberg 1991). At first, officials wanted to tape-record all interviews, but later interviews could be conducted if an intelligence officer simply stood by and observed the situation.

Reporters were not allowed, however, to forward their material until it had been checked—that is, censored. Officially, the purpose of these "security reviews" was to prevent the enemy from getting any facts of military importance. But journalists were more inclined to think these reviews were a political action, the purpose of which was to influence the image about the war that was mediated to home. For instance, young Kuwaitis could not be filmed while playing soccer because "it is not good to show them playing while others fight" (Meade 1991). According to the censor, Stealth bomber pilots returning from their first combat mission could not be "giddy"; they had to be "proud" (Schanberg 1991).

Between Two Evils

The work of the censors was made easier by the fact that journalists had to take into account the home audience and many pressure groups. For example, CNN was reprimanded for helping the enemy because it aired the weather forecast for the battlefield. CNN had to assure its viewers that Iraq already had the information. Many politicians and organizations scrutinized the media for possible traces of defeatism, breaches of security, or "understanding" of the enemy.

After the war many journalists, especially those from the United States, described being caught between two evils: the Pentagon and the enthusiastic home front (Boot 1991). At the Gulf, censors usually had little work. Most journalists there identified with the army spirit and goals, were eager to take part in the training and fitness tests provided by the army, started to wear uniforms, and adopted army slang (Millar 1991).

In Finland many journalists identified themselves with Western interests and efforts. But because no Finnish troops were taking part in the fighting, the atmosphere was more calm than, for instance, in Britain or in Czechoslovakia. Because Finland is far from the Gulf but near the Soviet Union, during the war the Soviet crisis, not the Gulf, was often the leading story.

Finland was a bystander. The war was quite generally accepted by the press and the public, but without any real enthusiasm and with no pressure against opposition voices. The mainstream press was mainly pro-U.S., but it allowed other opinions to be published.

Only a few journalists were enthusiastic advocates of the war. One of them was the editor of *Helsingin Sanomat,* the leading Finnish prestige newspaper, who described the war as "a classical victory of Good against the Bad" (January 3, 1991). But it is illuminating of the Finnish debate that this sentence was ridiculed more than taken seriously.

A New, Happy War

According to one source, the U.S. public wanted to believe that the government was telling the truth. A "fast and vigorous" war was needed, and thoughts of censorship could be postponed until after the battle. A momentary patriotic joy swept through the country. The foreign editor of the *Baltimore Sun,* Richard O'Mara, described the public's identification with the military expedition as "manic." From coast to coast the country was filled with yellow ribbons as signs of support. The U.S. flag could be seen at many houses, and people who did not fly it were sometimes intimidated or even threatened (O'Mara 1991).

David Gergen's opinion was expressive of the situation quoted in (Valeriani 1991, 27, 28). Gergen worked as the head of information in Ronald Reagan's government:

> I can tell you that television had an enormous impact on our policy in Lebanon. We withdrew those marines from Lebanon in part because of television. We asked the Israelis to stop bombing in part because of the television pictures that were coming back from Beirut. In this particular crisis, though, television has had precious little impact so far on the course of the American foreign policy. . . . It is not an independent force in the crisis. . . . I have growing

concerns about the balance that exists between our institutions. We got into this war, frankly, without having a vigorous national debate in the country.

On the Western periphery, solidarity is felt and political support is given to the countries that do the dirty work of protecting the West's interests. The media are dependent on the centers of power, on what U.S. information officials decide can be seen (or not seen). But because countries like Finland are bystanders, there is no need to homogenize the opinions of the press or the public. It also happens that the political interests of the countries on the periphery are not in line with the interests of the great powers. The spectrum of opinions is and will be more wide.

References

Boot, William (Christopher Hanson). 1991. "The Press Stands Alone." *Columbia Journalism Review* (March-April).

Getler, Michael. 1991. "Do Americans Really Want to Censor War Coverage This Way?" *Washington Post*. March 17.

Jaumain, Yves. 1991. "Getting Their Own Back." *Index on Censorship* (April-May).

Johnson, R. W. 1991. "Rebirth of the Right." *New Statesman and Society,* March 8.

Kaidy, Mitchell. 1991. "War Brings Anti-Arab Racists Out of the Woodwork." *Guardian,* January 30.

Knightley, Phillip. 1975. *The First Casualty: From the Crimea to Vietnam—the War Correspondent as Hero, Propagandist, and Myth Maker.* New York: Harcourt Brace Jovanovich.

———. 1991. "A New Weapon in the News War." *Guardian,* March 4.

Meade, Geoff. 1991. "Hard Ground Rules in the Sand." *Index on Censorship* (April-May).

Millar, Peter. 1991. "Facts, Lies and Videotape." *European,* February 22–24.

O'Mara, Richard. 1991. "In a Gulf of Darkness." *Index on Censorship* (April-May).

Ray, Ellen. 1991. "How to Lie." *Lies of Our Times* (February).

Saksa, Markku. 1991. "Kupla nimelta Kuwait" (The Fallacy of Kuwait). *Iltalehti,* May 6.

Schanberg, Sydney. 1991. "Censoring for Military/Political Security." *Washington Journalism Review* (March).

Schmeisser, Peter. 1991. "The Pool and the Pentagon." *Index on Censorship* (April-May).

Suhonen, Pertti. 1991. "Suomalaiset ja "Aavikkomyrsky" (The Finns and the "Desert Storm"). *Rauhantutkimus* (February).

Valeriani, Richard. 1991. "Covering the Gulf War: Talking Back to the Tube." *Columbia Journalism Review* (March-April).

Visuri, Pekka. 1991. "Suurvalta murskasi ylivarustautuneen kehitysmaan" (A Super Power Wiped Out an Armed-to-the-Teeth Developing Country). *Sotila-saikakauslehti* (April)

Wiio, Osmo A. 1991. "Televisiosota?" (A Television War?) *Uusi Suomi,* February 7.

CHAPTER TWELVE

◆

Truth: The First Victim of War?

Rune Ottosen

DURING THE PRELUDE to the Gulf War, the U.S. government stressed that this war was not going to be another Vietnam. This goal manifested itself in military strategy, in propaganda, and in restrictions on press coverage. The latter were accomplished by methods tested and refined in previous wars. The strategy of press restriction can be summed up as follows: Keep the media as far away from war activities as possible for as long as possible, and put maximum restrictions on their working conditions.

The highly efficient press censorship carried out by the British Ministry of Defence during the 1982 Falklands War became a school for subsequent conflicts. During the initial phase of the war, when the battle of public opinion is assumed to be won, great restrictions were put on journalists' ability to gain insight into the conflict. Because military authorities checked and controlled all information during the first phase of the war, a favorable atmosphere was created for justifying the war as well as for presenting the military's own version of why war was necessary. Journalists were effectively prevented from getting hold of "unpleasant truths" regarding, for example, civilian casualties.

These were doctrines the U.S. military put to use during the 1983 invasion, in Grenada. News bulletins were prohibited for the first hours of the invasion, and no journalist was allowed information on war activities at close quarters. To this day we have no independent reports, photos, or TV footage of the invasion itself. As a result, the official U.S. version of the invasion—that it was carried out to "secure American lives"—dominated the news, even though those Americans involved never said they had felt threatened.[1]

Panama: A "Success Story"

This strategy vis-à-vis the press was developed with even greater success during the December 1989 U.S. invasion of Panama. The invasion was scheduled to take place during the Christmas season, coincidentally also overshadowed by the civil war in Romania and the fall of Nicolae Ceauşescu. Journalists were kept as far away from the conflict as possible. A small pool was set up where several media were expected to work together and to share the small amount of available firsthand knowledge of war activities. The only TV footage released was presented uncritically by TV stations all over the world without any mention that this was the official U.S. version of battle activities.[2]

Independent journalists trying to get into Panama were not admitted. Partly because of closed airports and borders, there was no access to the country. Furthermore, the three hundred journalists who arrived by chartered plane from Miami were detained in military barracks and kept there with only four outgoing telephone lines and little information to send home. After forty-eight hours they were told to choose between staying on where they were under the same conditions or returning to Miami. Most of them opted for the second alternative.

The military was able to command the news with its official statements, which maintained that the purposes of the invasion were to safeguard U.S. lives and get the "narcotic drug criminal Noriega." No mention was made that the CIA had originally helped him to gain control and had protected him despite his drug crimes.

The media were left with little room to present alternative reasons for the invasion. That Noriega had brought up the possibility of nationalizing the Panama Canal when the U.S. lease expired in 1997 seemed to be forgotten. Panama's resistance to U.S. support to the contras in Nicaragua, Panama's opposition to U.S. policy regarding the debt crisis, and a number of other possible contributory causes were left out of the picture.

As with the Grenada invasion, hardly any independent information was provided on battlefield activity itself. U.S. disinformation regarding the low number of losses and the few civilian casualties was not contested. According to official U.S. figures, 516 persons lost their lives. But an independent investigation maintained that as many as 5,000 people were killed during the invasion. In addition to human suffering, the material damage proved enormous, given the bombing and the lack of police protection to prevent extensive looting.

Panama's own news agencies, which continued presenting news during the invasion, were also quickly silenced. Radio Nacional continued to transmit programs and reports on what happened but was precision-bombed by a rocket from a U.S. military helicopter. The newspaper *La*

República, published reports on civilian casualties after the invasion. The following day U.S. soldiers attacked and cleared the editorial offices, detained editor Escolástico Calvo, held him for six weeks without due process of law, and transferred him to prison for an unlimited period of time, still without due process. Two other newspapers were closed, and the television station was placed under U.S. military command. At least 150 journalists were fired. No free press remained to judge the invasion and the new rule of President Guillermo Endara.[3]

Censorship also shaped the U.S. enemy picture, which was partly based on a forgery and partly on prejudice with racist undertones. All over the world, TV pictures were shown of Noriega's kitchen, with one bucket of white powder, supposedly fifty kilos of cocaine, and another bucket with blood, apparently to be used in a voodoo ritual. Later on it turned out that the buckets contained cornstarch and animal blood, both meant for a traditional Panamanian dinner dish. The mug shot of a humbled Noriega and his pockmarked face dominated global coverage. All these pictures distracted people's attention from an action that U.S. experts admitted was contrary to international law and condemned as such by the United Nations.

What U.S. military authorities had learned from these experiences was put to good use prior to the Gulf War. By setting up a so-called news pool, the military administration set a limit on the number of journalists at the front, thereby securing control of news coverage though an effective censorship system. Some 192 journalists from various agencies, TV stations, and newspapers were divided into groups and assigned to different military units. In theory, this was done to make all information from pool members available to all stations and newspapers while also safeguarding journalists. In practice, however, the system proved a more effective control of the journalistic process. The International Journalist Federation, representing 175,000 journalists throughout the world, protested the pool arrangement: "The way the pool system now functions, it represents a clear violation of press freedom. Important information is stopped and the system discriminates against non-British and non-American journalists."[4]

A restrictive set of rules was developed. Journalists were permitted to interview or take photographs of wounded U.S soldiers only in the presence of a military escort and only with the consent of patient, doctor, and commander. Other restrictions from the ground rules included the following: "The visual and audio recording of personnel in agony or severe shock are not authorized. . . . Imagery of patients suffering from severe disfigurement or undergoing plastic surgery treatments are not authorized. . . . Interviews with or visual imagery of patients undergoing psychiatric treatment are not authorized."[5]

These restrictions were obviously meant to obstruct pictures that might reduce the U.S public's fighting spirit. Other rules obstructed access to the pool for "undesirable" journalists. Two female journalists were not allowed to enter the pool because military authorities found that their questions at a press conference had been "impolite."[6]

It was, in fact, easy to keep a check on the journalists allowed to enter Saudi Arabia, as visas were required. To begin with, the Saudi government suggested that 42 correspondents would be sufficient to cover the Gulf War for the entire world press. Gradually the Saudis allowed more to enter, maybe because they realized there was nothing to fear from the media. By the end of the war, 72 British journalists, almost 1,000 U.S. journalists, and several hundred from the rest of the world were present in Saudi Arabia.

Through the pool arrangement military leaders developed a tendency to consider pool journalists as "their" journalists, an integrated part of their own forces. This became quite clear when the head of an air base at the front provided pool journalists attached to the base with small U.S. flags that had been kept in the cockpit of the first plane bombing Baghdad. When he gave them the flags, he said, "You are warriors too."[7]

Once journalists had been granted access to the pool, their attitude toward news gathering became highly competitive. Many were more concerned with protecting their exclusive right to news from the front than with giving other journalists reasonable access to information.

At the end of January, when Iraqi troops attempted to gain control of the border town of Ra's al Khafji in Saudi Arabia, pool reporters were kept several kilometers from the front and fed erroneous information that the town had been recaptured. The British prime minister proudly announced that the town had been reconquered. Journalists from the British newspaper the *Independent,* having made their own way to the town, could see that fighting continued. When the paper's journalists met the pool reporters, the latter proved more concerned with protecting "their information sources" than with correcting the misinformation. A furious reporter from a U.S. TV company shouted out at an *Independent* journalist, "You asshole; you'll prevent us from working. You're not allowed here. Get out. Go back to Dahran." He then called over a U.S. public affairs officer, who announced, "You're not allowed to talk to U.S. Marines and they're not allowed to talk to you." In another episode a reporter from the *Sunday Times* located a British regiment in the desert. He was then confronted by an angry British major accompanying the British press pool, who claimed that if the reporter did not leave, "You'll ruin it for the others."[8]

This divide-and-rule system functioned to perfection. The major victim was independent reporting.

Censorship

Experienced reporters were concerned with the extent of military censorship, which was far greater than was necessary to prevent the leakage of sensitive military information. Censorship was used to eliminate information that might create a negative picture of U.S. soldiers. On board the aircraft carrier *Kennedy,* journalists reported that the crew had watched porno videos before action. This was deleted by censors. But there was no objection to U.S. pilots saying when discovering Iraqi soldiers in Kuwait, "It was like turning on the kitchen light late at night and the cockroaches started scurrying. . . . We finally got them out where we could find them and kill them."

In addition to censorship, Western journalists were obstructed by their own cultural biases. As a result, it was easy to fall back on stereotypes instead of dealing with the conflict within an historic/structural framework. Muslim journalists also met with prejudice. Large media enterprises and news agencies preferred free-lance contracts with journalists from the Third World to avoid paying high insurance premiums. The Danish *Journalisten* (organ for the Danish Journalist Federation) reported that a Lebanese free-lance female journalist employed by a European TV company was sent to the front without the gas mask issued to regular employees on the grounds that she was not one of them and was therefore not essential.[9]

CNN correspondent Peter Arnett was called a traitor in Congress because he stayed on in Baghdad throughout the war. CNN transmissions around the clock meant a revolution in war journalism, even though the information may have given the wrong picture. We remember the CNN transmissions showing Iraqi Scud rockets on their way to Israeli or over Saudi airspace. The touch of drama seemed fit for TV, adding to the enthusiasm for one of the war heroes: the Patriot missile that time and again hit the Iraqi rockets. Later it was revealed that the Patriots brought more harm than good as they exploded full blast on the ground, together with the remaining elements of the Scuds.

TV screens were full of pictures of "smart bombs" accurately hitting the military headquarters in Baghdad. These carefully selected pictures played an active part in creating the myth that this was a matter of a rapid and efficient war intended to strike military targets only. We hardly saw the result of smart bombs that did *not* hit their targets or the result of the massive carpet bombing carried out over Basra and other densely populated areas. And we shall probably never know how many Iraqi people lost their lives in the war (according to a Red Cross estimate, 150,000–200,000).

Disinformation

Norman Schwarzkopf was pleased to describe how press agencies were deceived into contributing to the disinformation on Iraq. According to Agence France Presse, Schwarzkopf was happy that the press uncritically repeated his own exaggeration of the number of Iraqi ground forces when the ground war was being prepared. From intelligence sources the U.S. military knew that the Iraqi ground forces consisted of 350,000 troops, not the 540,000 repeatedly announced as the official number. Military leaders also knew that many military units were understaffed and that in the early phase of preparations Iraq already had great problems regarding fighting morale and desertion. Furthermore, they knew that allied forces would not encounter great problems when crossing mine-fields and that Iraqi artillery could not boast of accuracy. Thus, they were probably well aware that the risk of losses among their own soldiers was greatly exaggerated.[10] Yet disinformation on the "powerful Iraqi war machine" continued, possibly to avoid endangering the perceived legitimacy of the ground war. Gallup results revealed that 61 percent of French reporters who covered the Gulf War did not find their own work satisfactory; 53 percent wondered whether their credibility would ever be the same again.

Norwegian Media

A report from a meeting of the Norwegian Association for Newspaper Editors cited a Danish newspaper editor's claim that in this century the Gulf War was the one with the least satisfactory reporting. The only Norwegian journalist who reported the war from within Iraq said that the reporting from the war was a catastrophe, that the mass media had itself to blame, and that the media were "drawn into propaganda service for the Pentagon.[11]

The Gulf War also affected the general program policy of Norwegian broadcasting. Satirical series from World War I and World War II, such as the British-produced "Allo, Allo" and "Black Adder," were taken off the air. This was not the case with the U.S.-produced documentary series "War and Memories," which had a strong emphasis on U.S. patriotism. The editor in charge denied that this policy had anything to do with the war and that it was the result of the death of the Norwegian king.[12] But the series mentioned were not reintroduced until after the Gulf War was over, whereas program policy in other areas was normalized just a week after the king's death.

After Iraqi soldiers had been thrown out of Kuwait, Norwegian TV news broadcast an interview on March 1 with a Kuwaiti nurse who by means of injections had poisoned and killed twenty-two Iraqi soldiers during their stay in the hospital.

NURSE: "I gave them injections, killed them."
REPORTER: "To kill them?"
NURSE: "Yes."
REPORTER: "Did you kill many?"
NURSE: "Yes, maybe twenty-two. I got the chance to kill them in hospital."
REPORTER: "How did you do it?"
NURSE: "With injections; if he checked up, I gave the injections at the feet. If he wanted to check down I would go up, anywhere even in his neck, anywhere. If he screams, he does not know if it's from injection; it could be anything."

The reporter went on to comment, "But among the ruins in the partly demolished capital, the Kuwaiti people celebrate their freedom, cheering their liberators." Killing patients with poisonous injections is hardly in accordance with the ethics of the nursing profession, but here the action was presented as a heroic deed.

A journalist in the political department of one of the biggest and most influential Norwegian newspapers, *Aftenposten,* wrote, "[The critics] seem to have forgotten that the most important thing in a war is not to send reports home but to win. Thus the truth will always be subordinated to victory. And that is how it should be. . . . This means that in a war there are greater tasks than news reporting, and you have to know which side you are on."[13]

Notes

1. Hugh O'Shaughnessy, *Grenada: Revolution, Invasion and Aftermath* (London: H. Hamilton, with the Observer, 1984).
2. *Nödvendiga Nyheter,* no. (1991).
3. Martha Gellhorn, "The Invasion of Panama," *Granta,* no. 32 (1990).
4. *Journalisten,* no. 4 (1991).
5. *Newsweek,* January 14, 1991, p. 19.
6. Ibid.
7. *Journalisten,* no. 4 (1991).
8. *Independent,* February 6, 1991.
9. *Journalisten,* no. 4 (1991).
10. *International Herald Tribune,* March 18, 1991.
11. *Aftenposten,* January 18, 1991.
12. *VG,* January 27, 1991.
13. *Aftenposten,* June 10, 1991.

CHAPTER THIRTEEN

◆

Public Opinion and Media War Coverage in Britain

Martin Shaw and Roy Carr-Hill

THE CONTROL OF THE MEDIA in Britain during the Gulf War was overdetermined by the efficient U.S.-organized coalition control of information, by the lack of domestic political legitimation for criticism of coalition policy, and by a desire on the part of both media and government to learn from their conflicts during the Falklands and produce an understanding that would preserve a degree of journalistic autonomy within a framework of military-political control. It is certainly arguable that British controls went beyond those of many coalition states: The BBC's banning of sixty-seven popular songs, comedy films, series with a vaguely military theme, and a minority-channel series on Vietnamese films indicated a level of general cultural control that went far beyond the political or military censorship that was evident in most or all of the countries involved in the conflict.[1] This control was reflected in the wider cultural establishment—for example, in the Victoria and Albert Museum's banning of the exhibition "The Art of Death," which included tombstones, mourning fans, and funeral loaves.

The denial of death in such policies may have reflected, as the organizer of this exhibition commented, a "peculiarly 20th century attitude."[2] It also reflected something more specific, however: the coalition's general desire—taken possibly to extreme lengths in the United

We acknowledge the generous assistance of the Joseph Rowntree Charitable Trust and the University of Hull in supporting our research. We also acknowledge the B&G Cadbury Trust in supporting Martin Shaw to give a paper at the conference of the International Association for Mass Communication Research on "News Media and the Gulf War," Istanbul, June 1991, on which this chapter is based.

Kingdom—to minimize the violence of the war by avoiding anything, from British or U.S. "body bags" to film of the Iraqi victims of air attacks, that brought home the reality of the war. In general, this objective was very successfully achieved, at least during January and February 1991, even if it could not be so easily maintained in the aftermath of the war.

British coverage of the early phase of the war emphasized its high-technology efficiency. Film was widely shown of U.S. fighter pilots' describing their assaults—"Exactly like the movies." "Baghdad was lit up like a Christmas tree. It was tremendous!" "It was kinda neat."[3] Television news frequently, but not always, matched this description of a BBC bulletin: "a very muscular and loyalist affair, straight out of Biggles:[4] our top guns on bridge-busting, Israeli jets zapping Palestinians around Sidon, the B-52s lumbering into Fairford and an almost black and blank screen from Baghdad, courtesy of CNN."[5] Even the land war, with its instant success, was widely presented in a glamorous light, at least until the extent of the carnage was revealed. The image of a local evening paper advertising "Land War: Sunday Colour Special" sandwiched between billboards for a "Big Fight Sensation" and "City Match Report" evoked the sporting metaphor for war.[6] Cutaway diagrams of Challenger battle tanks and F-15E fighters covered the centerfold of the children's supplement to a "quality" paper.[7]

A tension had begun to develop in the media coverage by the second week of February. The Independent Television News bulletin of the same evening as the BBC report just quoted "showed Iraqi pictures of civilian damage and spoke of children dying, with the corrective remark that the Iraqis had stolen the incubator from Kuwaiti hospitals." The media campaign faltered more decisively on February 13 when confronted with the bombing of a bunker, believed to be a military communications center, in which hundreds of civilians were killed. It was at this point that significant parts of the media departed in their coverage from the smooth track that the military had provided for them.[8] The BBC's coverage, which included film of the shrouded remains of the victims as well as a tour of the shelter's charred interior, led to charges of treachery from some Conservative members of Parliament, who dubbed the BBC the "Baghdad Broadcasting Corporation." Here there were shades of the conflicts between television and government that had characterized the Falklands War.

Apart from this incident, virtually no bodies or injured people (a few Israeli victims were probably the only exceptions) appeared on any television screens or in any newspapers until the war was practically over. There was certainly little intimation in much of the reporting of the real violence involved in the attacks. Video film of missiles approaching their targets was released—but not the film of the horrified face of an Iraqi lorry driver a split second away from death. The campaign was systematically presented as an attack on things—weapons, transporters, bridges, buildings—but not on people.[9] There was a deliberate denial of the violence actually being perpetrated on human beings. Only in the final stages of the land war did the massacre of Mutla Ridge lead to some brief snatches of gruesome realism. There was extraordinarily little speculation about the numbers of Iraqi military casualties until the war was over. Then U.S. and U.K. military sources began to divulge horrific estimates of anywhere from forty thousand to two hundred thousand killed, which made their way at least into the serious newspapers.

A further element of denial was the refusal, or transfer, of responsibility, which was faithfully reproduced by the British media. When U.S. planes bombed the bunker in Baghdad in which several hundred civilians were killed, there were many attempts to blame Saddam Hussein for this grisly mistake, arguing either that he should not have placed civilians in a place that also had a military function or, more extremely, that he had deliberately placed civilians there so as to make political capital out of their deaths. One British newspaper headlined this story "Victims of Saddam," denying the responsibility of those who had actually launched the missiles that killed civilians in the bunker.[10]

People in Britain, as in other Western societies, were insulated by the media coverage not only from the immediate reality and direct threat of violence (marginal and sporadic terrorist incidents apart), but also to a very large extent from information about and images of the ways in which these realities and threats were affecting people in Iraq. It was not surprising in this context, and given the plausible political case against Saddam Hussein's invasion of Iraq (which was condemned even by opponents of the war), that opinion polls in Britain showed massive majorities for the war. An initial 80 percent level of approval rose to around 90 percent in many polls, enabling one newspaper to claim "an extraordinary degree of unanimity, unprecedented in modern times towards any policy."[11]

Nevertheless, the lives of people in these societies were linked by abstract relationships to the violence of the war. As Anthony Giddens pointed out in his recent work on modernity, the transformation of relationships of time and space means the involvement of people in distant risks and dangers and in a well-distributed awareness of these. "Disembedding mechanisms" in social relations (the dislocation of social relations from given temporal and spatial contexts) have, he argued, "provided large areas of security," but "the new array of risks which have thereby been brought into being are truly formidable." The circumstances in which many of us live today have as a result a "menacing appearance."[12] In the Gulf War, many people who were not directly threatened nevertheless felt themselves to be living with the dangerous situation developing thousands of miles away. Abstract relationships and personal involvement are not, of course, opposed but interrelated.[13] Some people in Britain were living with this tension in a much more personal way than others. We expected that, despite their "support" for the war, many people would have responses of a more complex character.

The Survey Research

We planned two surveys, the first during the aerial attack phase of the war and the second after the commencement of the land war. This chapter reports chiefly on the data from the first survey but with some results from the second survey indicated.[14]

The first questionnaire included twenty-nine questions about the politics of the war, perceptions of the coalition attacks, attitudes toward violence and to the media coverage, and a set of sociodemographic and other identity questions. The substantive questions, framed in mid-January, were asked in a general way. (In the second survey, we were able to ask far more specific questions about events in the war.) The surveys were based on random samples of the local population in Hull (a Labour-voting northern industrial working-class city) and Beverley (its adjacent Conservative-voting middle-class suburban area). Our interest, moreover, was in establishing relationships among different aspects of attitudes to the war, and between these attitudes and a range of social variables, rather than to engage in precise, predictive opinion polling in the sense in which this is carried out in, for example, electoral contexts.

Our selection of a random sample from the electoral register avoided the recognized dangers of quota samples,[15] on which all national U.K. opinion polls are based. For our first survey, questionnaires were sent by post to thirteen hundred people between February 7 and 11; by February 22, when a cease-fire was imminent, we had received approximately five hundred replies, giving a response rate of nearly 40 percent. Especially given that the register we used had been compiled in October 1989, and so included many who had moved or died, this was a good response that compared well with other postal questionnaires in similar situations.[16] Most of the discussion in the remainder of this chapter, including all that dealing with the breakdown of the findings by age, sex, party, newspaper readership, and so on, is based on this survey.

For our second survey, questionnaires were sent to approximately four hundred of the original respondents, who had agreed to receive a second questionnaire, together with almost one thousand additional people drawn at random from the same electoral register. Questionnaires were sent out at the end of March, one month after the end of the war, and replies came in during April and the beginning of May—effectively the period of the Kurdish crisis in the media, although our questions (framed in advance) did not specifically mention this. Even though the urgency of the war itself had disappeared, our overall response rate was still a little less than 40 percent (although lower among the new element of our sample). Only some overall findings have been included in this discussion.

Attitudes Toward Media Coverage

Large majorities of our first sample regularly watched television news of the war (90 percent), read the local evening paper (72 percent), and read a national (or regional) daily newspaper (65 percent).[17] Clearly, most respondents obtained all their knowledge of the war from these three media (and from radio, about which we unfortunately did not ask questions in this survey). Five percent reported that a member of the immediate family was in the Gulf, so that there may have been some input of information directly from the theater of war. Only a small minority, therefore, may have directly obtained some local knowledge in addition to that provided by mass media, although of course many people may have processed their media-based information through discussion in face-to-face situations.

Overwhelmingly, people reported that they watched television news for information, although a substantial minority also said that they watched because they were worried. Only 5 percent, almost exclusively younger men, reported that they were fascinated or excited by the war. Among those not watching television news, worry was a majority factor (especially among a few of those with family involvement in the war), although boredom was also cited by a few.

We asked three sets of direct questions about television coverage. Overall, 60 percent of our respondents found it "informative," while 25 percent found it "too informative," and 16 percent found it "not informative enough." But dividing our sample between those who replied before the Baghdad bunker bombing (a landmark in the television coverage) and those who replied after this incident, we found a significant decline in the proportion agreeing that coverage was too informative. This could have been because the level of coverage was itself reduced from the early saturation levels.

We also asked about patriotism in television coverage. Overall, 68 percent found it "patriotic," with minorities of around 16 percent each finding it "too patriotic" or "not patriotic enough." The only significant change after the Baghdad bombing was a small increase, from 12 to 18 percent, in the proportion seeing television news as "unpatriotic."

We also asked, however, whether television news reflected "a sensible attitude to the war," "glorified the war too much," or was "too critical of the war." Overall, 59 percent of our sample found that it was "sensible," a figure that did not change over time. Nevertheless, the minority seeing television coverage as "glorifying" the war was as large as 40 percent before the Baghdad bombing, but it fell to 29 percent afterward. The minority seeing television as "too critical" was a minuscule 2 percent before but a more significant 13 percent later on. These figures represent strong evidence (1) of a substantial viewer tendency to see television as involved in an uncritical glorification of the war and (2) of the effect of the bunker bombing. Nevertheless, only a small minority endorsed the "too critical" position even after the bunker incident. Even among Conservative voters, more saw television as overglorifying the war than saw it as too critical, despite Conservative politicians' criticism of the BBC over this incident.

In responses to the same question in our second survey, 36 percent saw television as "overglorifying," and only 6 percent saw it as "too critical," indicating the strength of overall impressions once the impact of the specific incident had subsided. When asked specifically about the incident, however, 57 percent of respondents agreed that it was right for television to have shown the shrouded bodies of the bunker victims, compared to 35 percent who disagreed.

Asking the same basic questions about national newspaper coverage, we found that smaller minorities adopted critical positions than was the case for television. In particular, only 8 percent found the paper they read too informative, and 11 percent found it not informative enough; 19 percent found it too patriotic, and 7 percent found it not patriotic enough; while 30 percent found it glorified the war too much, and 5 percent found it too critical. This ambivalence was reflected in an overall "dissatisfaction" level of 16 percent, compared to 77 percent "satisfied" with their daily paper.

The differences between the findings for newspapers and television clearly reflected the fact that in the former case we were asking about a differentiated product; in the latter, about a uniform product. Although there were some differences between BBC and independent television coverage of the war, and among programs, these were not sharply defined, and our judgment was that it would have made little sense to ask people about programs or channels when coverage was largely uniform in character.

People generally sought a higher or lower level of information in choosing their newspaper, so that informativeness on particular issues was measured against varying bases. Issues raised by the Gulf War were liable, however, to increase demands for different levels of information from those normally accepted. In the case of the *Sun* and *Star,* the two most down-market (and Conservative/war-mongering) national tabloids, for example, 15 percent of readers found their paper "too informative," while 16 percent found it not informative enough. Among readers of the *Daily Mirror,* the *Sun's* Labour-oriented mass circulation rival, only 4 percent found their paper too informative, while 20 percent found it not informative enough. In contrast, among readers of middle-market tabloids and quality dailies there was much less dissatisfaction on either count. Readers of down-market tabloids were clearly far less satisfied with their level of information than those of other papers. (This finding was repeated in our second survey.)

A similar pattern can be seen in replies to our question about the patriotism of national newspapers. Almost 25 percent of *Sun* and *Star* readers found the paper too patriotic, as did almost 20 percent of *Mirror* readers (although 11 percent also found it unpatriotic); the figures for the middle-market and quality papers were lower. Levels of agreement that newspapers overglorified the war followed the same pattern. As many as 41 percent of *Sun* and *Star* readers agreed that their papers glorified the war too much,[18] as did 35 percent of *Mirror* readers, 25 percent of middle-market tabloid readers, but only 7 percent of quality-paper readers. Very few newspaper readers found their paper too critical of the war (10 percent of *Mirror* readers was the highest proportion). Given that tabloid readers, especially of the most down-market papers, choose their papers knowing of their sensational and generally (with the exception of the *Mirror*) right-wing attitudes, these levels of consumer resistance were significant. David E. Morrison and Howard Tumber's post-Falklands survey also found greater dissatisfaction among tabloid than among quality readers, but our survey, by asking about the tendency of media to "glorify" war, seems to have shown a larger critical tendency even among readers who overall did not actually claim to be dissatisfied with their papers' coverage.[19]

Our survey showed that more people read their local evening paper (the *Hull Daily Mail*) than a national daily paper. This paper was similar in level to a middle-market tabloid, and its coverage consisted of basic war information with a large number of stories about local armed forces personnel, their families, support groups for them, those people collecting goods and money for the troops, schools sending letters to them, and so on. (Less than 5 percent of the local population, according to our survey, had actually been involved in any of these activities in support of the troops; only 26 percent claimed even to have donated.) Local anti-war activities (which involved fewer than 1 percent) were covered, and editorials were at times quite somber. Fewer readers of national qualities than of national tabloids read the local paper; those who did were most dissatisfied with its level of information and found it too patriotic and glorificatory. Readers of national middle-market tabloids were most satisfied with the local paper's coverage.

Differences in reception of the three media emerged in response to questions in our second survey about coverage of the massacre of retreating Iraqi troops at Mutla Ridge. Almost 80 percent claimed to have seen pictures of dead Iraqis on television, but only 20 percent saw such pictures in a national paper and 3 percent (wrongly, to the best of our knowledge) in a local paper. Television news had indeed played the major part in providing (with the war safely won) visual evidence of these gruesome events, which many of the national newspapers neglected to provide. Moreover, despite the views of some right-wing critics of television, including those in the daily press, our sample was overwhelmingly in favor (67 to 23 percent) of showing bodies on television.

Media and Perceptions of the War

No fewer than 82 percent of our first sample (asked to choose the one or two most appropriate descriptions) endorsed the statement that the initial aerial attacks were "precise strikes against strategic targets with minimum civilian casualties," the dominant view propounded in television coverage. Forty-one percent agreed that the attacks were "sorties by brave allied airmen," a view supported by television coverage and enthusiastically canvassed by much of the tabloid press. Only 8 percent saw them as "intensive bombing with unacceptable civilian casualties" and 5 percent as "like video or computer games."

These figures seem to provide confirmation of media messages well received. Even after the war, our second survey found very similar perceptions: 81 percent still endorsed the "precise strikes" statement, and there was a small rise to just 13 percent in the numbers seeing the air attacks as "intensive bombing." At the same time, almost all the sample recognized that more Iraqi lives had been lost than those of any other nation. But when asked to choose the description of the Baghdad shelter bombing that they found most acceptable, no fewer than 36 percent agreed that Saddam Hussein had placed civilians in the bunker to make propaganda from their deaths, and 24 percent agreed that it had been a military shelter correctly bombed. A further 21 percent agreed with the statement that there are always casualties in war, and only 11 percent saw the bunker as a civilian shelter bombed by mistake. Thus, the issue that created most conflict over the role of television, the majority agreed with a statement that either attributed blame for the results of coalition attacks to the enemy (a line promoted by much of the tabloid press) or repeated the military justification of the attack. Only a small minority appeared to have clearly received the "critical" message that there had been a coalition mistake. Breakdowns of these findings according to newspaper readership were very revealing: Readers of quality newspapers were far more likely, for example, to see the bunker bombing as a mistake.

A similar pattern of perceptions applied to the killing of Iraqi troops during their retreat from Kuwait. Sixty-five percent of respondents saw this as justified to destroy the Iraqi military machine, in addition to 13 percent who saw it as necessary to win the war. Only 15 percent agreed that it was unjustified as the war was already won.

There was, moreover, clear evidence of the misleading effect of media coverage in the answers to a question about what proportion of the more than one hundred thousand sorties flown by the coalition had been flown by British airmen. Thirteen percent of our sample believed that the British had flown more than 50 percent, 29 percent said 30–50 percent, 21 percent said 20–30 percent, 19 percent said 10–20 percent, 16 percent said 5–10 percent, and only 3 percent said less than 5 percent. The correct answer was about 3 percent, but patriotically focused media had clearly given a very different impression. Certainly, most respondents recognized the United Kingdom's subordination to the United States, which was seen as the most important member of the coalition by 87 percent (only 7 percent putting Britain first). But the media clearly inflated Britain's role: 76 percent saw it as the second most important member of the coalition, compared to only 17 percent who named Saudi Arabia.

Perceptions also clearly reflected, however, individual interpretations of information. When asked, for example, which leaders had been "for" and which had been "against" the war, Labour voters, who were themselves more likely to oppose the war than were Conservatives, were also more likely to see Labour leader Neil Kinnock as having opposed the war. In fact, Kinnock's position had been a carefully nuanced, calculated support for the war combined with regret that sanctions had not been pursued longer. Interestingly, Labour voters were also likely to see other potentially ambiguous figures, such as the Liberal Democrats' leader and the archbishop of Canterbury, as having been antiwar.

Underlying perceptions of the issues in the war also appeared to reflect media coverage. The British national "myth of war," derived from World War II experience (according to which dictators should not be appeased but should be resisted by military force),[20] was widely applied to the Iraqi situation by tabloid newspapers even more than by Conservative politicians. Our research showed that far more tabloid readers believed that Saddam Hussein was like Adolf Hitler and/or that he was "mad" than did quality-newspapers readers. These differences were far greater than other differences (age, sex, class, party, etc.) and remained significant when we controlled for these factors.

Media and Attitudes Toward the War

Our research was designed to provide a broader base of information than that given by the national polls so that we could interpret "public opinion" on the war. We were concerned to identify aspects of people's responses to the war that were not revealed in superficial opinion research. We wished to go beyond the headline poll findings to examine the broader range of feelings about and attitudes to the war. The influence of the media on these attitudes was necessarily a major part of our concern.

One of the major dimensions which we wished to investigate was the way in which people were personally affected by the war. If the "spectator sport" and "armament culture" theories discussed by Asu Aksoy and Kevin Robins in Chapter 17 are valid, the media coverage of the war would have functioned to "screen off" the actual violence.[21] We found, however, that 13 percent of respondents claimed to be "worried about family or friends in the Gulf." Of these, 56 percent claimed that a member of the family (in more than half the cases, a child or teenager) had been "adversely affected by the violence of the war," compared to 21 percent in the sample as a whole. Larger numbers, moreover, of those who had no such personal involvement also claimed to be "worried about the violence of the war in general" (32 percent). Only a small proportion "[felt] good because of allied or British successes" (12 percent). Of the rest, 39 percent claimed not to have been personally affected by the war. Women, especially older ones, and readers of "quality" newspapers were particularly likely to say they were "worried" in general; readers of downmarket tabloids were both more likely to be worried about family or friends in the Gulf and to feel good about the war.

The general atmosphere of crisis seemed therefore to have given rise to widespread anxiety, which the media communicated along with the image of high-technology military success, and to have occurred despite the screening out of violence. As we have seen, people largely accepted official and widely diffused media explanations of the war. They were nevertheless highly concerned about violence, even if they had little concrete evidence of the forms it was actually taking. Our first survey showed that more than 60 percent of our sample claimed to be "concerned" or "very concerned" about loss of life among Iraqi soldiers, and more than 85 percent expressed worry about Iraqi civilians; more than 95 percent claimed to be concerned about loss of life among Israeli, Saudi, U.S., and British forces or civilians.

The reasons for the anxiety and the concern about violence, as well as for different stances on the political issues in the war, were clearly complex. Our analysis showed significant (and in some cases substantial) differences between men and women, young and old, social classes, supporters of different parties, and affiliates of different religious denominations. Personal involvement with the military and a historical experience of war also played significant (but not identical) parts in forming attitudes.[22] Clearly, even the role of the media should be looked at in a longer-term perspective (in their contribution to shaping attitudes to international conflict, the military, and so on). Short-term media coverage in the buildup to, duration, and aftermath of the war was only one factor in the formation of attitudes.

In looking at the role of the media, therefore, we distinguished their role in providing information and shaping perceptions of current events and in shaping underlying perceptions and attitudes. We took it for granted in our research that television was the prime source of information on the war for most people because of the chronological and the visual immediacy of the medium.[23] We did not take it for granted that television was as important as newspapers, or that the media as a whole was as important as other factors, in the formation of attitudes.

It has been widely assumed that television has replaced newspapers both as a primary source of information and as a source of attitudes toward political events. Our study suggested, however, that this is too simple a view. The differences in perceptions of and attitudes toward the war among readers of different newspapers were more extreme than any of the other variations measured in our study, and these differences remained significant when we controlled for age, sex, class, politics, and military/war experience.[24] We noted a wide spectrum of attitudes when we divided our sample into four sizable groups: readers of the *Sun* and the *Star,* readers of the *Daily Mirror,* readers of the middle-market tabloids (*Express, Mail, Today*), and readers of quality papers (*Guardian, Independent, Telegraph, Times*).

We suggest that newspapers, although generally unable to compete with television in terms of visual immediacy and instant communication of the war, were nevertheless able to offer much more ideologically complete interpretations of events and stronger advocacy of particular positions. A differentiated, ideologically and politically partisan press was able to offer far more explicit positions than the much more homogeneous television, which was legally regulated and politically monitored to produce a relatively neutral product. It is difficult to explain many of the variations without knowledge of the positions adopted by the newspapers themselves. We found, for example, that among *Sun* readers no fewer than 21 percent favored using nuclear weapons against Iraq. In no other subgroup in our sample on any dimension was the percentage supporting this option in double figures. It cannot be accidental that the *Sun,* alone among British newspapers, actually advocated the use of nuclear weapons. We also found strong, yet differentiated, support for the demonization of Saddam Hussein among down-market tabloid readers generally and *Sun* and *Star* readers particularly; this finding reflected the personalization of the conflict in these same papers.

Political and religious leaders did not provide their followers with detailed, let alone day-to-day, understanding of or positions on the events of the war. Indeed, some quietly and deliberately avoided such commitments: The leaders of the two opposition parties and of the Church of England were the three figures (out of the seven about whom we asked in our second survey) whose position on the war seemed most ambiguous to our respondents.

The media were thus left in the position of being the only institutions continually interpreting and judging a rapidly developing series of anxiety-producing, threatening, and contradictory events to members of society. Although television held the center stage, newspapers played a special role in this process. In times of crises, while television assumes primacy as a source of information (and of immediate interpretations of it), newspapers provide more general interpretations and positions linked more explicitly with differentiated sets of values that, in buying the product, readers have to some extent chosen for themselves.

The Gulf War, as Giddens pointed out, was "the most heavily mediated, reflexively monitored war in human history."[25] Most members of most societies obtained knowledge of the war only through mass media that controlled the supply of information and interpretations to unprecedented degrees and were in turn controlled in doing so. Our survey of a local population in the United Kingdom confirmed that perceptions of the war followed closely from the dominant patterns of television and newspaper coverage.

Even while they approved of the war, respondents expressed anxiety about it, and few confessed either to fascination with it or to good feelings about the successes of the victorious coalition. Even while they endorsed the dominant perceptions of the war gained from the media coverage, a very large minority of television viewers saw British television coverage as "glorifying the war too much." Even after the image of a clean, efficient, high-technology campaign had been partially undermined by some fairly visually explicit and ideologically questioning coverage of the Baghdad shelter bombing, few respondents agreed with right-wing criticism of the media.

Although most people accepted the versions of this event provided by the military, political leaders, and the press, most also agreed that television had been right to show the shrouded remains of the victims. Similarly, although most people accepted the justifications given for the slaughter of retreating Iraqi troops, a large majority supported the more explicit television coverage of the killing's effects. Even more interesting, perhaps, was the fact that although tabloid newspaper readers' views clearly reflected their papers' orientations on the war, very large minorities also saw their papers as "glorifying the war too much."

Notes

1. Much of the information about British censorship, with comparative accounts from the United States, France, Germany, Turkey, Israel, and so on, is compiled in the *Index on Censorship*'s special issue, "Warspeak: The Gulf and the News Media (April-May 1991).

2. Maev Kennedy, "The Forgotten Art of Death Rituals," *Guardian,* April 6, 1991.

3. "Sound Bites," *Weekend Guardian,* January 19–20, 1991, p. 7.

4. Biggles is the fictional pilot hero of the interwar boys' adventure stories created by Captain W. E. Johns.

5. David Pallister, "Gulf Mediafile," *Media Guardian,* February 11, 1991. CNN itself was not received directly in British homes, although its coverage was frequently utilized by the British channels.

6. *Yorkshire Evening Press* billboards, York city center, February 24, 1991.

7. *Funday Times,* supplement to *Sunday Times,* quoted in *Guardian,* February 7, 1991.

8. Significant numbers of British television viewers recognized the shift in coverage, according to my survey.

9. This presentation was remarkably similar to that of *Kristallnacht* by its perpetrators: "By portraying the pogrom of November 9/10, 1938, as the night of broken glass, Nazi propagandists meant to fix attention on this material damage. They went out of their way to stress that Jews were neither looted nor physically harmed" (Arno Meyer, *Why Did the Heavens Not Darken?* [London: Verso, 1989], p. 169). There was no comparison between the politics of the Gulf coalition and that of the Nazis, but propaganda methods were close in this respect.

10. *Daily Mail,* quoted by Edward Pearce, "Auxiliary Boys' Brigade," *Guardian,* February 14, 1991. Less than a week later, the Irish Republican Army (IRA) bombed Victoria Station in London, killing one person, and then issued a statement blaming the police for this death because they failed to clear the area. The police responded with a statement that the IRA's attempt to abdicate responsibility for the killing it had caused "almost beggars belief" (Metropolitan Police statement, February 19, 1991, quoted in *Guardian,* February 20, 1991). No one noticed the irony.

11. *Sunday Times,* March 2, 1991.

12. Anthony Giddens, *The Consequences of Modernity* (Stanford, Calif.: Stanford University Press, 1990), p. 125.

13. Ibid, pp. 120–121.

14. Martin Shaw and Roy Carr-Hill, *Public Opinion, Media and Violence,* Report no. 1 (Hull: University of Hull Gulf War Project, 1991). This is available for £3 from the Gulf War Project, University of Hull, HU6 7RX, England; make checks payable to the University of Hull. This report contains the full questionnaire.

15. *Newsletter* (London: Survey Methods Centre, February 1991).

16. See Claus Moser and Graham Kalton, *Survey Methods in Social Investigation* (London: Routledge and Kegan Paul, 1975); and P. Dixon, "Response Rates in Postal Surveys" (York: University of York Centre for Health Economics, 1991, mimeo).

17. There is a national market for daily newspapers in the United Kingdom; most titles are published in London and circulated nationally. Nearly all our respondents who read a daily morning paper (more than 60 percent of the sample) read a national title, although a few read the *Yorkshire Post.*

18. This proportion rose to 55 percent in the second survey.

19. David E. Morrison and Howard Tumber, *Journalists at War: The Dynamics of News Reporting in the Falklands Conflict.* (London: Sage, 1988).

20. Martin Shaw has discussed this myth more fully in *Post-Military Society* (Philadelphia: Temple University Press, 1991), Chapter 4; also see Chapter 6.

21. See Chapter 17.

22. These factors are discussed more fully in Shaw and Carr-Hill, *Public Opinion, Media and Violence;* and in Martin Shaw and Roy Carr-Hill, *Attitudes to War: A Political Sociology of Responses to the Gulf Conflict* (forthcoming).

23. Research conducted in the United States by Bradley Greenberg, University of Michigan, and presented to the IAMCR, Istanbul, 1991, corroborated this assumption in great detail. The research examined, for instance, the relationship between various media and word of mouth in people's first information about the outbreak of war.

24. Charts comparing the breakdowns of our data by various factors are given in Shaw and Carr-Hill, *Public Opinion, Media and Violence.*

25. Anthony Giddens, Paper presented at the conference on "Nationalism in a Post-Marxist World," London School of Economics, London, March 1, 1991.

A SOVIET SNAPSHOT
Eugeni Mikitenko

The Soviet media covered the war in the Gulf objectively and fully. Under the present conditions of freedom of expression, references to Western sources and others were no longer subject to censorship. The times have also passed when Soviet journalists were required to cite only those information sources that emphasized the successes of Moscow's foreign policy. The Soviet media contained innumerable articles, interviews, and opinion pieces, including pieces from military specialists, on the developments of the war. Soviet journalists did not have to follow any party line or change events and opinions to conform to the official version.

Nevertheless, the strong anti-Iraqi campaign carried out by some media, along with other stories of this nature taken from Western publications, gave rise in the Soviet Union to a "Saddamphobia" that threatened to turn into an "Arabphobia" and to degenerate into strong anti-Arab prejudices. It is the task of scientists, journalists, and experts in the Near East to neutralize these tendencies and reestablish the "good image of the Arabs" in Soviet society. In this task the Soviet Union needs help from the United States and the Arab countries.

COVERAGE OF THE GULF WAR
BY THE SPANISH AND CATALONIAN MEDIA
Héctor Borrat

As was the case with colleagues in other European countries, Spanish and Catalonian special correspondents were discriminated against by the U.S. military during the Gulf War. None of them was allowed to be part of the "pool" of journalists who traveled directly to the front. Only U.S. and British journalists, previously selected and given an almost military training, were selected. When Spanish and European journalists protested their exclusion, the response was that their countries were not making a military effort in the war comparable to that of the United States and Britain.

(continues)

(*continued*)

Eduardo Sanjuan (special correspondent from TV3 to Saudi Arabia) underscored how frustrating it was to depend on members of the pool for information. Working under these conditions was "extraordinarily difficult." Antoni Castel (special correspondent from *El Observador*) stated unequivocally that the Gulf War was a "war of disinformation" in which everything depended on the pool, members of which had been selected for purely political motives. Alfonso Rojo (special correspondent from *El Mundo*) complained that Peter Arnett would not let Rojo use the direct telephone line because, Arnett said, "he was the competition." Belen Ayala (special correspondent from the radio chain Sociedad Española de Radiodifusión) reported that she was discriminated against in Saudi Arabia because she was a woman—"the women are treated like suitcases"—a problem she solved only by dressing herself as a man.

In his evaluation of the war coverage of the Spanish special correspondents, Said Alami observed that almost no one spoke Arabic, contrasting this lack of language skill with the fact that no Spanish news media would contemplate sending a correspondent to Paris, much less a special correspondent, who did not speak French.[1] Alami described "most of the reports, especially those from radio that were broadcast in Spain" as "merely reading the wire service reports that had already been received in Madrid." With some notable exceptions, such as those of Alfonso Rojo, Eric Fratini, and Franc Sevilla, these reports were U.S. and British information read in Spanish. Alami criticized the "endless copying by Spanish journalists of Anglo Saxon and French media when reporting about regions about which they had little information, for example the Near East."

Nevertheless, what Alami called copying was probably little else than the spontaneous coincidence of the Spanish journalists holding perceptions of the conflict similar to those of the many generalists sent by the U.S., British, and French media. The same professional styles and the same weaknesses shared by the media of many countries could well have led to the same type of information and reporting.

At the beginning of the conflict, the Spanish media were forced to share with many other countries the services of the only cable

(*continues*)

(*continued*)

television channel that had been provided by the government of Iraq to CNN. Either because of their own communication styles, or the hazardous situation in which they were forced to work, the three CNN reporters, Bernard Shaw as anchorman, Peter Arnett as correspondent, and John Holliman as reporter, became the protagonists of their own stories. The information about the war accentuated from the beginning the war as a spectacle, and the television coverage itself became the news of the next day. CNN beat the announcement of the outbreak of war by presidential spokesperson Marlin Fitzwater by half an hour. Defense Secretary Richard Cheney declared that the best information about what was going on in Baghdad came from CNN.

The Spanish press took part in the widespread praise of CNN. An enthusiastic *El País* editorial ("Pregunte a CNN," January 18, 1991) called it a "true spectacle: the 1991 war will be remembered not only as the first war of computers, but even more as the first warfare witnessed directly by the whole world. This time the war will not be covered by partial reports of correspondents in the war zone and transmitted after the battles, but by a blow-by-blow description of the events." *El País* also praised the "impartiality of the TV cameras and the fidelity of the events they transmitted."

The praise was entirely out of proportion to the actual situation. CNN's coverage was limited to a very small part of the events and was seen from the subjective and limited angle of a team of reporters who were as much "generalists" as were the Spanish correspondents. *El País* rightly found it "worrisome" that CNN was the "only media that could transmit," a situation that "limited the richness of contrasting information."

In addition to the kudos gained for its coverage, CNN was also the object of various critiques. An *El País* editorial offered the most extensive criticism: "CNN is no longer an instrument of information. It has become another weapon [against Iraq]." María Carrión agreed: "It is understood that Washington uses CNN to communicate with the enemy and study their reactions."[2] Luis Mariñas, the director of news at Telecinco, was even more critical of CNN's role: "It has become a hegemonic channel, an open window between Iraq and the United States. The result is that

(*continues*)

(*continued*)

here we receive the images that they want us to see. This is not
new; it has always happened in wars. But it leaves us with the sole
possibility of commenting on what they send us and trusting in
the intuition and courage of some other journalists to tell other
points of view."[3] At the same time, Marlin Fitzwater understood
that CNN was being used as part of the Iraqi disinformation campaign. Others simply asked, "What is the secret of CNN in Baghdad's war?"[4] (Despite censorship, Spanish media did report the
February 13 bombing raid on Baghdad that caused a great number
of civilian deaths.)

At the beginning of February, the Spanish journalists who were
working on the Gulf War were able to gauge to what extent the
Spanish government had instituted its own form of censorship.
They did not have to be sent to the Gulf to run into obstacles to
freedom of information. Rosa Conde, the spokesperson for the
government, announced that "for reasons of security and efficiency," the government has imposed an absolute blackout on
information on "the logistical support to the allied forces."

Complaints about the government's restrictions on information
had been appearing since the beginning of the war. On January
21, 1991, *El País* observed that whereas "the United States, the
United Kingdom, France, and Holland had admitted correspondents," Spain was "among the few countries that did not allow any
information about its forces in the Gulf" (one battleship and two
escorts). The only information available was that coming from the
Ministry of Defense spokesperson in Madrid.

On February 1, 1991, a survey carried out by Demoscopia for *El
País* demonstrated that the complaints did not come only from
professional journalists: "Seventy percent of Spaniards think the
government is not informing them adequately about the Gulf conflict, the Spanish position, or the consequences of the war for
Spain." (Only 28 percent believed the contrary.)

But this same day the information blockade was broken by a
revelation, coming first from foreign sources and rapidly transmitted by the radio chains that the Spanish base of Moron was being
used by U.S. B-52 bombers for their air raids on Iraq. According to
the *New York Times,* the decision to use the bases had been kept

(*continues*)

(*continued*)

a secret because of its politically sensitive nature. Citing Pentagon sources, the *Times* revealed that the B-52s had flown their missions secretly from Spain since before the war began.

On February 2, every newspaper except *El Observador* published this information on its front page. *El País, El Periódico,* and *El Diario de Barcelona* ran a banner headline; *La Vanguardia* and *Avui* lead the paper with the story. The importance of the revelation generated a series of editorials (on February 2 in *Avui* and *El Diari de Barcelona,* on February 3 in *El País* and in *El Diari de Barcelona,* on February 4 in *El Periódico,* on February 5 in *La Vanguardia,* and on February 6 in *El Observador*). Of all the editorials, the least critical of the government were those in *El Periódico* and *La Vanguardia.* The harshest criticism came from *El País.* "The secrecy in this issues is not an isolated incident; it forms part of a deliberate information policy that is against the democratic use of the media." This secrecy demonstrated that Moncloa (the government) "is convinced that it should treat the Spanish people as if they were irresponsible children to whom the truth should not be told," and "it represents a deception by omission" that "can suppose a breakdown in the relationship of confidence that a president should maintain with the citizens of the country and with the parliament, which has protested against this almost unanimously."

External and internal censorship conditioned the efforts of the Spanish media, the limitations of the generalists, and the fallacies of the "information stars." Since the referendum over NATO membership, no other story had gained the attention given the Gulf War by the Spanish media. The investment in news resources was enormous. But these investments went more toward the reproduction of professional practices and communication strategies—especially those that imitated U.S. practices—than toward the creation of new, innovative forms of news coverage. Given that the media provide excellent occasions to review history, there is still hope that the information censored and blocked during the war will come to light and will be narrated and analyzed by journalists dedicated to unraveling the myths of the discourse of power and rewriting the pages of history.

(*continues*)

(*continued*)

NOTES

1. Medios españoles y guerra del Golfo, "Communicación," *El Mundo,* March 23, 1991, p. C3.
2. "La guerra en el cuarto de estar," *El Observador,* February 4, 1991, p. 7.
3. Roque F. Pacheco, "La información sobre el conflicto bajo control. Televisiones públicas y privadas afirman que existe una clara censura informativa," *El Independiente,* January 22, 1991, p. 60.
4. Eduardo Haro Tecglen, "Algo no se entiende en Twin Peaks," *El País,* March 18, 1991.

THE WAR AS *TELENOVELA*
Omar Souki Oliveira

After the 1964 (U.S.-supported) military coup in Brazil, large amounts of tanks and missile launchers were sold to Iraq. Commercial cooperation was increased in the 1970s, and since then Brazilian building companies have played a significant role in the construction of highways and major buildings—which were bombed during the Gulf War.

The catastrophe of the war was made into a show. The little historical context provided to Brazilian audiences was overwhelmed by the glorification of the computer-operated machinery and its so-called fantastic accuracy. CNN supplied a continual flow of images to the Brazilian networks, but they provided very little interpretation of what was happening. When they did, it was to confirm the messages of U.S. television—that Saddam Hussein was a mad man who had to be assassinated and that the Arab countries had no other contribution to make to the West than their oil. These ideas reinforced the view, often promoted by the media, that Third World countries were not reliable. Thus, the West had to be prepared to control them by force if needed. The colossal power used to smash Iraq and send it back to a preindustrial age, may have been intended as a warning to other, equally "unruly" Third World countries.

(*continues*)

(*continued*)

A Brazilian company in Iraq brought back its employees, and they were interviewed by the media as they returned home. Their messages consistently denied many of the assertions made by national and international news programs. The last ones to arrive in Brazil assured the audience that the human costs of the war were dramatically higher than what was broadcast in the West. Some showed no patience during the interviews, saying that the reporters had no idea of what was actually going on in Iraq.

Minimal effort was made to provide more media exposure to the views of those Brazilian workers who in general showed great sympathy for the plight of Iraq's people. The logic of the war and the righteousness of the Western alliance, under U.S. leadership, were seldom questioned by the Brazilian media.

Throughout the five months preceding the actual clash, Brazilian audiences were programmed to accept violence as the only possible resolution. Computer-generated war games were constantly shown on the major networks. The war was discussed even before it happened, but often the human element was left out of the picture. Possible fighting strategies were conveyed to the Brazilian people as though there would be minimal suffering, and the media gave the impression that the sooner real fighting began, the better.

Negotiations that could lead to a peaceful solution of the crisis were quickly dismissed. Interviews with war strategists were given preference over those with leaders of peace movements in Brazil and abroad. Instead of searching for alternative views or peaceful possibilities, most reporters basically translated what they received from Western news agencies, thus reinforcing stereotypical perceptions.

Even President Fernando Collor de Mello contributed to the overall confusion. In an attempt to curb his dwindling popularity, he took advantage of this momentous media event and appeared on national television to convey to the public the seriousness of the situation and the need to conserve fuel and cooking gas. But this move backfired pitifully: For many days after his speech, television newscasts showed immense lines in front of gas stations and stores that sold bottled cooking gas. The population did ex-

(*continues*)

(*continued*)

actly the opposite of what was asked, precipitating an artificial shortage as a result of hoarding.

This ridiculous turn of events was more akin to a sitcom and suggested a comparison between Brazilian soap operas and the war as covered by the media. In the *telenovelas* everything is possible. Often they show dramatic improvements in the characters' lifestyles that can find no parallel in real life. The favorite scripts are variations of the poor boy's story: He leaves the countryside, comes to the city, meets a rich girl, falls in love, marries, and lives happily ever after. Belief in such fantasies may help people deal with the harsh realities of a country where 220,000 children, aged zero to five, starve to death every year ("Alceni" 1991) and where, in the state of São Paulo alone, an average of three street children are violently killed every day (Franca 1991).

If these monstrosities, which happen right under the noses of the networks' headquarters in Rio and São Paulo, are not thoroughly discussed on television, one should not expect an honest coverage of a war taking place on the other side of the planet. The networks see no commercial advantage in broadcasting such horrors. Instead, a mystified view of Brazilian daily life is provided, as happened with the coverage of the Gulf War.

Images and testimonies that could have shocked the audience and generated indignation against all wars were carefully edited out. The death of Iraqi children in the aftermath of the war was not broadcast by CNN links with the Brazilian networks. The same has happened with the murders of street children in Brazil, which are seldom, if ever, dealt with on the evening news. In sum, the Gulf War as portrayed on Brazilian television had as little to do with actual events in the Middle East as *telenovelas* do with Brazilian reality.

REFERENCES

"Alceni diz que crianças desnutridas são 6 milhoes." 1991. *Jornal do Brasil,* June 12, p. 4.

Franca, Mauricio. 1991. "A face oculta da modernidade." *Visão,* 35 (August 28): 44–46.

CHAPTER FOURTEEN

◆

A Sampling of Editorial Responses from the Middle Eastern Press on the Persian Gulf Crisis

Hamid Mowlana,
with Danielle Vierling and Amy Tully

DURING THE PERSIAN GULF CRISIS and war, the Middle Eastern press took an active role in reflecting the cultural opinions, attitudes, and moods of the region. As events unfolded, various media sources attempted to analyze different aspects of the crisis. In addition to coverage through news reporting, which was dominated by the Western news agencies, an assessment of the public disposition toward the war can be obtained from editorials. This chapter attempts to capture trends in opinion found in a survey of approximately 250 editorials from respected Iranian, Egyptian, and Jordanian newspapers.

A comparison of these various editorials reveals both common concerns for the region as well as differences based on the specific geopolitical positions and indigenous makeups of the countries in close proximity to the Persian Gulf crisis. Two main concerns voiced by many editorialists throughout the region were the illegitimacy of Iraq's invasion of Kuwait and U.S. intervention in Middle Eastern affairs. In the months prior to the war, editorialists expressed hopes that the Arab or Islamic countries would unify against U.S. intervention and resolve the conflict on their own. But as President George Bush's January 15 deadline approached, these editorialists became more pessimistic. The U.S. dismissal of Soviet efforts to formulate a peaceful solution with Iraq reinforced the idea that the United States really wanted war and had all along.

Even though countries, including Iran and Jordan, wanted Saddam Hussein to withdraw Iraqi soldiers from Kuwait, they did not all advocate waging war against Iraq. For example, although Iran considered itself neutral, neither siding with Iraq or the U.S.-led coalition in the Persian Gulf crisis, it, too, wanted an Iraqi withdrawal but stood against U.S. intervention and war against Iraq. Jordan followed a similar trend in opinion but emphasized the pertinence of the Palestinian question to the crisis. Egypt was split between government support of the U.S.-led coalition and public opposition to Western interference and war against Iraq.

Differences among editorialists can be distinguished by their particular political histories and agendas. In the case of Iran, an emphasis on the significance of the Islamic movement in relation to the Persian Gulf prevailed among its editorials. An examination of editorials from several newspapers over the nine-month period immediately following Iraq's invasion of Kuwait revealed the primacy of Iran's Islamic approach to politics. This approach, viewed by its indigenous people as a positive force, sustained a neutrality toward a war unrelated to their spiritual goals. Iranian editorialists also recognized that the United States viewed their Islamic viewpoint as a negative force obstructing and threatening the pursuit of Western political and economic goals. Hence, most Iranian editorials expressed a highly critical reaction to Iraq's invasion of Kuwait, U.S. intervention, the U.N. Security Council's approach to the crisis, Middle Eastern nations such as Turkey and Saudi Arabia, and Western censorship and control of the media.

Immediately following Iraq's invasion of Kuwait, Iran came forward as the first nation to criticize this act. Although in some respects Iran and Iraq paralleled each other in their rejection of any foreign interventions or foreign solutions to the Persian Gulf crisis, editorialists from Tehran quickly recalled Saddam Hussein's aggression during the Iran-Iraq War. Hence, editorialists noted that Iraq "is an opportunist and its ideas are motivated by extreme Arab nationalism, its resort to Islam goes back to its opportunistic nature" (*Kayhan International,* August 5, 1990). Iranians did not consider the Iraqi appeal to Islam genuine, given that Iraq had been "trained by Western media as well as unrestricted military, economic, and diplomatic support to become an invader country." Despite this critique, some editorialists noted that "condemnation is not the general and undisputed feeling among the Iranian public. Some people look with a sign of relief at the invasion, arguing that the Iranians are being avenged for the bankrolling of uncountable number of missiles by Kuwait and other Persian Gulf countries that were dropped on their heads by Iraq." In any case, editorialists generally encouraged the public to be wary of Iraq's diplomatic maneuvering in order to protect their own integrity.

Although editorialists believed that diplomatic collaboration with Iraq could keep a foreign presence out of the Persian Gulf, they pressed for continuing condemnation of Iraq's invasion of Kuwait. In this vein of thought, an editorial stated that "the Western countries use a double standard; one for themselves and an another for all other countries. Iraq must have figured it could take advantage of this duality. But, alas, Iraq is wrong and its aggression upon Kuwait can never be legitimized, no matter how elaborate the pretexts it tries to come up with" (*Kayhan International,* August 5, 1990).

Moreover, although Iranians acknowledged the threat of Saddam Hussein acting against Islamic interests, the increased presence of the United States in the Gulf posed an even greater threat. To this end, an editorial commented, "The Iraqi regime's miscalculations and adventurism inflicted heavy blows on the Muslim world, undermining the Palestinian cause and giving the West a pretext to maintain its foothold in the region" (*Kayhan International,* March 13, 1991). Criticism of the United States also came forth in this way:

"Under no condition can the presence of U.S. troops on Arabian territory be justified. If Iraq's Kuwaiti invasion deserves condemnation of the highest order, the presence of foreign troops and their intervention in regional conflicts have no legal basis and should be opposed in every possible manner. Despite the historic differences between littoral states, there do exist options and Arab compromise formulas that can be thrashed out without inviting foreign interference. (*Kayhan International,* August 11, 1990).

Many Iranian editorialists scrutinized U.S. motives for interfering in the Persian Gulf crisis. For instance, one editorial assessment of U.S. objectives in the Persian Gulf noted that in addition to wanting to "force Iraq out of Kuwait, check the Iraqi power and organize its long-term policies accordingly, and gain a close access to the black gold, 'oil,' the United States also wanted to "check the Islamic movements and Iran as the heart of the Islamic world" (*Kayhan International,* January 30, 1991). Thus, Iranian editorialists acknowledged pressure coming from the West along with a confidence that neither the Iranian public nor government would acquiesce to that pressure.

Although Iranian editorialists commented on the uncertainty of the outcome of the Persian Gulf crisis, they observed the "establishment of an Islamic powerful union among the regional countries to keep peace and security" in the region (*Kayhan International,* January 9, 1991). Editorialists viewed Baghdad through a dual lens: as a counterforce to Western pressure and as a springboard from which the United States could launch its propaganda.

To justify its actions before the U.S. public and gain the support of other nations, the United States was perceived by Iranian editorialists as manipulating the media. "The heavy censorship of war reports, and the publishing of slanted news reports by the U.S. and the Western media, is a prominent feature of the Persian Gulf war," observed one editorial (*Kayhan International,* January 23, 1991).

One perceived victim of U.S. propaganda was Saudi Arabia. From the start of the Persian Gulf crisis, Iranian editorialists argued that the large number of U.S. forces in the Gulf suggested the inevitability of a conflict and the continuation of a U.S. presence in the region. Nevertheless, Saudi Arabia partook in this buildup because of its own political and military insecurities, thereby jeopardizing its own cultural integrity. On this matter, an editorial observed that "Washington will milk rich Arab sheikdoms in the name of defending them against external threats" (*Kayhan International,* November 25, 1990).

Editorials in Iran also showed skepticism toward the U.S. use of the United Nations to resolve the Persian Gulf crisis. A newspaper editorial pointed out that "the structure of the U.N, specially the Security Council, as one of its key elements, has been based on injustice in the hands of the victors of World War II" (*Kayhan International,* January 23, 1991). According to another editorial, the United States was manipulating the United Nations for its own ends. "Mr. George Bush is attempting to use the U.N. as a front for achieving unquestioned hegemony over the world's energy lifeline" (*Kayhan International,* August 16, 1990). The neglect of U.N. Resolution 665, which condemned the aggression and asked Iraq to withdraw from Kuwait peacefully and return to the international borders, appeared to be the result of U.S. pressure to force Iraq out of Kuwait and a breaching of the Security Council's pledge of neutrality. One editorial remarked, "The contrast with what is happening to Iraq five months after swallowing Kuwait is an object lesson in just how the U.N. and specifically the Security Council are used to legitimize imperialist aims. In the so-called post–Cold War era's first major crisis the world body, whose mandate is to solve crises through pacific means, has been bent to the purposes of the White House in turning Iraq into a vast parking lot . . . in the name of liberating Kuwait" (*Kayhan International,* February 2, 1991). In this view, "the concept of upholding international rules and regulations in the framework of the U.N. charter is more in tune with the evil designs of military and economic powers rather than the lofty goal of maintaining law and order."

From the standpoint of Iranian editorialists, U.S. intervention served to confirm U.S. military power and to regain a sense of U.S. pride and superiority as the United States continued to lose the economic race with Germany and Japan and to wallow in its own domestic problems.

As early as the month following the invasion, Tehran editorials commented that the future of the United States as a superpower depended on its ability to force Saddam Hussein out of Kuwait. For Iran in particular, this awareness meant that the United States would use its Persian Gulf security plan as a "superpower device for checking the Islamic Revolution" (*Kayhan International,* January 23, 1991), among other ends.

Hence, Iranian editorialists viewed many of Persian Gulf crisis events within the Islamic and historical context. Reference to the Iran-Iraq War, which pitted both Saddam Hussein and the United States against Iran's Islamic movement, raised questions about the sincerity of U.S. motives for being in the Gulf. The United States essentially was described as having a hidden agenda of premeditated war behind the guise of "liberating" Kuwait and restoring peace in the region. In effect, the United States was seen as leading a Western conspiracy to gain control of the economic and political climate of the Middle East for its own gains and prestige. Part of this hegemonic action would be to create regional tension over sensitive issues such as the Kurds and the Palestinians that would divide the Arab and Islamic worlds. By breaking the unity among Arabs and Muslims, the United States could then effectively claim the role of stabilizer and thereby maintain its clutch on oil resources.

Similarly, Jordanian editorialists described the Persian Gulf crisis and war as a scenario manipulated for Western ends. A Jordanian editorialist commented:

> Put simply, this is a war by which the American-led cash register coalition wishes to preserve the neo-imperial order which Great Britain and France instituted in the Middle East three-quarters of a century ago. The battle for Kuwait is and was a fake because we always knew and said that Iraq single-handedly could not stand up to the military forces arrayed against it. But the military battle is not what this conflict is all about. The battle for the new world order is real, and it has just begun. Like Vietnam, this shift from militarism to political struggle is marked by overwhelming American supremacy in weapons technology, but also overwhelming American ignorance and naivete about the political and mental landscape of the Third World. The video game is almost over. The real political and human battle is now almost engaged. (*Jordan Times,* February 23, 1991)

Jordanian views, however, varied in emphasis from Iranian ones because of Jordan's different geopolitical position in the Persian Gulf. Specifically, they focused on the Palestine question and the need to avoid war. Given a position between the cross-fire of Iraq and Israel and the U.S. bases in Saudi Arabia, these editorialists highlighted the regional need to avoid bloodshed. Thus, one editorial stated that militarily, the outcome of the war was determined in advance. No one should or could have expected Iraq to prevail over thirty countries led by the United States in an all-out shooting war.

Furthermore, Jordan, being largely composed of Palestinians and being a neighbor of Israel, naturally focused on the implications of the Persian Gulf crisis for the Palestinian-Israeli conflict. On this topic an editorial explained:

> From the first day of the crisis, and during the war, Jordan stood by its principles and behaved as a responsible member of the international community. Jordan neither responded to bribes nor to blackmail, and opposed the coalition's intent to destroy Iraq. But Jordan has a crucial role to play in resolving the Palestinian question, reestablishment of Middle East stability, and above all in helping to heal the wounds of the war. (*Jordan Times,* March 24, 1991)

Jordanian editorialists posed several questions for the "Western conscience." "Why is it when Saddam occupies Kuwait he is called a Hitler and when Bush and his colleagues occupy oilfields in the Gulf they are liberators? When Saddam sends 38 Scud missiles into Israel he is a terrorist and when the American coalition makes over 90,000 sorties in one month and throws more than 100 thousand tonnes of explosives, mostly over Iraqi and Kuwaiti civilian targets, they are champions of justice?" "Why for the past 40 years and in spite of all the injustice, torture and humiliation endured by the Palestinians under Israeli rule, has there never been (and never will be) an American human rights committee to investigate their plight, while barely two months after the Iraqi invasion a Senate Human Rights Committee convenes to listen to Kuwaitis testimony against Iraq and the hearing are aired on all the national networks?" (*Jordan Times,* February 26, 1991).

The questions that Jordanian editorialists provoked in the minds of their readers led to the conclusion that "the age of the new international disorder is upon us, brought about by the western culture of violence whose coin and currency is the use of force" (Kamel S. Abu Jaber, "Shattered Myths," *Jordan Times,* March 2, 1991). Another article summed up this view: "The West achieved all its strategic aims on or even before Aug. 2, 1990, when this present crisis ostensibly began. By that date, the oil was already secure in Western hands, Saudi Arabia protected, and an Iraqi commitment to withdraw from Kuwait secured" (Kamel S. Abu Jaber, "Back to the Future," *Jordan Times,* February 23, 1991).

Egyptian editorials differed from those of Jordan and Iran primarily because of the split between a government policy that supported the

U.S.-led coalition against Iraq and indigenous groups that opposed U.S. intervention in the Persian Gulf crisis. Some editorialists, such as those in *Al-Ahram,* sympathized with those who backed Iraq, not because Saddam Hussein invaded Kuwait, but rather because he stood up against Western powers (*Mideast Mirror,* March 5, 1991). *Al-Ahram* further contended that although Arab and Western interests initially converged in the effort to liberate Kuwait, differences in long-term goals for the region were occasioning a split.

Other Egyptian editorials focused on and critiqued Iraqi aggression, and editorialists who aligned with the Egyptian administration emphasized the need to squelch that aggression by any means, including force and all-out war. This attitude toward the war came forth in the official media coverage that emphasized the allies' military superiority and inevitable victory.

A group of Egyptian intellectuals against the Persian Gulf War spoke out in editorials. In regard to U.S. and U.N. measures to use force, they commented, "It should be starkly obvious, we believe, that this kind of military logic constitutes a clear violation of the Geneva Conventions on the rights of civilian populations during war, and that it is no different from the logic that lay behind that most shameful episode in human history: the nuclear bombing of Hiroshima and Nagasaki" (*Mideast Mirror,* February 22, 1991).

They went on to state:

> It is also a war aimed at establishing the exclusive supremacy of the United States in a new unipolar world order. In its massive—directly televised—show of U.S. and Western military force, it hopes to make of Iraq an example to the rest of the Arab people and indeed to the peoples of the whole Third World, whereby—and regardless of the particular pretext in this case—the real message is that any form of resistance to U.S. Western interests will be severely punished, even if this punishment involves the destruction of whole Third World nations. It is for this reason, and not for the naive claims of military security, that misinformation and an unprecedented information blanket have been such a distinctive feature of this war.

These types of editorials captured the mood of protest toward the war sweeping the Egyptian masses. One editorial remarked, "By pitting the rich Gulf States against Iraq, the West was turning Arab wealth against Arab might with the aim of destroying both together" (*Mideast Mirror,* January 30, 1991).

PART THREE

◆

Coming Back to Reality

CHAPTER FIFTEEN

◆

Twisting the U.N. Charter to U.S. Ends

Richard A. Falk

WITH THE ONSET of the actual war in the Gulf, the role of the United Nations diminished almost to zero. It became evident to all that, for better or worse, this war was the outcome of decisions made in Washington by U.S. political leaders acting on their own. The United States succeeded in building a coalition of countries that nominally cooperated during the war. Unilateral U.S. control over combat strategy was virtually unchallenged. And yet in a formal sense this was a U.N. war, the approach and results voted on by the Security Council over a period of months and approved by such major governments as those of the Soviet Union, France, and Japan. But was this the way the United Nations was expected to work on behalf of international peace and security? Was this Gulf War a fulfillment of the dream of a powerful United Nations taking over the task of protecting countries from aggression, or was it the perversion of that dream?

For decades, during the whole of the cold war, peace-minded persons lamented the political paralysis in the organization that made the United Nations little more than a spectator in relation to the most serious eruptions of international conflict. With the ending of the cold war, especially accompanied by Mikhail Gorbachev's enthusiastic support for a global approach to war/peace issues, the United Nations received a new lease on life. The Gulf crisis seemed to present the perfect opportunity to take full advantage of these favorable developments—clear aggression against a small state, with the aggressor, for the first time in U.N. history, purporting to annex a member and then intensifying the criminality of the undertaking by holding foreign residents hostage and committing severe crimes against humanity in the occupied country.

Given such provocation, and with East-West conflict abated, it seemed entirely possible and beneficial to fashion an appropriate, strong, and concerted U.N. response. Iraq's aggression against Kuwait also threatened the security and price structure of the world oil market, engaging powerful interest. Endorsing a firm response at the global level under U.N. auspices was not, however, equivalent to suggesting either that war should have been authorized or that the United States should have been allowed to run the show on its own. War should not have been authorized by the Security Council, or even threatened by way of the January 15 deadline. If war erupted in any event, the United Nations had an obligation to control the definition of war goals and the means chosen to achieve them and to use its authority to impose a cease-fire. The Security Council had no authority whatsoever to delegate these responsibilities to one or more of its members, and its own legitimacy in relation to the overall membership of the United Nations, especially with regard to the Islamic world, was drawn into serious question by its response to the Gulf crisis. The General Assembly and the secretary general should have been far more active in preventing war, more vigilant in upholding the integrity of the U.N. Charter in the face of the failure of the Security Council to act in accord with either its letter or spirit, and more vigorous in avoiding the impression and reality of double standards with respect to U.N. authority. (Israel, with U.S. backing, had been defying U.N. authority for years in its refusal to withdraw from the territories occupied during the 1967 war as well as in its rejection of all reasonable approaches to the satisfaction of Palestinian claims of self-determination.)

The people of the world were subjected to a series of misleading arguments to justify the U.S./U.N. approach in the period between August 2, the date of the invasion of Kuwait, and the initiation of warfare on January 15. Whether these arguments were put forward sincerely or hypocritically remains difficult to tell, although a mixture of belief and expediency is the most likely assessment. It is disturbing that such large portions of the public and the media swallowed these arguments with so little critical reaction, especially in the weeks leading up to the outbreak of war. It remains important to contest and expose the U.S. arguments that persuaded the Security Council to issue a blank check.

There is no doubt that the United Nations formally authorized the U.S. approach. President George Bush can correctly claim that the U.N. Security Council endorsed twelve resolutions to condemn Iraq's invasion and occupation of Kuwait, implemented tough economic sanctions against Iraq, and authorized the use of force to compel Saddam to comply. But behind this formal mandate lie extremely serious questions about whether the United Nations was true to its own charter and to the larger purposes of peace and justice that it was established to serve. And there is the disturbing impression that the United Nations was converted during the Gulf crisis into a virtual tool of U.S. foreign policy, thereby compromising its future credibility.

There was, above all, the granting of an unrestricted mandate to use force after January 15. U.N. Security Council Resolution 678 authorized "all necessary means" without guidance or clarification. It was widely understood in advance as giving Washington a green light to wage the war of its choice under U.S. command so long as the war began after the deadline had passed. Resolution 678 did not even contain limits as to duration or impose an obligation to keep the Security Council informed; it contained no restrictions as to the level of destructive means and failed to establish any accountability for civilian damage. The resolution did not even include a prohibition against reliance on weapons of mass destruction. To issue such an open-ended warrant to the United States to wage unrestricted war contradicted the fundamental U.N. undertaking "to save succeeding generations from the scourge of war."

President Bush's purported willingness "to go the extra mile for peace" added up to little more than his so-called offer of meetings at the foreign minister level. Secretary of State James Baker was instructed to meet with Foreign Minister Tariq Aziz in Geneva on the basis of Bush's conviction that there should be no negotiations, compromises, attempts at face-saving, and rewards for aggression. This was hardly an instruction that encouraged diplomacy.

The full extent of this perversion of the U.N. role and purpose became painfully evident as January 15 approached. Virtually all diplomatic attention was fixed on the interaction between Washington and Baghdad, with some minor confusing byplay on the part of the European Community, especially France. The United Nations virtually disappeared as an actor. If this had been a genuine U.N. undertaking, then one would have expected the Security Council to be in virtually continuous session as a situation of this magnitude moved toward its dangerous climax and Secretary General Javier Pérez de Cuellar to be feverishly engaged in stimulating a negotiated withdrawal from Kuwaiti territory. Instead, in the weeks prior to the war, there appeared to be no disposition whatsoever to allow even further discussion in the Security Council (evidently out of a fear of weakening the threat of war after January 15). The secretary general became almost invisible.

In what was no more than a last-minute gesture apparently designed to create an illusion of peaceful intentions, Baker announced from Geneva after his futile talks with Aziz on January 9 that because direct contact between the United States and Iraq had produced no results, the United States would now welcome a subsequent last-ditch effort by the secretary general and other members of the U.N. coalition. This encouragement was belated and halfhearted and was explicitly restricted to the Bush guidelines that deliberately provided no room whatsoever for diplomatic maneuver. Pérez de Cuellar visited Iraq and Saudi Arabia on this meaningless basis shortly before January 15, an undertaking he should have refused. This feeble and insincere initiative seemed part of the effort to build the case for war rather than to facilitate peace. We now know that President Bush and his "war cabinet" (of close advisers) had definitely decided on war at Camp David during the Christmas period. It is quite astonishing that even Saudi Arabia and Kuwait, the countries most affected, were not allowed to participate in this decision-making process, nor were they seriously consulted. Nothing was done in this period by other members to challenge the use and abuse of the United Nations.

The difficulties with the U.N. handling of the crisis go deeper. Article 33 of the U.N. Charter imposes on states a fundamental obligation to seek a negotiated solution to any international dispute that is war threatening. Of course, one can rhetorically maintain in relation to the Gulf crisis, as did Prime Minister John Major of Britain, that it is wrong to negotiate with a burglar. But such an analogy is simplistic and faulty. An international crisis cannot be usefully compared to a civil crime. Far more complex issues and interests are at stake. The peace and well-being of many millions of innocent people were jeopardized by the refusal to find a peaceful solution. This refusal was all the more inexcusable given that the anti-Iraq sanctions seemed effective.

The U.N. rush to mandate war totally ignored the sanctions process. Again, no one can claim with certainty whether and at what time sanctions could have succeeded, but it was far too soon to conclude that they had failed. Ironically, the two countries most reluctant to pursue the sanctions approach in this crisis, the United States and United Kingdom, were the very same states that had lectured the world community to take the time to enable sanctions against South Africa to exert meaningful pressure. The evidence suggests that sanctions were exerting heavy pressure on Iraq, a country whose viability was tied to foreign exchange earnings from oil exports. William Webster, then director of the CIA and no critic of U.S. policy, testified before Congress that sanctions had cut down Iraqi exports by 97 percent and imports by 90 percent; other prominent former U.S. government and military officials supported the general proposition that sanctions had been surprisingly effective. Journalists on the scene also confirmed in late 1990 that sanctions were taking their toll in Iraq. In the face of such evidence, it was a scandal for the U.N. to abandon sanctions. And the scandal was compounded by the parallel rejection of diplomatic approaches to a negotiated Iraqi withdrawal.

There is also a serious technical difficulty with the fundamental resolution of the Security Council that set the January 15 deadline. According to Article 27(3) of the charter, decisions by the Security Council on this sort of issue require "an affirmative vote of nine members including the *concurring* votes of the permanent members." China abstained from Resolution 678, and an abstention is not a concurring vote. There is, however, a shaky precedent for ignoring China's abstention that goes back to the Korean War, when the Security Council was allowed to authorize force during a period when the Soviet Union was boycotting its sessions. Then, at least, a constitutional argument was set forth that attempted to explain and justify the apparent evasion of the charter by rationalizing it as a response to the Soviet *boycott*. It was argued that the boycott was an expression of a refusal to participate in the activity of the Security Council and hence provided grounds for saying that for the sake of world peace Soviet nonparticipation in the voting could be overlooked. A parallel argument could no doubt be put forward in the setting of an abstention, but it was never attempted, and it would have been difficult to make such a line of reasoning convincing. It might be desirable to abandon the veto, given the more cooperative East-West relationship that now exists, and such a course might be helpful for the future growth of the United Nations. This would, however, require an amendment to the charter.

It is further distressing that such an obvious breach of the U.N. constitutional structure did not occasion challenge and discussion both in the organization and press. Silence on this matter indicated how complete the U.S. control over the use of U.N. machinery had been since August 2. Even the two states that voted against Resolution 678, Yemen and Cuba, failed to raise any constitutional objection to this way of proceeding. Overlooking the constitutional framework of the United Nations compromised the independence and future of the organization. It was neither healthy nor politically acceptable for the United Nations to become the creature of the only remaining superpower in the world, especially in the area of peace and security.

It should be clear, then, that the U.N. authorization to unleash the Gulf War rested on an extremely weak foundation. Recourse to war demonstrated the weakness of the United Nations in relation to its own charter far more than it added to the U.S. claim that its policies were a justifiable solution to the Gulf crisis. Because the United Nations gave its blessings to the war does not mean this course of action was legitimate.

The U.S. assertion went basically unchallenged that to work for overall stability in the region would reward Iraqi aggression. Any mention of justice for the Palestinians, even the proposal of a conference to consider Palestinian claims, was waved off by Washington with the single word *linkage*. The Palestinian card was delivered into Saddam's hand only because the West had taken such a hostile and imbalanced approach to the Israeli-Palestinian conflict. Diplomatic movement toward the creation of a Palestinian state was long overdue and should have helped resolve the suffering and continual warfare experienced by the peoples of the region, including the Israelis, for more than four decades. Beyond this, the U.N. response to Iraq's illegal occupation of Kuwait should have been balanced by a belated but necessary rectification of Israel's illegal and prolonged occupation of the West Bank and the Gaza strip. Beyond this, it would have been desirable to take steps to restore full Lebanese sovereignty, a country cruelly victimized for almost two decades by periodic Syrian, Israeli, and/or PLO interventions and occupations.

These regional concerns should still be addressed with urgency. Such initiatives never needed to be packaged as a deal with Iraq, but if a war could have been prevented because they incidentally provided some kind of face-saving benefits for Saddam Hussein, it would have been a bargain price to pay for Iraq's unconditional withdrawal from Kuwait.

That war came to the Gulf was to a large extent a consequence of governments and public opinion being lulled toward submissiveness by a U.N. diplomacy of illusion crafted by the U.S. government. Most states learned passivity during the cold war, leaving global peace and security almost totally in the hands of the superpowers. The Gulf War made it plain that the persistence of this passivity was likely to produce a dangerous new version of Pax Americana. One consequence of such a development would be to make the United Nations into a rubber stamp and its secretary general into an errand boy.

The present era even now offers opportunities for a new world order that is less militaristic and more centered on respect for international law and on an increased U.N. role. But such a possibility cannot happen until more governments take greater responsibility for shaping and implementing global policy. The Gulf War vividly demonstrates the acute dangers to world peace that arise from a refusal of those countries with economic and political leverage to throw their weight in the direction of peaceful settlement of conflict; common standards of law, morality, and justice; and an acceptance of the will of the global community as expressed through the main organs of the United Nations.

CHAPTER SIXTEEN

◆

CNN: Elites Talking to Elites

Richard C. Vincent

Just as General Powell tuned to CNN for news from Baghdad, so Iraq officials tuned to it for news from around the world and also used it to transmit news that it wanted to get out. . . .

A tired-looking President Bush, meeting with his Cabinet and Congressional leaders, told reporters there was "a lot of prayer going on." As if to confirm the point, Saddam Hussein shortly appeared in clips from Iraqi television doing some silent solitary praying (to the shriek of a siren in the background), while Mr. Bush attended church with an entourage that included the Rev. Billy Graham.[1]

CNN COVERAGE IS UNIQUE because of the network's twenty-four-hour newscast format and its commitment in covering the Persian Gulf War almost exclusively for nearly two months in early 1991. Hence, CNN became the newscast of record for the War and as such made a significant contribution to contemporary trends in electronic journalism.

Having attracted worldwide attention in the past (Beijing in 1989, the San Francisco earthquake, the *Challenger* space shuttle disaster), CNN positioned itself as a key news player soon after the Iraqi invasion of Kuwait. Two months after the invasion, CNN had already spent some $15 million on coverage of the crisis. The gamble paid off!

At the time of the war, CNN was legally received in more than one hundred countries. Unlike other news networks, CNN enjoyed a more lucrative financial situation because it collected advertising and cable fee revenues in addition to news service fees. Its worldwide visibility had also given CNN extremely good access to world leaders for stories and interviews. While CNN depended on these elites for its news and information, elites also relied on CNN. As Jay Rosen observed in the *Nation,* in "newsrooms, international airports, foreign ministries and financial houses around the world, CNN is left on all the time."[2] Even the Pentagon was reported to be watching CNN for late-breaking developments that its intelligence sources might not yet have received.

Domestically many viewers also relied on CNN for information on the Gulf War. During the first week of battle, the full-day average audience was 7.5 percent of the 56.7 million U.S. cable television households—by all counts fairly high. ABC was the next closest network, and it attracted only 4.4 percent of the viewers. Even though CNN's second-week full-day average dropped to 4.4 percent, that was still more than six times higher than CNN's typical audience before the war.[3] Its advertising rates jumped from $3,500 per thirty-second spot before the war to more than $20,000 after the war began. This occurred at a time when other major U.S. networks were reporting a loss of advertisers (as little as 20 percent of commercial time sold for specials). Clearly, then, CNN enjoyed a commanding domestic and international presence during the Gulf War.

Given that CNN played such a seminal role in conveying events of the war to so many people, it is fitting to examine how the network portrayed the war and what symbiotic relationship obtained between elite viewers and CNN presentation of elite news sources. By featuring news elites, CNN may have helped perpetuate various social norms and official viewpoints and may have functioned as a source of propaganda and disinformation. Hence news accuracy was potentially affected by both the news organization and newsmakers. We saw many examples of both during the Persian Gulf War, and charges of manipulation and bias were at times strongest against CNN.

The elite media and the news media's use of elite sources have already been topics of analysis. In a particularly interesting work looking at historical relationships among power, social order, and communications during the central Middle Ages (and other later time periods), James Curran demonstrated how various preindustrial society media—buildings, paintings, statues, coins, banners, stained glass windows, songs, medallions, and rituals—served either to help establish or to reinforce classes of the ruling elite during the rise of the papal government.[4]

The use of elite news sources by contemporary media has also been examined by the Glasgow Media Group. In one analysis, the group observed that "interviewees are drawn from an extremely narrow section of the social and political spectrum" and that "a large number of the statements quoted and referenced come from the same individuals in the narrow group that were interviewed most frequently."[5] The group concluded that particular worldviews are reinforced by journalistic practices and that this situation "prestructures what the news is to consist of and in a sense what the journalists themselves actually see as exciting, or as being significant in the world."[6]

Use of news elites was a concern in an analysis of U.S. television network news stories on air crashes. The authors found that such coverage may lend itself to maintenance of the "status quo."[7]

This emphasis on news elites becomes increasingly relevant because news images are now being transmitted faster than ever before, leaving less time for investigation of facts and evaluation of stories. For a long time, attention focused on the power of Western news media to control the flow of information throughout the world. Now we find that newsmakers have increasing power because the technology seems to lessen the abilities of news organizations to scrutinize and evaluate the images they transmit.

How Did CNN Present News on the War?

To facilitate this examination of elite news and news source presentation by the U.S.-based CNN, I categorize the various stories found in its telecasts during the war. There are eight categories in all.

1. Press briefings, speeches, and other staged news events by political and military leaders
2. Tapes and interviews supplied by military or government sources
3. Press pool stories
4. Reports recapping events, supplemented with sound bites from press briefings and staged news events (speeches by elites, government/military-supplied tapes, press pool footage, etc.) reported from the studio or on location (including media-controlled interviews with newsmakers or potential newsmakers)
5. Use of consultants and other "experts" to amplify or analyze events
6. Interviews of non-elite sources
7. Original stories based on current or related events (based on staff research)
8. Events in which news personnel are allowed to become the story

Press Briefings, Speeches, and Other Staged News Events

Press conferences and similar programming are an approach most viewers recognize and remember from television's Gulf War coverage. Common were daily briefings from the U.S., British, French, and Saudi commands in Riyadh, from the Pentagon, and from the White House. Many of these, carried live by CNN, provided direct access to information on daily casualties, strategies, and military maneuvers.

Going "live" is fairly routine in television news. Breakaway live reports and continuous live coverage of news events have been common throughout its history. Since the early days of the medium, U.S. networks have brought key correspondents together to report from the floors of U.S. political conventions, presidential inaugurations, and so on. Most of the nation watched when in 1963 ABC, CBS, and NBC canceled all regular programming and provided four-day continuous live coverage of John F. Kennedy's funeral. In the 1970s U.S. news audiences sat by their televisions to watch full coverage of the Senate Watergate hearings and other breaking news stories.

It was this class of coverage that took center stage in CNN's programming objectives–to offer twenty-four hour coverage of the Persian Gulf War. With so much time to fill, it made sense to supply live coverage whenever feasible. After all, live, continual coverage was something the competition could not provide given the multiplicity of its programming schedule, particularly when the war did not conveniently end within a few days. And it was in crises and disasters such as the space shuttle *Challenger* disaster that CNN had demonstrated the advantages of a twenty-four-hour news service in the past. CNN regularly carried live coverage as interest warranted.

Live reporting lends itself well to television. Television equipment has become extremely portable, and satellite transmission technologies have severely reduced the costs of sending footage coast-to-coast as well as around the world. Opinion polls have found that the U.S. public now names television as its primary news source. Immediacy is undoubtedly one reason for this circumstance.

From a narrative viewpoint, the use of live press conference and dignitary speeches helps set the stage for a conflict, aids in viewer identification of the major players, and allows the principals to tell their story. Unfortunately, such a method also provides the opportunity for those conducting the briefing or giving the speech to more or less set the agenda. It was in such an environment that Saddam Hussein requested that U.S. television networks carry a ninety-minute address to the U.S. public during the conflict. CNN complied. Although some faulted CNN, there may be little difference between this footage and comparable addresses from U.S. dignitaries. How can we evaluate the degree of propaganda in one versus the other? By carrying such events, CNN in effect partially shifted the burden of analysis from newscaster to viewer, even though analysis and summaries still typically followed such telecasts.

One objective of these well-orchestrated events was to feed certain information, or disinformation, to the opposition forces. Such a function was hinted at in the following military briefing excerpt:

REPORTER: General, you've referred today and on previous occasions to Saddam in personal terms. And you've talked about his air force and his forces today. Do you think Saddam is listening to your words now and are you trying to psychologically intimidate him?

GENERAL H. NORMAN SCHWARZKOPF: I've been trying to psychologically intimidate him from long before the beginning of this conflict. I think we have pretty well predicted for Saddam Hussein exactly what would happen if he went to war against us and he didn't choose to believe it. And I think he is—I don't know whether he knows what's exactly going on. But I have no intention of psychologically intimidating him, as much as I have of spelling out the simple facts of what's happening and what's going to go on happening.[8]

Let us look at a potential problem of such televised press conferences/briefings. The speaker may wish to be less than straightforward when relaying information on defenses or casualties. One side may wish to inflate while the other may wish to deflate. By never specifically addressing Iraqi casualties numbers, for example, these press briefings neatly shifted attention away from the grim fact than more than one hundred thousand had died. The rationale could be to intentionally mislead citizens, politicians, or members of the opposition or to affect world opinion. Whether misdirection or avoidance is the objective, the public loses.

At times, the maintenance of national security may be a very legitimate concern. But who is to determine that not to divulge information really supports a nation's interest? In one exchange a reporter asked briefer Colonel Greg Pepin about the weather. "When the weather is clear, it's good. When it's cloudy, it's bad." In frustration the reporter noted, "You were asked a direct question about the weather, not necessarily tomorrow's weather or today's weather. It has passed. The Iraqis know what today's weather is. We were asking has the weather improved, enabling your operations to function better because we know these have been problems in recent days with the weather? Why are you unable to answer that question?" Pepin replied, "I'm not a weatherman. I wasn't up there flying." The reporter then asked, "Today's weather?" Pepin relied, "Today's weather—past history."[9]

In another case, we witnessed actual disregard of reporters' questions.

REPORTER #1: Have you gone through, sir? Is that why it's [the casualties] light?
SCHWARZKOPF: One more question.
REPORTER #2: General, have you encountered the Republican Guard yet?
SCHWARZKOPF: Over here, last question.
REPORTER #3: General, are you going to pursue the Iraqi soldiers into Iraq, or are you going to stop at the Kuwait-Iraq border?

SCHWARZKOPF: I'm not going to answer that question. We're going to pursue them in any way it takes to get them to get out of Kuwait. Thank you very much.[10]

In such circumstances the only solution may be to just continue probing. There were many stories of reporters being denied answers from one briefer when the same information was divulged by another. The press cannot serve as a fourth (or in the case of television, fifth) estate if it so readily succumbs to these avoidance techniques. By not asking questions, the press is merely serving as a public relations arm for the status quo. If the press had refused to carry these staged events, chances are that the formats would have changed. But CNN was as guilty as others for continuing to give credence to these staged-for-media demonstrations.

Still another situation falling under this category was the live coverage of events such as public "support" demonstrations for troops, peace marches, and protests. Now it was over the coverage of peace marches/ activities that the news media were criticized for failing to provide substantial time both before and after the war began, and CNN seemed to share in that blame. But the category of public support demonstrations bears closer examination, and there is no better example than the "homecoming" ceremonies that came soon after the cease-fire was announced. In these telecasts large amounts of time were devoted to scenes of crowds anticipating the arrival of troops, to an assortment of patriotic speeches, and to highly emotional family reunions. In at least one case, CNN even planted a microphone on an anxiously waiting woman so that viewers could share in the meeting with her returning husband (she did discuss the microphone planting with him before he landed to ensure that the dialogue would be usable). In footage from another homecoming ceremony, a static single camera recorded a speakers' platform from which euphoric and patriotic speeches were to be delivered. Of interest was certain foreground activity whereby someone could be observed encouraging a flag-holding audience member to move a bit closer to screen center. The result was a more symmetrically composed shot with U.S. flags flanking both the left and right sides of the screen. Even though the manipulation was minor and the intended effect may have been solely esthetic, the result nonetheless was to enhance the patriotic messages being delivered in an already emotionally charged situation.

One of the problems with telecasts of live footage is that they often tend to be specifically designed and orchestrated by elites to supply information and promote a particular point of view. Even Western leaders frequently speak of the media's potential impact when opposition governments or terrorist groups seem to monopolize news coverage. The problem arises when television news, by virtue of the relative proportion of time allotted, assigns undue weight to information gathered and televised in this manner. CNN, of course, is not solely responsible for this, and one can argue that CNN and most other media organs were left with little choice. Government and military leaders were holding the cards.

Supplied Tapes and Interviews

Like the previous category, this one, too, provides for optimal elite control. Military-prepared tapes can be supplied to the media, and interviews can be prearranged. (A highly selective process can be assumed in the latter, for few organizations would knowingly supply poorly prepared subjects who might present a picture contrary to the organization's objectives.) The U.S. military in particular has focused a great deal of energy on training personnel in the nuances of the press interview since the Vietnam War. As retired army colonel Darryl Henderson has acknowledged, the military has worked for years to master and train personnel in methods of "marketing the military viewpoint," with an emphasis on "upbeat" public reports. He had admitted that he, too, underwent such training when serving as commander of the Army Research Institute for the Behavioral and Social Sciences.[11]

When it comes to the use of "packaged" videotapes, the embedded messages can be highly refined, polished, public relations vehicles in which the potential effect has been maximized by the message creator. From the public's view, preproduced and edited tapes have the drawback of not allowing direct questioning by the press. Videotapes also have the power to be very highly persuasive, given the multiple channels of information and the air of authenticity associated with documentary-type footage. Clips may include testimonials from personnel involved in "action" or simply "slice-of-life" interviews. Official points of view are not relayed here, just rank-and-file personnel performing either ordinary or somewhat heroic acts. We can be sure, however, that the intention is to show military actions in as positive a light as possible and to glorify daily and special missions. Consider one such interview aired on CNN in early February when Iraqi pilots were found flying their planes into Iran.

LT. COLONEL RANDY BINGAM, U.S. AIR FORCE: I was leading a force ship up to the east side of Baghdad, where we were to set up a combat air patrol. Ah-, we were rotating two ships back and forth, the two ships, man-, meaning the ah-combat air patrol. And, the other two ships on the tanker, refueling, air-to-air refueling, ah- we were going back and forth, and ah- during one of those cycles, wow, I happened to be on the tanker. Ah-, my wingmen were manning the cap, east of Baghdad, and the Awax controller called um-, and ah- told him that he had some hits. Unknown bogeys, ah- north of Baghdad, eastbound. Ah-, and um, number three and number four man snapped in that direction, got their radar on um. Ah-, did an excellent job of running the intercept and caught um, ah-they appeared to be running for Iran. And I got um just short of the Iranian border and had the engagement there and there went 4 and 0.[12]

Given the instant nature of reporting the Gulf War, there were long periods of time when nothing much was happening. Earth-shattering stories did not break every day. Hence, the news media generally, and CNN in particular, were a fairly easy target for a public relations–minded military striving to supply images reaffirming that allied forces were fighting a just battle and, even more importantly, that they were winning.

This category also includes the video testimonials of "smart bombs" and missiles hitting their targets. So mesmerized was the press over this computer chip arms technology that journalists often seemingly lost sight of the true story they were covering. And by virtue of its continuous coverage format, CNN may have been guiltier than most. The black-and-white grainy footage always showed pinpoint accuracy of this high technology as the target entered the cross hairs of the camera and moments later the screen went blank. The released footage was always of a perfect hit. Rarely could human activity be seen on the ground prior to the explosion. It was all so sterile. Yet people undoubtedly were inside some of the buildings that were obliterated. The destructive power of these bombs and missiles was appalling—people unfortunate enough to be caught at the center were not identified, their arms, legs, and flesh scattered in small pieces. Yet all these realities were easily overlooked in the concentration on the technology alone.

Press Pool Stories

Much controversy surrounding news coverage of the Gulf War centered on the press pool system, which was designed to give a limited number of print and electronic journalists access to allied operations and keep them under the watchful eye of the military. Stories produced under this system were then available to all. Because of its restricted membership (initially about sixty chosen from the few hundred assigned to cover the Gulf), mostly large media organs were represented in the pools. This restriction prompted a number of organizations to complain about being passed over for membership. Within the pools there was also a good deal of controversy. Journalists who tried to venture out on their own were threatened with credentials suspensions. In one case, *New York Times* reporter Chris Hedges, after earlier interviewing Arab shopkeepers, had his papers withheld temporarily when he attempted to conduct an unaccompanied interview of a military hospital's public relations officer. In other instances, Wesley Bocxe, on assignment for *Time* maga-zine, reported being blindfolded and searched spread-eagled and a Reuters photographer was apprehended—both by national guard troops.[13]

Although the official rationale for such tight control was security and safety, the true objectives were presumably to help maximize control of information flow to the public. The outcome was very positive and extremely sterile footage. The pool format was skewed against profound revelation. Normally, the stories reviewed the allied store of military weapons and gadgetry or offered interviews of front-line personnel who operated some of the high-tech weapons or were simply perfecting combat skills.

Although pool stories normally showed routine military activities, some of the footage was nevertheless quite revealing, particularly when stories were run before they could be carefully reviewed by the network. This occurred frequently because CNN was trying to get material on the air quickly. A good example was an interview on February 11 (the complete interview was run in its entirety only once; later airings used sound bites):

> POOL REPORTER: What's the best thing you've gotten so far? Can you tell us?
> PILOT OF U.S. AIR FORCE, A-10 SQUADRON PLANE: Got a lot of good secondaries, lotta good explosions. Just kind fun. It's *great!* It's a great, ah ya-, it's like an amusement park, almost, but- except they're shootin back at ya so you gotta be real careful,- *smart* about what you do. But there's ah-, in a strange kind of way, there's a *fun-ness* about it.[14]

In another story CNN anchor Sharyl Attkinson introduced a pool story on U.S. Air Force A-10 ground attack jet fighters. The story followed a live report from Israel where air raid warnings had just sounded and antiair-craft artillery was lighting up the skies.

> PAT DAWSON: Among the first to arrive here when the crisis broke last August, the 355th fighter squadron reflected growing confidence. Young, almost stud-ied in their cockiness, the A-10 pilots say they have markedly improved their kill ratios of Iraqi ground targets as the quick lessons of combat have set in. A different war in just three weeks.
> LT. MIKE MCGEE, U.S. AIR FORCE: The th-thrill of it will still be there, but we can still go up into ah-, and go into enemy territory and go up and ah- drop our bombs and fire our mavericks and, and come home, ah-. We feel, no problem now.[15]

Although one may wonder about the decision some military censor made to allow the release of stories that relegated combat to a game-like activity, in context the emotions apparently were viewed as positive. After all, this footage documented the high morale pilots were enjoying (intended audience—military personnel and civilians at home as well as the other allies and the Iraqis) and provided a positive assessment of military maneuvers even though exact casualty figures were usually withheld. This footage seemed to complement those video arcade–type images in which devastating bombings were reduced to a surreal viewing experience. And journalists were undoubtedly affected. It was difficult not to rally around the flag. As Michael G. Gartner, president of NBC news observed, "It's just unreal to be watching a war unfold like a football game. . . . You get so wrapped up in covering it that you forget it's a war and you have to stand back and [sic] sometimes and say, 'My God, this is a war.' "[16]

Reports Recapping Events

This category of coverage frequently recapped news of the day. Stories reviewed and summarized latest events and those the network typically had been following over the course of the day. Recaps and news summaries often tended to center around major events as defined by "great men" and "great politics." (This approach was quite similar to the "great man" tradition discussed in Western historiography; the French *Annales* school was a reaction to such a trend.) Newspeople as "gatekeepers" helped perpetuate this tradition.

> MOLLY MCCOY: Good morning everyone. Eighteen and one-half hours to the deadline. The U.N. Security Council meets this morning for another attempt to avert war in the Persian Gulf. Last November the U.N. set that deadline for Iraq to get out of Kuwait or to face military action. The U.N. secretary general now says that extending the deadline is, as he put it, "out of the question." The Security Council were at New York until 2:45 this morning after hearing a report from Secretary General de Cuellar's unsuccessful peace mission to Baghdad. When council members reconvene about four hours from now, a new peace initiative from France will be one topic. U.S. Ambassador Thomas Pickering has already said that he does not like the French plan.[17]

The news summary is a staple of broadcast journalism. Reporters and anchors regularly summarize key events when relaying a news story and use information from many video and audio inputs. News summaries aired during the Gulf War regularly utilized footage—interviews, speeches, news briefings, reports filed by reporters, pool stories—originally supplied for other purposes. Such footage helped make stories more interesting by providing visual and aural variety. Such footage might have also served another purpose.

An examination of the information-processing/news-learning litera-
ture reveals that audience retention of information is quite low in regard
to television news. Just half of the viewers who watch television news
have even a cursory recall of 50 percent of the stories seen, for example.[18]
By reusing footage throughout the day, newspeople help viewers recall
and possibly retain information shared earlier. Remember that although
CNN is not exactly structured as a "headline" news service, many viewers
still join the telecast for only short periods of time. They "check in" with
the news channel frequently over the course of the day. The repetition
of stories is built with these audience flow patterns in mind.

Just as television commercials are scheduled to maximize viewer effect
through repetitive airings, so, too, can news footage serve to reinforce
itself when rebroadcast. Hence, newscasters are reiterating earlier reports
while also lending credibility to the footage as it takes on a reality of its
own. This became a problem that even Washington acknowledged when
a Bush adviser noted that intelligence reports included CNN material
with follow-up reports seemingly confirming the first report. "It turns
out that they're just using a later CNN broadcast. CNN confirming CNN."[19]

During the Persian Gulf War, we saw ABC and CBS move its anchors
to report from the Middle East. Utilizing its satellite technology, CNN
also relied heavily on this style of reporting but used its stateside anchors
to help coordinate the multiple news inputs. In all, such techniques of
news delivery may simply heighten the feeling of immediacy while
offering little in the way of substantial gain. As former news anchor Walter
Cronkite observed, "There's no real reason for live coverage. What
purpose does it serve, except some dramatic purpose? It doesn't serve a
real journalistic purpose."[20]

Consultants and Other "Experts"

By seeking multiple sources for news analysis, journalists increase the
possibility that they are reporting the true story, not just one that some
leaders want the public to believe. Potential inaccuracies may also be
uncovered. Reliability is maximized when the press fights for access to
sources.

It is the use of consultants and experts that can offer special insights,
particularly when the military is so reluctant to share information. The
danger, however, is that these individuals may often be considered elites.
Many military experts are themselves successful military men who may
have even helped plan aspects of current military information policies
or have helped design the weapons systems being used. In addition,
consultants by their very nature tend to be problem solvers. This is how
they make a living. The Gulf crisis, however, may not have been a crisis

that lent itself to simple solution strategies and perspectives. Thus, the frame of reference of some interviewed consultants may have been too narrow. Rather than providing diversity of viewpoints, these interviews sometimes ran the risk of simply reinforcing the status quo, something viewers were apparently receiving in great volume.

> QUESTION: . . . What should be America's war aims? Let me give you an example: Suppose after 10 days we smash this guy's military machines, his tanks, and he's got no surprise coming in and his ballistic missiles and his air forces and the rest of it. Is there any necessity then for us to immediately send a land army in Kuwait? Why not wait him out, rebuild our air ordnance, and come back with more air strikes if he hadn't quit.
> ROBERT HUNTER (IN SAN FRANCISCO): If he hasn't come at us in a way that we have to respond, that is, come at us with his armor or try to extend the war into Jordan, Israel, or try to draw on Iran—sure that's the wise thing to do. Though I must say if we are going to war, I also want to go after his nuclears while I'm at it, his nuclear potential.[21]

One alternative would have been more interviews with academics and authors. Although CNN did attempt this to a degree, we certainly did not see it enough during Gulf War coverage. And even though such experts were interviewed, they were used much less frequently than the alternative. Presumably the professional consultants came with better screen "presence" or other qualities with which the general public could better relate. But consider an example from CNN International that aired a few months after the war formally ended. The story was an extremely long one on Ethiopian poverty and included a five-minute or longer interview with author Graham Hancock. Hancock was informative but did not talk down to audiences. He provided great detail while being blunt and realistic. He outlined the problems and then noted obligations of a "responsible, thinking, world community."[22] During the Gulf War, such interviews were infrequent and were typically kept short. CNN seemed to favor interviews with other journalists when attempting to offer a diversity of views. This ranged from newspaper editors throughout the Middle East to those based right at home. Such interviews were certainly welcome, but even they were in the minority. By and large professional consultants were employed, and they usually supported the status quo.

Non-elite Sources

Although diversions from Pentagon briefings and addresses by political leaders may have seemed a welcome alternative, this footage was often trivial and frequently helped support or reinforce the basic goals of the status quo. These peripheral, human-interest stories almost always offered ancillary support to pro-allied efforts so prominently promoted throughout the war. Themes for these secondary support stories commonly centered around behind-the-scenes military personnel always prepared or coping with adversities, support services performed by military personnel stationed in the United States, or activities of family members, neighbors, and friends who were "keeping the faith" at home.

> RALPH WENGE, ANCHOR: In New Waverly, Texas, the jobs are pretty scarce these days for many of the town's high school graduates; the military was their best hope for the future. But as CNN's Mike Capps reports, the Persian Gulf War is clouding that future.
>
> MIKE CAPPS: American flags and hundreds of yellow ribbons fly proudly in New Waverly, Texas. Residents consider themselves extremely patriotic.
>
> [We see shots of pickup trucks moving down a small-town main street and yellow ribbons tied many places.]
>
> GRADY CHANDLER, NEW WAVERLY MAYOR AND RESTAURANTEUR: It's like one big family—if one family has problems—if they—if one cries, they all cry.

From here the story went on to include interviews of customers in a restaurant, then children and teachers in a school. The story ended with a shot of a picturesque little church followed by one with townsfolk on a porch with a large U.S. flag in the background. Reporter Mike Capps noted, "Residents say strength from God will pull their young men and women through the war in the Gulf."[23] Another story centered on a nursery school where many Saudi-based military had children in attendance. Still another glorified one of the first U.S. dead as the soldier's father, a former marine himself, rationalized the loss in an interview from his Utah home. Even though the mood in this final clip was somber, the dead marine was portrayed as a true hero. Never were U.S. political motives questioned, nor did the father doubt that his son was doing the "right thing."

Occasionally a story on non-elites did raise questions about the war, even if only subtly. One story from the Saudi Arabian desert focused on a U.S. Marine saxophone player playing his instrument from the sand dunes at sunset and emphasized the imminent danger the men and women at the front lines were under and how frightening that sometimes felt. The young marine commented, "It is an escape, it's an escape, it's a—hear that, kinda—none of that, I don't like to hear that, so when I'm playing I don't hear it, the people around me when I'm playing, they don't hear it. We just hear that [saxophone music in background playing throughout interview], we hear the pity pats of home, kids running around the street, the soft tune of [music verbalized by player], we hear our families calling us [aircraft noises in the far background], just an escape."[24]

In all, stories that emphasized non-elite sources supported the status quo more often than they raised questions about elite decisions and actions. This category represented vast untapped potential.

Original, Related Stories

Another category of Gulf War news was the original, investigative story based on current or related events. It was here that a journalist could explore key issues or look for answers not offered in formal briefings, press releases, and other orchestrated footage. The journalist could pose probing questions and collect evidence from any available source.

Some of these stories fell into the category of patriotic journalism. Take David Burnkoff's report on the Tomahawk missile, for example. While exploratory in terms of background material (how the missile worked), the piece was basically a public relations release glorifying allied technology superiority.[25] But other stories did indeed provide a true alternative from the standard rhetoric of Gulf War reporting, as can be seen in the following excerpt from a February 8 special report in which Frank Sesno provided an early analysis of George Bush's so-called new world order.

SHARYL ATTKINSON: You've probably heard U.S. president Bush say many times that he has a vision of a new world order, nations working together in harmony. Critics say the term *new world order* is just a catch phrase, a cliché. CNN's Frank Sesno reports.

FRANK SESNO: Of the many reasons given for going to the war in the Persian Gulf, one rings out for its soaring, if vague, ideals. . . . President Bush calls it the "new world order."

PRESIDENT BUSH: It is a big idea-, a new world order-, where *di*verse nations are drawn together in common cause- to achieve the universal aspirations of mankind: peace- and security-, freedom-, and the rule of law.

SESNO: The president first spoke of a new world order amid the collapse of communism in Eastern Europe, the revolutions of 1989. But critics observe it is more than the absence of just the cold war. It is building new institutions to manage crisis and change. In Paris last November thirty-five countries signed on to the challenge. But the new world order is often invoked, seldom defined. Its lofty principles can change with the landscape, sometimes reminiscent of Woodrow Wilson's League of Nations utopia.

BUSH: Now my vision of a new world order, ah-, foresees a United Nations with a revitalized peace keeping function.

SESNO: Sometimes reminiscent of Theodore Roosevelt's "big stick" diplomacy.

BUSH: And when we win, and we will-, we will have- [applause], we will have taught a dangerous dictator, and *any* tyrant, tempta, tempted to follow in his footsteps, that the U.S. has a new *credibility*. And that what we say, goes. [crowd noises, cheers, general approval]

CHARLES LICHTENSTEIN, FORMER DEPUTY U.S. AMBASSADOR TO THE UNITED NATIONS: I think the danger of saying that sort of thing, without knowing *exactly* what you mean by it is that a lot of people, including *friends* of ours, are probably beginning to be a little bit worried about what begins to sound almost like, and here again I use capital letters, Pax Americana.

SESNO: The world's policemen. U.S. officials *insists* [*sic*] that's not what America wants or intends.

DICK CHENEY, U.S. DEFENSE SECRETARY: To play policemen to the world implies that somehow you're going to get involved in every conflict, everywhere, wherever it arrives. We have *no* such idea of trying to do that.

PETER RODMAN, FORMER NATIONAL SECURITY COUNCIL OFFICIAL: We would not be succeeding if we didn't have the cooperation of many others. And I think people rightly pay tribute to the president for, for multilateral, ah, diplomacy that can be conducted in pulling this coalition together. That I think is a model for the future.

SESNO: But that future is clouded. The Soviet Union, pivotal to the new world order, has lurched to the right—its ethnic tensions, bleeding sores, its economy collapsing, its people, like its politics, strained almost to the breaking point. It is a shaky foundation on which to build a new international structure. The concept's vagueness lends itself to hyperbole.

JAMES BAKER, U.S. SECRETARY OF STATE: We are really at ah, at a hinge of history, if you will, in terms of the possibility of a new order.

SESNO: And to criticism.

LICHTENSTEIN: I think it is a cliché. It is, it is a catch phrase to describe something that's emerging.

SESNO: To many, a new world order also implies far more than the president is willing to embrace. Fundamental change with a debt-ridden developing world. A new economic equation based on free trade and open markets. A far more active approach to problems of the global environment. [gunfire]

In the environment of this war, it's clear the world has changed. But how much, and how durably, remains a question. President Bush's new world order is very much an evolving idea. He may be keeping it vague deliberately. In any case, it is easier to invoke than it is easier to explain—or to implement. Frank Sesno, CNN, the White House.[26]

This commendable video essay squarely took on one of the principal idioms of the Bush campaign. To highlight the shallowness of such a phrase was a true departure from tendencies among the Western press, including CNN, throughout the war. Even though the story may have been largely ignored by the administration, the question was nevertheless asked. Sesno's piece demonstrated how journalists could have helped set the news agenda rather than simply follow one already set by the status quo. But many other questions, such as the cost of the war and the consequential "resource drain" effect it had on domestic social programs, went largely unasked.

Personnel-Focused Stories

This category has the potential to be the most dangerous, for attention gets shifted from news events to news-gathering and news personalities. CNN management in some ways may have recognized this danger when early on it decided to refrain from hiring "name" journalists (although the move was probably more heavily influenced by financial considerations).

In their zeal to break a story, U.S. television news networks came under stiff criticism for misreporting. Examples included ABC's and NBC's reports that the first Scud missiles launched against Israel carried chemical weapons. CBS aired reports of Israeli retaliation following this attack. Although CNN did not go as far, it noted that retaliation was almost inevitable. On another occasion it was widely reported, quoting Pentagon sources, that six Iraqi helicopters defected to Saudi Arabia prior to the start of the air battle. Still another was the story of how Iraqis threw newborn babies out of incubators, stole the incubators, and left the babies to die. It turned out that these reports were either untrue or grossly exaggerated. Few efforts were ever made to correct the record.

It was in one CNN telecast that we first learned of the start of the Gulf War. Through it, Holliman, Shaw, and Arnett became household names; CNN gained credibility; and CNN got a jump start that other U.S. networks never could equal.

The footage has been played and replayed. With these words John Holliman broke the news: "The war has begun in Baghdad." Holliman, Shaw, and Arnett then took turns narrating what they were observing from their Rashid Hotel windows. "There has been an attack," Holliman said. "The antiaircraft fire began twenty minutes ago. There were loud explosions, obviously bombing, perhaps near the airport and a military barracks. The attack started at 2:30 Baghdad time. Perhaps they are seeking out Iraqi radar sites." Holliman later added, "The sky is lighting up to the south with antiaircraft fire." CNN crew members could be heard reacting to nearby explosions. "An airburst." "The telecommunications center. Bombs are now hitting the center of the city. War has begun in Baghdad."

This was perhaps the highlight of Gulf War journalism. The dedication CNN's crew displayed by remaining on air when all competition was shut down was commendable. But there were other times when CNN decisions were questioned. In one instance, U.S. broadcast networks charged that CNN had made certain concessions to Iraq in exchange for special access to news during the first few weeks of the war. CNN dismissed the accusation as "desperate."[27] Another situation had Peter Arnett, the sole U.S. news correspondent based in Iraq, reporting on the allied jet bombing of what appeared to be a residential neighborhood of Al Dour, some one hundred miles from Baghdad. Twenty-four civilians were reportedly killed. As for their homes, "they were flattened as though shaken by an earthquake," Arnett reported. The U.S. military contended that an Iraqi "military munitions depot, a chemical warfare production and storage facility, and a military communications site" were all located nearby. Arnett was criticized for promoting an Iraqi viewpoint. Similar controversy surrounded the allied bombing of an alleged Iraqi baby formula plant, a civilian bomb shelter, and a bridge in the city of An Nasiriya, to name some.

> The Iraqi's say these bridges are used primarily for civilian traffic and should not be targeted. Doctors at the [inaudible] Hospital at An Nasiriya say hundreds of persons were walking across the bridge which crosses the Euphrates River that bisects the town of a million people. The three o'clock bombing came near the end of the working day, they say. . . . They say others are believed pinned under the wreckage or drowned and swept away. Doctors said they have treated one hundred and sixty-three people in recent days for injuries received at the bridge and from bombing elsewhere in the city.[28]

The Arnett controversies raise an interesting question regarding journalistic practices. On the one hand, he was the only Western news source in Baghdad for many of those early weeks, and his access was obviously controlled by the Iraqis. On the other hand, few in the United States seemed to mind when CNN was able to supply information useful to allied military intelligence. Even Israel barred reporters from naming landmarks and directions when reporting on Scud missile hits. As I have argued, the pendulum swings both ways. And the fact of the matter remains that Iraqi civilians *were* killed by allied bombs. Presumably Arnett rarely had the resources to verify that allied bombs had indeed done the specific damage he was privy to, but allies unquestionably killed civilians sometimes. The record of accuracy for unguided bombs was said to be a mere 25 percent, and they constituted 93 percent of all explosives dropped on Iraq and Kuwait.[29] Arnett did investigate when he could; he reported that the baby formula sign was conveniently printed in English and that exposed bunker communications cables did not appear to be those characteristically found in a civilian shelter. CNN was correct in downplaying the criticisms. The accusations were trivial within the context of war. Yet, the debate helps raise larger questions regarding journalists' involvement in the stories they cover. In the era of modern technology and instant news, these concerns become even greater.

The concern raised here is simply that journalists must recognize the fine line between stories being followed and stories being personally initiated. If one subscribes to the Western notion of journalistic objectivity, press manipulation of news events is unacceptable. Although there were many tales of such practices during the yellow journalism days of William Randolph Hearst and Joseph Pulitzer, such practices are commonly frowned on today. Yet manipulation can be subtle as the journalist is pulled into a story.

Anthropologists have long been concerned with the potential effect the camera has on the maintenance of reality. Some hold that the very presence of a camera helps change the behavior of those being observed. Direct manipulation is an even graver concern because then the event can be entirely affected. The presence of the camera changes the event. This concern applies to Gulf War coverage in which the story was allowed to shift to "journalist as patriot" or news organization feuding. This emphasis reduced the access journalists should have been granted to allied-controlled events and territory. Most media did encourage debates on press censorship, but when journalism became the principal story, attention shifted away from elite activities. As Bernard Shaw observed shortly before the bombs started falling on Baghdad, the role of the reporter is "to be eyes and ears, and to observe, to analyze, to gather facts, and to report on what is happening."[30]

Conclusions

A great deal of what happens in a normal day's news reporting falls under the classification of "press release journalism." These are stories prepared by newsmakers and shared with the news media via press releases and other orchestrated events such as press conferences, scheduled speeches, and news briefings. In all these, newsmakers attempt to capture the attention of the public or at least control how and to what degree the public learns of certain events, intentions, and actions. Common users of this approach are government bodies, corporations and other institutions, and public-interest groups. Such tendencies were most prominent in the delivery of official information to the public on the latest offensive, or just casualty updates, during the Gulf War.

The media, of course, are powerful vehicles of persuasion and have long been effectively used to help influence public opinion. Many examples can be cited of governments using the mass media to help promote war causes. Most recently, there has been grave concern surrounding news restrictions enacted in the Falklands, Grenada, and the Persian Gulf War.[31]

Commenting on Vietnam War coverage, Roger Grimsby of KGO television, San Francisco, observed that "there are almost no correspondents who speak Vietnamese or who are really up on the political situation. The military are very cooperative and will take you anywhere. . . . So the military angle wins out."[32] In such an environment, newsmaker manipulation can be subtle but extremely effective and can divert public attention from the real issues of war.

Knowingly or unknowingly, CNN all too often helped perpetuate the status quo point of view of the Gulf War, as did other news media. CNN may have been particularly vulnerable given the large amount of programming time to be filled; the "instant" nature of its news format, which makes for less prior review and editing; and the network's relative inexperience as an international news organization.

Obviously, CNN news coverage had different appeal for different viewers. For many, it offered the opportunity to stay informed. It allowed viewers to feel like participants in the events, even though the tight control and censorship meant there was little chance to really be very well informed. Because information was so effectively controlled, viewers accepted almost any information they were allowed to receive. After all, anything was better than nothing, and viewers had no recent war reporting as a basis for comparison. Even though reporters enjoyed much greater liberty during the Vietnam years, few viewers would have remembered these telecasts clearly. CNN did run reports on press coverage in this and other wars, and it certainly sponsored many dialogues and debates, but the news community generally tolerated news reporting conditions "under protest." Some journalists continued to remain in news pools when colleagues were excluded, and they continued to carry military-orchestrated events rather than refuse to participate.

One problem CNN faced was that it fell victim to the very circumstances that helped make it popular. News coverage of the Gulf War became an immediate experience as viewers were offered the opportunity to feel like participants in the events they witnessed. Such coverage helped define CNN's news format and made it the news network of record. The instantaneous nature of coverage additionally meant that reports would be aired with minimal editing. Hence, the selection process was left to viewers unaccustomed to sifting through footage for relevant facts and information and not necessarily prepared for this opportunity.

So although CNN's problems were not unique, the network may have fallen victim to its own popularity. The Gulf War effectively directed world attention to CNN's telecasts and placed it at center stage. Moreover, we can learn much from CNN's experience for these problems will undoubtedly arise again. The changes in news-gathering technology have helped to guarantee this. The task the news media now have is to engage in introspective analysis. The best way to avoid falling victim to manipulation is to more critically examine how the media have responded to crises in the past.

Notes

1. Walter Goodman, "A Day of Good News; Then Urgency," *New York Times,* January 18, 1991, p. A15.

2. Jay Rosen, "The Whole World Is Watching CNN," *Nation,* May 13, 1991, pp. 622–625.

3. "War Continues to Boost CNN's Ratings," *Broadcasting,* February 4, 1991, p. 32.

4. James Curran, "Communications, Power and Social Order," in Michael Gurevitch, Tony Bennett, James Curran, and Janet Woolacott (eds.), *Culture, Society and the Media* (London: Routledge and Kegan Paul, 1982), pp. 202–235.

5. Glasgow University Media Group, *More Bad News* (London: Routledge and Kegan Paul, 1980), p. 11.

6. Ibid.

7. Richard C. Vincent, Bryan K. Crow, and Dennis K. Davis, "When Technology Fails," *Journalism Monographs,* no. 117 (1989).

8. Briefing, Riyadh, Saudi Arabia, January 27, 1991.

9. U.S. military briefing, January 22, 1991.

10. CNN, February 24, 1991.

11. Tom Wicker, " 'Marketing' the War," *New York Times,* May 8, 1991, p. A23.

12. CNN report, February 6, 1991.

13. R. W. Apple, Jr., "Correspondents Protest Pool System," *New York Times,* February 12, 1991, p. A8.

14. CNN, February 11, 1991.

15. CNN, February 6, 1981.

16. Alex S. Jones, "Feast of Viewing, But Little Nourishment," *New York Times,* January 19, 1991, p. A10.

17. CNN, January 15, 1991.

18. Doris Graber, *Processing the News,* 2d ed. (New York: Longman, 1987); John P. Robinson and Mark R. Levy, *The Main Source: Learning from Television News* (Beverly Hills, Calif.: Sage, 1986); Dennis K. Davis, "News and Politics," in David L. Swanson and Dan Nimmo (eds.) *New Directions in Political Communication* (Newbury Park, Calif.: Sage, 1990), pp. 147–184.

19. Maureen Dowd, "Washington Goes to War, Besieging the TV Set," *New York Times,* January 29, 1991, p. A13.

20. CNN, February 6, 1991.

21. From "Crossfire" program, Michael Kinsley and Pat Buchanan, hosts; CNN, January 14, 1991.

22. CNN International, June 18, 1991, 9:55 A.M. (Paris time).

23. CNN, February 7, 1991.

24. CNN, February 7, 1991.

25. CNN, February 6, 1991.

26. CNN, February 8, 1991.

27. Bill Carter, "Networks' Anger with CNN Deepens," *New York Times,* February 12, 1991, pp. B1–2.

28. CNN, February 6, 1991.

29. Tom Wicker, "For Pentagon Censors, an Easy Victory, Too," *International Herald Tribune,* March 22, 1991.

30. CNN, January 15, 1991.

31. See Johan Galtung and Richard C. Vincent, *Global Glasnost: Toward a New International Information/Communication Order?* (Cresskill, N.J.: Hampton Press, 1992), Chapter 7.

32. "The Press: Room for Improvement," *Newsweek,* July 10, 1967, p. 76.

CHAPTER SEVENTEEN

◆

Exterminating Angels: Morality, Violence, and Technology in the Gulf War

Asu Aksoy and Kevin Robins

THE WAR IN THE Persian Gulf was cast as a global confrontation between humanity and bestiality, a battle between civilization and barbarism. This was a war to defend the principles of modernity and reason against the forces of darkness. It was in this cause that the smart weapons of the West meted out what was projected as a moral kind of violence. In this cause, the angels became exterminators.

Crusade Against the Evil Empire

When nearly 2 million troops, 10,000 tanks, more than 5,000 pieces of artillery, 3,900 warplanes, 1,800 helicopters, and 175 warships were preparing for the conflict in the Gulf, President George Bush declared to the U.S. Congress that the ensuing war would be a "just" one in which all moral questions would have been resolved and it would be simply a matter of black versus white, good versus evil. The United States was "on the side of God." It had a "unique responsibility to do the hard work of freedom" against a criminal and monster who dared to disturb the "moral order" of the world. The driving force behind the massive buildup of armaments was the notion that an aggressor "who uses force to replace the rule of law" must be punished. "We are ready," said Bush, "to use force to defend a new order emerging among the nations of the world, a world of sovereign nations living in peace." There was no question about the justness of this war. It was a matter of stopping "another Hitler" in time.

Bush's belief in the moral rightness of his crusade was not surprising. But the wider support that the Western cause received from most opposition parties and from much of the intellectual community in the West was. Here, too, Saddam Hussein was demonized as a "new Hitler" poised to take over the world. Hans Magnus Enzensberger (1991) put it most bluntly: "The description of Saddam Hussein as the new Hitler is not merely journalistic license, not the hyperbole of propaganda, but is actually deadly accurate. . . . The behaviour of the new enemy of humanity is no different from that of his predecessor." Such an aggressor—this "enemy of the human race"—had to be "removed from the surface of the earth."

In the words of Fred Halliday (1991), the stark choice was "between indulging a state and its associated international movement (Ba'athism) that, for all its progressivist decoration, is akin to fascism, and accepting the need for war." According to Bernard Lewis (1990), it was "an awesome choice: either to discipline Saddam Hussein and restore the status quo, or to abandon the world to the violent and the ruthless." In other words, unless one wanted to support the rise of fascism in the Middle East, there was no real choice to be made. The pulverization and humiliation of Iraq were unavoidable. As Margaret Thatcher put it, the assault had to go ahead in the name of making the world a better, safer place. Those who were opposed to this mission could be seen only as the "indecent" supporters of fascist rule.

Saddam Hussein was the Great Satan. Bush referred repeatedly to Saddam's immoral and unconscionable brutality; to rape, assassination, cold-blooded murder, and rampant looting; and to the violation of every civilized principle. Saddam was a violent monster who did not bat an eyelid when he was killing, whether it was the Iranians or the Kurds, the Saudis or the Palestinians, the Kuwaitis or the Israelis, or even his own unfortunate people. According to Bush and his publicists, Saddam's troops were supposed to have killed at least three hundred premature babies by removing them from their incubators (though this accusation was subsequently proved to have no foundation). A "U.S. girl Marine" prisoner was described by the *Sun* (February 1, 1991) as being "at the mercy of the beast." According to the *Daily Star* (March 2, 1991), "Brutal Iraqi soldiers became real-life vampires during the occupation of Kuwait. They drained the blood of innocent civilians until their victims were dead." Almost any degree of force necessary to destroy Saddam was therefore seen as permissible. As *Newsweek* (March 11, 1991, p. 48) put it, "The chain had to be pulled, to flush Saddam away."

It quickly became clear that Bush's war aims were more ambitious than just liberating Kuwait. U.S. generals were out there to go deep into Iraq, to destroy Saddam Hussein's "monstrous military machine," and maybe even to "take out" the man himself. As Edward Said (1991) suggested, it was "as if an almost metaphysical need to rout Iraq had sprung forward" and this "because a small non-white country had disturbed or rankled a suddenly energised super-nation imbued with a fervour that can only be satisfied with compliance or subservience from 'sheikhs,' dictators, and camel-jockeys." For Bush, the upstart Arab embodied the forces of irrationality and barbarism. And Bush was ready, in the name of civilization, in the name of reason and humanity, to discipline those alien forces, to defeat them "decisively and rapidly." That was the almost metaphysical dimension of the U.S. crusade.

So convinced were the Western forces of the moral justness of their mission to "neutralize" Saddam that they were prepared to put no limits on the drive to accomplish this objective. In this just war against this new evil empire, all kinds of advanced weapons would be enlisted. Why, asked General Norman Schwarzkopf, should the allied force have to stand up, allow themselves to be shot, take on overwhelming numbers, and not use the weapons they had available when the Iraqis could do anything they wanted, such as gas innocent women and children, loft Scuds against civilian populations, and use human shields? Why should they not get a taste of their own medicine? This time Western soldiers did not intend to go into battle, as they felt they had done in Vietnam, with one hand tied; this time they would use all the weapons they had available.

General Colin Powell warned Saddam at the beginning of the war that Iraq had not yet seen the tools in the U.S. Army tool box. Through the course of the war, it came to see just what the tools were in that box: the "daisy cutter" (the biggest U.S. conventional bomb, whose blast effect is comparable to that of a tactical nuclear weapon); fuel-air explosives (which have the same explosive capacity as a small atomic bomb, though without the same radioactive or political fallout); the cluster bomb; the Stealth bomber; the Tomahawk cruise missile; the multiple-launch rocket system; and more "conventional" weapons such as B-52 bombers, which can carry up to fifty five-hundred-pound bombs, each capable of devastating an area three miles long by a half mile wide. All these were deployed in the Gulf. Through the use of high-tech instruments of terror, Western armies turned the war into a twenty-four-hour killing field from which nothing could escape.

Saddam Hussein's scuddish violence was always seen as vicious and brutal. His weapons appeared to be imprecise and undiscriminating as they were blindly launched against Israel and Saudi Arabia. In contrast, the allies were, paradoxically, able to project their bloody assault as clean and clinical. The desert was to be a theater in which the Western forces would play out the fantasy of a war made bloodless through scientific and technological expertise. From the outset, the scientific warriors stressed that their aim was to "take out" legitimate targets through "professionally executed strikes" by allied aircraft using precision-guided munitions. Precision weapons would enable troops to identify and then remove chosen targets at will.

Moreover, these "supersophisticated systems"—stealth weapons, sea-launched cruise missiles, Strategic Defense Initiative–like defenses and space systems—would save the lives not only of allied pilots but also of ordinary Iraqis because they enabled precision attacks that limited civilian casualties. This was to be a "push-button, remote-control war" won without visible casualties. U.S. accomplishments in science and technology would be used as instruments of targeted punishment and in the process would legitimate that punishment.

It was through this capacity to believe in a well-managed and rationally conducted war that the allies could come to have no moral qualms about the destructive and horrific power that they had unleashed. Even when it became clear that the "phenomenally accurate" weaponry could kill civilians in the hundreds and thousands, as happened with the allied bombing of the Al-Amiriya air raid shelter in Baghdad, the moral certainty remained intact. As General Richard I. Neal said after the bombing, it defied logic that the missile, which had been so well targeted at the bunker in order to destroy military communications equipment, could have led to the slaughter of so many civilians. Douglas Hurd was quick to emphasize that Saddam Hussein would have to take the blame if any civilians died accidentally and that this was another devilish plot from Saddam. As General Neal commented, the air force planners continued to feel "very comfortable" with their choice of target.

Defending Civilization

But how could they be, and remain, so very comfortable? How could military high technology be so closely associated with absolute virtue? How could "logic" justify the technological violence that was bombing Iraq and its people "back into the dark ages"? These are the key questions. And it was not only the Western leaders who were disavowing responsibility and projecting guilt onto the "devilish" Other; the process of moral dissociation was a more general phenomenon.

To different degrees it affected us all. As we were engulfed by images of the Western military machine, we seemed to forget how murderous and destructive those weapons were. It was as if our moral senses had been taken out and neutralized. The "smartness" or "brilliance" of computer-controlled rocket systems and of Tomahawk missiles seduced us into thinking that Iraq's murderous violence was being confronted by efficient and rational systems whose objectives were, not to murder, but simply to "clean out" enemy targets. As the allied bombing proceeded to fire the skies of Iraq with ammunition far exceeding the amount used during the whole of World War II, we in the West were being lured into a blind and complicit fascination with the high-tech arsenal.

Why did our moral sense not provoke a sense of outrage and shame? We became deaf, as John Berger (1991) declared, to the atrocities committed by our own civilization, and that deafness became exponential. We watched the war on our televison screens, but our screen culture had come to sustain our moral blindness and moral passivity. "CNN is live and alive," one Turkish writer lamented, "as our humanity is about to die." We were expected to remain silent when told that the videotapes from the gun cameras of the Apache helicopter raids on Iraqi soldiers revealed the horror of their deaths and showed how they were blown to bits.

How could we watch our civilization turning into a terminator? To ask this question is to consider what the war can tell us about ourselves and also what the war has done to us. It is also to consider the relationship among technology, violence, and morality in Western culture.

The very distance of the campaign made it almost impossible to realize the awful truth of the carnage. We did not see the suffering at the other end, which made it difficult to identify with the sufferers. Those potentially subversive glimpses we were given of the human consequences of the "greatest aerial bombardment in history" were of faceless others. The enemy were objects, far removed from us, as Francis Fukuyama (1990) put it, "in a desolate Middle Eastern desert," and those objects were seen as undesirable. It seemed entirely reasonable, then, to apply Western techno-rationality to teach them their place in the world, their inferior place in our civilized world.

What emerged in most of the Western commentaries on the war was the belief that there was a profound moral difference between the violence of Saddam and that of Bush. After the war, Bush could declare that it had been a victory for the United Nations, mankind, the rule of law, and what is right. Bush's deeds of violence were always assumed to be morally defensible, to be self-evidently just acts in defense of civilization, reason, and sanity and against the "dark practices" of an alien force. On what basis, we must ask, was it possible to sustain this belief and these assertions?

The key to this question is the polarization between Western civilization and its Other—represented in this episode by the endemic "barbarism" of Arab culture—and the contrast between our enlightened modernity and their benighted dark ages. "Their twentieth century is not ours," wrote Alain Finkielkraut (1991). "They have allowed honour to prevail over democracy, and force and machismo over freedom."

According to Martin Woollacott (1991), Arab life suffered from "a problem of irrationality and fantasy, a "sickness" centered on the "failure of thought." Associated with this confrontation is a false dichotomy between the rational and the irrational. The choice, quite simply, is between reason and unreason. And then the choice is implicitly made between the moral and the immoral, for it is on the power of its reason and rationality that Western morality is reputedly grounded.

The symbolic damnation of Saddam reflected this logic. In positioning itself against the barbarity of "medieval practices," the United States solicited moral support. Insofar as its modern identity was defined against the irrationality and barbarism of the Other, the United States sought to legitimize its rationalized violence in the name of civilized reason and progress. This legitimation was grounded in the belief that the allies' "modern" violence was of a different order from the "medieval practices" of Iraqi violence. It was smart violence. When "smart means good," it becomes possible to maintain a distinction between good and bad kinds of weapons and then to differentiate between morally right and morally wrong kinds of violence.

Smart, Therefore Good

The starkest expression of modernity and reason is technological rationality, and this rationality in turn becomes associated with the moral superiority of Western culture because the very idea of rationality seems indissociable from the idea of worthwhile aims. It was on this basis, and only on this basis, that the awesome and devastating firepower of the Western war machine could actually seem to be an expression of moral virtue. It was on this basis that the advanced nature of Western military technologies could guarantee their moral rightness. According to Sidney Perkowitz (1991), a military researcher, "The allied forces' stated goal of minimising innocent casualties, along with minimising casualties for our own soldiers, has moral weight. And it is the technical means to select targets that make the moral decision possible, and therefore meaningful."

This researcher, like many others, honestly believed that he had "contributed to good technology." What the technology did was "to put a sharp spearpoint on war's bludgeon." The guilty feelings associated with being engaged in military research were than lifted as he "watched the breathtaking TV images of our missile attacks" and realized that these weapons were smart; they did not kill civilians.

We were continually told about the marvelous intelligence of the new high-tech weapons: how they used night hours "efficiently," how they could "look deep behind enemy lines" and "cut through the fog of war," how computers tracked the trajectory of incoming projectiles so fast that counterfire could wipe out the enemy's artillery "before they got off a second shot." All this was a great display. We were impressed with the Stealth fighter-bomber's sleek invisibility and its smart bombs that could be guided "down the air shafts" or "through the front doors" of targeted buildings. We were amazed at how the Tomahawk missile had "a mind of its own" and at how it could wend its intelligent way to its "terminal end point." And we watched the Patriot missiles and the M-101 tanks and the Apache helicopters as if we ourselves were arms-buying connoisseurs.

The clear message was that smart was good and brilliant was virtuous. Smart weapons, it was being claimed, could actually save the lives of soldiers and civilians alike in the Gulf. To reduce error, to be so deadly accurate and efficient, was a reflection of the virtuous triumph of Western technology.

The Gulf War demonstrated that the power and dominance of the technological order had become so well secured that it was now the criterion of what was moral. The power of Western techno-rationality was not questioned. When the Al-Amiriya shelter was destroyed, or when an allied aircraft missed a targeted bridge during a bombing mission and devastated a shopping area in Falloujah instead, there was never any question of Western responsibility or guilt. A certain Group Captain Irving claimed that he had never seen any bombs veer off course before in this campaign and that there was no question of the crew being in error." (The inhabitants thought that the pilot "must have been Saudi.") We witnessed starkly that when morality is legitimated by efficiency, questions of efficiency tend to become a surrogate for ethical decisions and choices. And when efficiency fails, there is no means to cope with the human and moral fallout. The technology is designed not to go wrong; therefore it cannot be morally in the wrong.

On this basis, it became possible for the allies to dissociate themselves from the pain and death that their modern weapons brought about. Because the weapons were so smart, proponents could believe they were delivering Western forces from moral dilemmas. In reality, these belief systems functioned to desensitize the troops and to delink their actions from their human consequences. Smart technologies allowed action "at a distance": Soldiers pushed the buttons of Tomahawk missiles and then watched, if at all, the consequences of their action later on videotapes.

As Zygmunt Bauman (1990, 7) argued, "distance technologies . . . eliminated face-to-face contact between the actors and the objects of their actions, and with that naturalised their morally constraining impact." The causal connection between the act and its human consequences were broken, and the ultimate effects of actions remained invisible to the actors. One U.S. military source admitted to having "absolutely no clue" about Iraqi casualties. It was as if the enemy had no human existence.

But how different, really, was this modern violence of the Western military machine? What did the smart technologies actually deliver? As we now know, when the ground war started smart quickly turned to hellish: With our very modern technologies we brought Armageddon to people we scarcely knew. The horrific nature of the Western assault was exemplified as the allies "went in for the kill" at the start of the ground war and slaughtered the routed Iraqi army. The ensuing victory, as John Pilger (1991) said, was "a one-sided bloodfest."

During the brief land war launched by Washington, the allies shot thousands and thousands of fleeing Iraqi soldiers and civilians in the back. The shooting was described as being like "a giant hunt." The Iraqis were driven ahead, "like animals," by the allied air and land attacks. U.S. pilots were said to have likened their attack on the convoy to "shooting fish in a barrel." The retreating Iraqis were said to have presented a "bounty of targets." "We hit the jackpot," one pilot said. "It was like a turkey shoot."

After the bombing, a U.S. officer said that he found it distressing to describe the scene on the main road between Kuwait City and the Iraqi city of Basra: "Dead, mutilated and charred bodies were everywhere." At another scene of carnage, it was reported that "for sixty miles, on the road to Umm Qasr, hundreds of Iraqi tanks and armoured cars, howitzers and anti-aircraft guns, ammunition trucks and ambulances were strafed, smashed and burned beyond belief. Scores of soldiers lay in and around the vehicles, mangled and bloated in the drifting desert sand" (*Guardian,* March 11, 1991).

The killing that went on was no less violent than it had been at Dresden or in Vietnam. As a U.S. Marine lieutenant conceded, in distress, "They had no air cover, nothing to defend themselves. It was not very professional at all." U.S. pilots had used Rockeye cluster bombs in the attack. Each Rockeye bomb dispersed 247 bomblets containing needle-sharp shrapnel designed for "soft" targets, in other words, *people.* The "great victory" of the allied forces smelt of naked and brutal violence. A reporter traveling with the leading tanks of the "hounds of hell" battalion described the scene as "something out of a medieval artist's vision of hell, a great backdrop of leaping flames against which we could see the tiny figures of men frantically trying to escape the fire" (*Newsweek,* March 11, 1991, p. 46). It was like a "demolition-derby circuit" in which "huddled groups of green-uniformed soldiers waving white rags of surrender stood, bewildered, while tanks rolled by." Where was the smartness in this? Where was the justice?

Reason and Violence

What we must learn from the experience of the Gulf War, once again, is how the "us good, them bad" logic hides the fears, anxieties, and guilt buried deep in Western consciousness. Saddam was projected as a monster and a beast. Like Frankenstein's monster, he was an outcast from the "moral order" of the world; he was a "race apart." As in Mary Shelley's *Frankenstein,* the symbolic drama was between a "race of devils" and the "species of man." All the evil was projected outwards into that "desert." In projecting all evil onto the monstrous alien, the Western psyche was seeking to protect the integrity of its own reason and rationality. As Bush made clear, it had to be black versus white, good versus evil.

Through this splitting process, the Western psyche was then able to avoid confronting the sources of its own violence. The fervor with which Saddam was accused of being criminal and bestial was fired by the desire to protect the "species of man," to absolve Western culture and civilization from the guilt associated with its own violence. It is difficult for us to acknowledge that violence and destruction on both sides are expressions of "rational" behavior, that "reason" may be at the heart of violence.

As Franco Moretti (1982, 136) argued, the story of Frankenstein's monster is about a two-sided process in which formation entails deformation, in which civilization carries barbarism within itself. In this process, science and rationality contain the possibility of destructive violence. The monster—"the pedestal on which Frankenstein erects his anguished greatness"—turned out to be a distortion and "negation" of that greatness. The deformed monster then had to "become the object of an instinctive, elemental hatred; and 'men' need this hatred to counterbalance the force unleashed by the monster." This is what happened in the Gulf. Saddam's "monstrous military machine" was simply a distorting reflection of the West's anguished greatness. It was the West that created this "monster," and then extinguished it when the monster turned on its creator. And the West did so with a violence surpassing that of the monster.

So the West was "on the side of God," and Saddam was in the camp of the devil, the "enemy of the human race." For that reason, the humiliation and destruction of Iraq seemed both desirable and inevitable. But there are those who do not now see this as a victory "for all mankind" and for "what is right." And there were those who did not support the side of Bush's God. Journalist James Buchan (1991) described how in Jalazan—a Palestinian refugee camp in Israel—"when the Scud missiles come over, everybody goes out on the roof to shout and dance." There were those who did not see Saddam Hussein as "another Hitler." There

were even those, such as writer Driss Chraibi (1991), who found themselves applauding Saddam Hussein and doing this because "he defied
the United States, and millions of people don't like what the United
States stands for in the world."

Simone Weil wrote in her journal on June 13, 1940, as the German
army marched into Paris, "This is a great day for the people of Indochina."
As David Rieff (1990, 85–86) commented "Weil reminded us that the
history that we in the West care about . . . is neither the history of
everywhere nor of everyone. She invites us to undertake that most
uncomfortable of reasoning, the realisation that an event which for us is
cause for mourning may be celebrated by other people every bit as decent
as ourselves at the moment when hope first dawned."

Perhaps we should consider why a challenge to the power of the
United States was experienced by some as a moment of dawning hope.
Does that seem to "belie logic"?

> *Phantoms out of the dark ages,*
> *Their claws aflame*
> *Pounce on what makes man human,*
> *What makes him sacred—all teeth.*
> —Fazīl Hüsnü Dağlarca

References

Balzar, J. 1991. "Video Horror of Apache Victims' Deaths." *Guardian,* February
2.

Bauman, Z. 1990. "Effacing the Face: On the Social Management of Moral
Proximity." *Theory, Culture and Society* 7.

Berger, J. 1991. "In the Land of the Deaf." *Guardian,* March 2.

Buchan, J. 1991. "The Arabs in the Middle." *Independent on Sunday,* February
10.

Chraibi, D. 1991. "Vous avez dit liberation?" *Liberation,* February 15.

Enzensberger, H. M. 1991. "The Second Coming of Adolf Hitler." *Guardian,*
February 9.

Finkielkraut, A. 1991. "The Gulf of Backwardness." *Guardian,* March 1.

Fukuyama, F. 1990. "The World Against a Family." *Guardian,* September 12.

Halliday, F. 1991. "Awkward Facts Won't Toe the Line of Dodgy Politics." *Guardian,* February 11.

Kivanc, U. 1991. "CNN Live, biz olu." *Birikim,* 22.

Lewis, B. 1990. "At Stake in the Gulf." *New York Review of Books* 37, no. 20.

Lifton, R. J. 1991a. "Techno-bloodshed." *Guardian,* February 14.

———. 1991b. "Last Refuge of a High-Tech Nation." *Guardian,* March 12.

Moretti, F. 1982. "The Dialectic of Fear." *New Left Review* 136.

Perkowitz, S. 1991. "The Scientist at War." *Guardian,* March 7.

Pilger, J. 1991. "A One-Sided Bloodfest." *New Statesman and Society,* March 8.
Rieff, D. 1990. "European Time." *Salmagundi,* nos. 85–86.
Said, E. 1991. "Empire of Sand." *Guardian,* January 12.
Woollacott, M. 1991. "Iraq Was Simply an Especially Extreme Case of Arab Sickness." *Guardian,* March 4.

BACK TO THE FUTURE
Kamel S. Abu Jaber

It is not only President George Bush of the United States of America who is interested the future. Our concern is not that he is concerned with his future; rather, it is because he is concerned, it seems, with our future. And however we may be dismayed with this new pastime that he is developing, in addition to jogging, fishing, and golfing, it does not seem likely that we can dissuade him from his aim.

Unlike most other humans, even some world leaders, Mr. Bush is not consulting with palm readers, coffee- or teacup diviners, or even with the more sophisticated tarot cards explainer, but with statistics fed into a computer and attitudes shaped by a well-placed remark or advice made here or there. His soothsayers are not gypsies in a carnival tent but cold-blooded, single-minded specialists and experts closeted in the underground bunkers of institutions such as the Pentagon, the Department of State, and the Central Intelligence Agency. It is their business to "make" the future for others, or at least highly influence its course. In their executive summaries, details, and plans, there is no warm smile or knowing wink designed to make one more comfortable.

We may indulge ourselves in blaming Mr. Bush or Shamir—maybe we should amalgamate the two together because they seem to have developed an organic relationship between them and call them shortly "Bushamir"—for their uninvited concern with our future, but the blame must really rest with us. What have we done for ourselves? The crisis is now at its zenith, and Iraq, still alone on the battlefield, is fighting the Arab fight, though the vast majority of the Arabs are on the other side. And once again, we prove to ourselves, as to the rest of the world, that our biggest enemy is still within ourselves.

Judging from our performance in modern times, the future looks like more of our past. We seem, once again, not to have learned anything from the lesson that life, Bush-Shamir, or others have been trying to teach us. One would think that somewhere, something would have changed or at least would promise to. Yet as we stare deeper into the bowels of the present crisis, we see only a continuation of the same. Arab leaders still talking at their

(continues)

(*continued*)

peoples rather than consulting with them and the sum total of most of their activities have been in the spirit of distraction rather than action. And so it has again come to pass that a historic opportunity is missed.

Whatever the sins of Iraq may have been, no one else is innocent. Surely Iraq should not have occupied Kuwait, but just as surely those who are now mere onlookers or those ganging up to take a stab to complete the kill are just as guilty. For while the world is holding its breath anticipating the grand finale, one would expect that we would be consulting among ourselves about the days to come.

If it is a sin to drop a rock into a cesspool to stir up the rottenness that exists there, then Iraq is a sinner, and anyone who can may cast a stone. The tragic fact is that we have nothing to lose but our shackles and somehow someone, no one knows how, realized that fact and dropped the rock.

And now, while most of us are sitting in these dark and odd days wringing our hands, not only is no one thinking of the days to come, but we also seem to be enjoying an orgy of self-flagellation by criticizing and even attacking Iraq. The truth of the matter is that the West achieved all its strategic aims on or even before August 2, 1990, when this present crisis ostensibly began. By that date, the oil was already secure in Western hands, Saudi Arabia protected, and an Iraqi commitment to withdraw from Kuwait secured. Nevertheless, the crisis escalated so as to ensure that future for Shamir by sealing the future of Iraq. One would think that everyone, at least among the Arabs, knew that and would act accordingly. While some are intimidated, others dragged by the herd mentality developed by the West, and others bought, none could act, as if the whole Arab body politic is totally drugged. The Seven Sleepers awoke, and as the story goes they remained awake thereafter. Since the advent of modern times, we seem to have awakened for brief moments and then have been induced to slumber once again, and thus our life has come to be a series of missed opportunities and broken hearts. At this rate we may never know who is doing what to us. What they are doing and our existence will remain as tangential in the future as it has been in the past, being moved like pawns at the will of others.

(*continues*)

(*continued*)

Is it true that only a few of us realize that this is a historic bend in the road? If that is the case, then we should blame no one but ourselves, for God knows we have had enough experience, and that Bushamir taught us enough lessons and created for us enough facts. When will we ever learn?

In looking over the future designed for us throughout this century, I am struck by the fact that it was an American president, Woodrow Wilson, who sponsored the idea of the League of Nations while the Balfour Declaration and the Sykes-Picot agreement were revealed; that it was an American president, Franklin Roosevelt, who sponsored the United Nations while the partition of Palestine was advanced; and that it is an American president, George Bush, who is sponsoring the so-called new world order while the slaughter of the Arabs, through the slaughter of Iraq, is being carried out.

It is we, not the United Nations, who are in perfect ill health. We cannot go on forever so mindlessly vulnerable, nor can we go on forever so out of step with the requirements of our time. Cruel as the adjustments must be, they must be made. In the Holy Koran it is said the God does not change a people unless they change first within themselves. Either we change or we perish, as others are planning for us. Can this choking silence maintained by our political systems be maintained?

This piece was originally published in *Jordan Times,* February 23, 1991.

CHAPTER EIGHTEEN

◆

More Viewing, Less Knowledge

Michael Morgan, Justin Lewis, and Sut Jhally

THE MEDIA ARGUABLY PLAYED a more visible and critical role in the Persian Gulf War than in any other in history. During the entire "crisis in the Gulf," from Iraq's invasion of Kuwait in August 1990, to the rapid surrender of the Iraqi army in late February 1991 and beyond, immense public debate was focused on the role of the media. In much of the period building up to the war, news coverage was both lengthy and intense, and during the war itself this escalated into long periods of saturation coverage. Rarely does any event receive such media attention, and rarely is so much attention focused on the media themselves.

Although most polls found that the U.S. public was generally favorable to the coverage and easily accepted the "need" to censor it (Dennis et al. 1991), the coverage was virulently attacked by many. War opponents claimed that military censorship meant that the U.S. public saw only "good" news or that the media acted more as lapdogs than watchdogs and in effect served as "cheerleading" public relations arms for the government. War supporters claimed that the media gave too much attention to the antiwar movement and ran the risk of supplying critical tactical and strategic information to the enemy that could endanger U.S. troops.

Critical analyses of the media coverage have been plentiful, especially of that provided by television news, along with much speculation about the media's role in establishing and maintaining the extraordinary level of support for the war by the U.S. public. Accounts of the coverage appeared not only in alternative media (Anderson and Carpignano 1991; Bennis 1991; Boston Media Watch 1991; Cockburn 1991; Herman 1991a, 1991b; *Index on Censorship* 1991; Larsen 1991; Nathan 1991; Naureckas

1991; Ray 1991; Sklar 1991; Solomon 1991; Wallis 1991), but also surprisingly often in the popular mainstream press (Browne 1991; DeParle 1991a, 1991b; Gelb 1991; Goodman 1991; Hickey 1991; James 1991; LeMoyne 1991; Lewis 1991; Winter 1991), in various trade publications (Karem 1991; Ruffini 1991; Schanberg 1991), and in conservative publications (e.g., Bernstein 1991).

Yet people in the United States did not just suddenly begin watching television during the Gulf War. Whatever impact the media coverage had on public opinion and beliefs took place in a cultural context whose mainstream was dominated by the stable and consistent messages of television entertainment, with its clear-cut good guys and bad guys, quick and violent solutions, and images of nefarious Arabs (Shaheen 1984).

This chapter reports some results from a survey we conducted to explore the contributions of both the war coverage itself and overall amount of television viewing to people's beliefs and assumptions about the Gulf War. What, we wanted to know, had the U.S. public learned from the media? With all the coverage, did people become better informed about events in the Middle East and about U.S. foreign policy? The answers to these questions were, we discovered, both dramatic and revealing.

More generally, the study was also prompted by concerns about the way the U.S. media present (or fail to present) what is going on in the world, in both news and entertainment. Many studies have documented television's impacts on people's beliefs about the world. Television, especially in its entertainment programs, provides millions of viewers with a constant stream of images and portrayals that are a source of widely shared assumptions and conceptions (Gerbner et al. 1986). Thus, we wanted to see how overall viewing of television, which is turned on in the average U.S. household for more than seven hours a day, and not just news viewing, contributed to people's beliefs about and support for the war.

These are not idle questions; they go to the very core of a democratic system because the quality of our democratic decisions depends on the quality of the information on which those decisions are based. Our study therefore tells us something about the health of democracy in the United States. Moreover, the high level of public support for the war in the Gulf translated directly into historically unprecedented approval for the president and for a particular style of foreign policy. Therefore, there is far more at stake here than the success or failure of ABC or CNN.

With this in mind, the research we undertook had three main goals: (1) to measure how much people knew about events in the Middle East, (2) to investigate how knowledge levels varied as a function of support for the war, and (3) to examine the extent to which both knowledge levels and support for the war were related to media exposure.

Methods and Measures

Telephone interviews were conducted with a random sample of 250 adults aged eighteen or older in the greater metropolitan area of Denver, Colorado, between February 2 and 4, 1991. Random-digit dialing procedures were used. The sample was stratified by sex, giving an equal number of males and females (125 each). The response rate was 60 percent.

Most respondents (89 percent) were white, and almost a quarter (23 percent) had served in the military; a tenth of the respondents had a close family member serving in the Persian Gulf. Respondents ranged in age from 18 to 86, with a mean of 43.6 years. For analysis, they were trichotomized into three age groups of roughly equal size: 18–32, 33–47, and 48–86. Education was measured in terms of years of schooling. Less than a third (29 percent) did not go beyond high school; just less than half (45 percent) graduated from college. The sample was split at the median (fourteen years of education) into low and high education groups.

"Level of support for the war" was constructed from two questions (the first two in the survey): "Do you support President Bush's decision to use military force against Iraq? (yes/no)," and "Would you describe your opinion on this subject as strong, fairly strong or not very strong?" Of the 250 respondents, 144 (58 percent) said "yes" to the first question and "strong" to the second; these respondents were categorized as "strongly supporting" the war. The 65 respondents (26 percent) whose support for the war was either "fairly strong" or "not very strong" were classified as having a "medium" level of support for the war. The 41 others (16 percent) were coded as "opposed or unsure." Support for the use of force against Iraq and strength of opinion were significantly related; those who supported the war were more likely to feel "strongly" about their opinion.

Television viewing was measured by asking, "How many hours per day do you estimate you watch television?" The mean was 3.1 hours, quite similar to data from national samples. Respondents were divided into three groups based on how much television per day they reported watching—light viewers (less than 1.5 hours a day), medium viewers (1.5 to 3 hours), and heavy viewers (more than 3 hours). There was, not surprisingly, little variation in news viewing. Almost 80 percent of respondents reported watching the news at least nightly (designated as heavy news viewers); more than 50 percent of those classified as light news viewers were watching TV news between three and five nights a week.

The survey was designed to be as simple and straightforward as possible. Most questions were open-ended in order to avoid pushing people into categories of response that they might not, on their own, have thought of. The factual questions we posed were, like most facts, not politically neutral. We did not intend that they should be. Some, like the State Department's failure to warn Iraq of the consequences of attacking Kuwait, could have reflected badly on the administration's war policy. Others, like knowledge of Saddam Hussein's use of chemical weapons, could have justified the need for war. In this regard, we were interested in discovering whether the overwhelming public support for the war was based on an acceptance of President Bush's moral rationale for the liberation of Kuwait (the defense of freedom, democracy, and international boundaries and law) or whether the support was contingent and conditional (based on considered and rational thought about the specifics of the Middle East, past and current U.S. policy toward the region, and U.S. strategic interests).

The Untold Story

Our survey, like most others taken during the period, showed a vast majority of respondents (84 percent) in support of President Bush's decision to use military force against Iraq. As noted, most respondents described their opinion on this subject as strongly held, and a majority (58 percent) were even prepared to pay higher taxes to pay for the war. It might be expected, or at least hoped, that such firm views on such a politically contentious issue were based on a knowledge of the pertinent facts. In this case, we discovered, they were not. Despite the months of television coverage devoted to this story, most people, we found, were alarmingly ill informed.

It was quite surprising to find a relatively low level of recognition of some of the major actors involved in the war. For example, less than half the respondents (42 percent) could identify General Colin Powell—the chair of the Joint Chiefs of Staff who had been the object of extensive media attention. But the lack of knowledge we found went far deeper—and had much more serious implications—than whether people could identify generals.

The most striking gaps in people's knowledge consistently involved information that would have reflected badly on the administration's portrayal of this as a moral or just war. Whatever Ambassador April Glaspie did or did not tell Saddam Hussein in July 1990, none of her shifting versions claimed to have warned Iraq that an invasion would be countered with force. At the very least, the administration's subsequent aggressive posture toward Iraq reflected a shift, rather than a consistency, of resolve. The overwhelming majority of our respondents were not only unaware of the administration's initial murky position; they assumed a consistency in policy that was entirely fictitious.

For example, we asked people how the U.S. State Department responded before the invasion, when Saddam Hussein indicated he might use force against Kuwait. Only 13 percent responded "correctly" (i.e., in terms of the available news at the time) that the United States indicated it would take no action, while 74 percent said the United States threatened to impose sanctions, and as many as 65 percent said the administration vowed to support Kuwait with the use of force. This amounted to a remarkable rewriting of history in the collective consciousness, the beneficiary of which was the Bush administration. It was, after all, much easier to strongly support the administration's decision to go to war if one thought the president was consistent throughout and that Saddam Hussein had been "warned."

Critics of the war policy said that it was hypocritical for the United States to react so violently to one occupation in the Middle East while ignoring—or supporting—others in the region. In terms of public support for the war, this point was critical because a majority of our respondents (53 percent) stated that the United States should intervene with military force to restore the sovereignty of any illegally occupied country (compared with only 18 percent who supported intervention to protect oil interests). This reponse suggested that most people (unless they were advocating a whole series of military interventions) were unaware of other occupations in the Middle East—or anywhere else. Such an awareness could have undercut the moral cornerstone of the war policy.

Only 31 percent of respondents were even aware that Israel was occupying land in the Middle East, and only 3 percent were aware of Syria's occupation of Lebanon. Despite repeated U.N. resolutions condemning both occupations, some may argue that Israel's occupation is more "justifiable" than Iraq's. What was clear from our survey, however, was that most people were in no position to make such an evaluation because they knew about one occupation but not about the other. The Bush administration's vigorous rejection of a "linkage" between the two issues was therefore endorsed by a population that had little or no idea what it meant.

Similarly, while the plight of Kuwait quickly became common knowledge, only 15 percent were able to identify the Palestinian protest against occupation, the *Intifada*. Moreover, only 14 percent were aware that the United States was part of the tiny minority in the United Nations to have voted against seeking a political settlement to the Palestinian/Israeli conflict. This was almost the same number (12 percent) as those who suggested that Iraq was voting on the same side (we scarcely need to point out the irony of this misconception). This limited understanding, once again, made it much easier for the president to appear morally consistent and to invoke "international law" as a basis for the attack on Iraq and occupied Kuwait.

This notion was also sustained by the idea that Saddam Hussein, like Adolf Hitler, was a madman who had to be stopped. Although we cannot comment on Saddam Hussein's inclinations toward megalomania, it is worth noting that the Iraqi invasion of Kuwait was motivated, at least in part, by an unremarkable economic rationale. One of the most well-documented reasons for the Iraqi invasion was Kuwait's insistence on lowering oil prices, a policy that was severely straining Iraq's economy following the war with Iran; yet only 2 percent of our sample could identify this as a reason for Iraq's action. While knowledge of this recent history would not, for most people, have justified the invasion, it would have been more difficult to portray the Iraqi leader as an irrational, power-hungry lunatic with a relentless, unprovoked lust for power. The failure to understand this history made the administration's attempt to portray him as the most evil leader since Hitler (as opposed to, say, Pol Pot, Augusto Pinochet, or newfound Gulf War ally Hafiz al-Assad, who might also have a claim to this infamous distinction) seem much more plausible.

Even though most respondents had difficulty with questions about the Middle East and U.S. foreign policy there, people were more confident about a few areas. Most of our sample (81 percent) knew the name of the missile (the Patriot) that (supposedly) shot down the Iraqi Scuds so effectively. Most people (80 percent) were also aware that Hussein had used chemical weapons against Iran and/or members of his own population (although more recent reports have cast some doubt on this "fact"; see Wines 1991). This knowledge suggests that the public is not generally "ignorant"; rather, it is selectively misinformed. There are some facts, in other words, that most TV viewers do know, and just as the unknown facts are not neutral, neither are the known ones.

Knowing details about weapons—particularly one that, like the Patriot, has been celebrated for its presumed defensive capabilities—may well help those who wish to promote the idea that the enormous Pentagon budget is money well spent. Either way, it is extremely disturbing that this public expertise in aspects of military technologies was not matched by any clear understanding of the circumstances behind their deployment.

Similarly, knowledge of Saddam Hussein's past atrocities (which, though brutal, are not uncommon in a world littered with dictators with scant regard for human life), clearly supported the administration's moral case against him. So, for example, when asked whether the United States should forcefully intervene against leaders that slaughter significant numbers of civilians, 58 percent responded positively (less than half this number, 27 percent, said no). If this moral position were applied consistently, the United States would have invaded many countries that it has actually supported (e.g., Cambodia, Indonesia, East Timor, El Salvador, and Guatemala). These data suggest that people's awareness of Saddam Hussein's abuse of human rights was combined by unawareness of other comparable human rights abusers.

These findings amount to a highly selective understanding of contemporary history, with all the awkward information neatly removed. They constitute a worldview that allows people to construct an extremely misleading impression about U.S. foreign policy based on a naive faith that the United States is on the side of the "good guys." This context of information made it far easier for President Bush to legitimate the war in moral and absolute terms. A moral reading becomes harder the more knowledge there is of other occupations (such as Israel's) and past U.S. policy toward Iraq.

Knowledge and Support for the War

The relatively low levels of knowledge about critical aspects of the Middle Eastern situation and the actual patterns of what information the public did and did not know together suggest that support for the war may have been built on highly selective and distorted assumptions. That is, many of these unknown facts could have undermined key parts of the administration's moral argument. In fact, our data showed a strong relationship between knowledge and opposition to the war: The more people knew, the less likely they were to support the war.

We are not saying that people against the war were right and people in favor of it were wrong. Rather, we are simply noting that because our study showed a clear relation between knowledge and opinion, and because what people did not know tended to undermine the administration's moral position, it is plausible to assume that an increase in knowledge could have led to an increase in antiwar sentiment.

There are many examples of this pattern, some of which are shown in Table 18.1. Strong supporters of the war, for example, were more than twice as likely as were nonsupporters (29 percent to 12 percent) to wrongly assert that Kuwait was a democracy (before the invasion). The tendency for war supporters to believe that Kuwait was a democracy held up in all subgroups (except among younger respondents, who, regardless of their position on the war, were more likely to believe that Kuwait had been democratic). Among males, 27 percent of the war supporters but

TABLE 18.1
Relationships Among Selected Beliefs, War Support, and Media Exposure

	Support for the War				Television Viewing				TV News Viewing		
	Strong	Medium	Opposed	Gamma	Light	Medium	Heavy	Gamma	Light	Heavy	Gamma
Percent who could identify the Patriot missile	81	83	78	−.01	85	84	74	−.21[a]	78	82	.12
Percent who could identify the *Intifada*	12	15	24	.25[a]	22	15	10	−.30[a]	11	16	.21
Percent who said, "The U.S. said they would take no action."	10	11	27	.32[a]	17	15	8	−.25[a]	9	14	.24
Percent who said, "The U.S. said they would support Kuwait with the use of force."	72	63	46	−.32[a]	59	65	70	.15	69	64	−.09
Percent who said, "Kuwait was a democracy (before the invasion)."	29	19	12	−.34[a]	16	21	32	.29[a]	22	24	.06

[a] $p < .05$

none of the opponents believed that Kuwait was democratic. In some cases (e.g., among middle-aged and older respondents), supporters of the war were more than four times as likely as opponents to believe that Kuwait was democratic.

Thus, those supporting the war were more likely misled into supposing that this was a "fight for democracy." This does not mean that the Bush administration actively promoted the falsehood that Kuwait was actually democratic, but all the talk about the "legitimate government of Kuwait" and the U.S. employment of military force to "liberate" it may have led quite a few to that conclusion.

Similarly, very few respondents (about 13 percent) knew that the United States told Iraq it would take no action if Kuwait were invaded. Table 18.1 shows that those opposed to the war were substantially more likely to know this; only 10 percent of strong supporters were aware that the United States had failed to warn Iraq of a military response to an invasion, compared to 27 percent of nonsupporters. This pattern held across the board, and the margin of difference was usually significant. Less than 10 percent of younger respondents and of those with less education knew this was the case.

Additionally, Table 18.1 shows that 72 percent of strong supporters, as opposed to 46 percent of opponents, erroneously thought that the United States said it would support Kuwait with the use of force. This difference held up sharply and significantly in almost all subgroups. Among males, war supporters were more than twice as likely as opponents to believe this (71 percent to 29 percent). The smallest difference between supporters and opponents of the war was a full twenty-three points (among older respondents).

Finally, in relation to the Palestinian uprising on the West Bank, Table 18.1 also shows that opponents of the war were twice as likely to be able to identify the *Intifada* than were strong supporters (24 percent to 12 percent). This pattern persisted in all subgroups except (again) for the younger respondents.

In regard to "opinion" questions, there were also some striking differences between supporters and nonsupporters. When asked on what hypothetical bases the United States should intervene in other countries, supporters of the war were much more likely to countenance military action. For example, 63 percent of strong supporters, compared with only 27 percent of opponents, thought that the United States should intervene militarily to protect human rights in the case of a guerrilla army taking power and slaughtering civilians. Similarly, 65 percent of supporters, compared with 15 percent of opponents, thought that the United States should intervene militarily in the case of illegal occupations of foreign countries. Even in the case of fighting for oil, supporters were more than twice as likely as opponents to support military intervention (21 percent to 10 percent). Given the association between knowledge and opinion, the antiwar respondents' reluctance to endorse military intervention may have been partly due to their awareness that agreement would imply widespread military actions (given that these situations applied to many other countries apart from Iraq).

It is also worth noting that supporters of the war gave much lower estimates of the loss of life in the war at that point, particularly on the Iraqi side. The average estimate of Iraqi casualties was between three and four times higher among those who did not support the war. Although it is still difficult to verify which estimate was more accurate, there was clearly a very different perception between the two groups about the effects of the war.

The Media, Knowledge, and Opinion

One explanation that may account for the low levels of information about the Middle East (particularly about information that could have undermined the administration's war policy) is that people were simply not paying much attention to the media. But as this and other surveys have discovered, people watched a great deal of television, and news exposure was very high during the war. They may not have been watching the news carefully, but they were certainly watching it. How did amount of exposure, both to news and television in general, relate to knowledge and opinion about the war?

Our data suggested that television seemed to confuse more than to clarify. Even after controlling for other variables, we discovered that the correlations between TV watching and knowledge were mostly negative. In short, the more TV people watched, the less they knew. Some examples of this pattern can be seen in Table 18.1. As amount of television viewing went up, so did the percent who believed that Kuwait was a democracy before the invasion. Heavy viewers were more than twice as likely as light viewers to (wrongly) believe this; 16 percent of light viewers, 21 percent of medium viewers, and 32 percent of heavy viewers said that Kuwait had been democratic. This pattern held up in all subgroups. Light viewers were also more than twice as likely as heavy viewers to know that in the preinvasion discussions between Iraq and the United States, the latter had indicated that no action would be taken against Iraq should Kuwait be invaded; this association, too, held up almost across the board.

Conversely, 70 percent of heavy viewers, versus 59 percent of light viewers, thought that the United States had informed Iraq that it would protect Kuwait with the use of force. This was even stronger for males, among whom about half of light viewers (53 percent) and about three-quarters of heavy viewers (74 percent) held this belief. Finally, light viewers were more than twice as likely as heavy viewers to be able to identify the *Intifada* (22 percent of light viewers compared to only 10 percent of heavy viewers could do so). Among those with less education, about 22 percent of light viewers but only 2 percent of heavy viewers knew what the *Intifada* was.

The same pattern emerged again and again. In regard to a question about other occupations, 40 percent of light viewers, versus 23 percent of heavy viewers, were able to identify Israel's occupation of other lands in the Middle East. Concerning past U.S. relations with Iraq, heavy viewers were less likely than light viewers (67 percent to 46 percent) to know that the United States had supported Iraq during the Iran-Iraq War.

One of the most striking findings concerned the perception of how much damage the intense bombing of Iraq and Iraqi troops had caused. When we asked people to estimate the number of Iraqi deaths thus far, light viewers gave a mean estimate of 9,848 deaths (by February 4, 1991), while heavy viewers gave a mean figure of 789 (8 percent of the light viewers' estimate). The question here was not about accuracy but about relative perceptions—clearly heavy viewers were more inclined than light viewers to buy into the idea that the war was being fought cleanly and efficiently with smart bombs that were damaging only buildings. The lack of visual pictures of actual dead people no doubt helped to cultivate this image of cleanliness.

In contrast to overall viewing, news viewing contributed very little to knowledge and opinion. Heavy news viewers were slightly more likely to be able to identify the *Intifada,* slightly more likely to know the United States said it would take no action, and slightly less likely to believe that the United States warned Iraq it would protect Kuwait with force (by about five points, and not significantly, in each case). Similarly, heavy news viewers were more likely to be able to identify the Patriot missile and Colin Powell and to know about other occupations in the Middle East.

Yet heavy news viewing did not always go with a slight tendency to give "correct" answers; heavy news viewers were also slightly more likely to think that both Iraq and Kuwait (before the invasion) were democracies. And the mean estimate of the number of Iraqis killed given by heavy news viewers (3,930) was significantly less than the mean estimate of light news viewers (8,380), which may confirm the view that the news media underplayed the extent of the carnage in Iraq.

On the whole, however, differences deriving from news exposure were consistently negligible. Only one question produced differences of any noteworthy magnitude: 83 percent of heavy news viewers, compared to "only" 65 percent of light news viewers, agreed with Bush that the United States had fought in Vietnam with "one hand tied behind its back." Dennis et al (1991, p. 42) noted that in all the coverage, from August 1, 1990 through February 28, 1991, the word *Vietnam* appeared far more often than any other (7,299 times, about three times as often as the runner-up, *human shields*). Thus, far more than anything else, it appears as though news viewers had indeed learned the "lesson" of Vietnam—at least as the media and the administration presented it.

The lack of observable differences deriving from news exposure was certainly partially a result of lack of variation in the measure—again, nearly everyone was watching a great deal of news in January and February 1991. But that in itself made the low levels of overall knowledge all the more striking. "Responsibility" for this lack of knowledge lies with both the media and the public. It is too simplistic to say that it was the news media's "fault" that people did not know basic facts about U.S. policy and the Middle Eastern situation; selective perception, attention, and evaluation played a critical role as well.

The problem was thus one of proportion. All the facts that we asked people about had been reported at one time or another. But their overall presence in the news coverage was very low. When compared to the presence of information about the mechanics of war or the administration's view of the situation, the foregoing information clearly got lost.

Media Use and Support for the War

Given these relationships among media use, knowledge, and support for the war, we would expect amount of television viewing itself to be associated with support for the war. Overall, there was an extremely strong positive relationship between general amount of television viewing and support for the war. Table 18.2 shows that less than half (47 percent) of light viewers, compared to three-quarters (76 percent) of heavy viewers, strongly supported President Bush's decision to use military force against Iraq. This relationship was highly stable across subgroups, although it was weaker among those with more education and did not hold for older respondents.

The association was especially strong among the "middle-aged" respondents (those between thirty-three and forty-seven) and those with less education; in those groups, only 36 percent of the light viewers, in contrast to 79 percent of the heavy viewers, expressed "strong" support for the war. Younger heavy viewers with less education were the most likely group to express strong support; nearly 90 percent of that group "strongly" supported the war, and the remaining 10 percent expressed a

TABLE 18.2
Percent Who Strongly Supported the War, by TV Exposure

TV Viewing	Both	Gender		Age			Education	
		Female	Male	Young	Middle	Old	Low	High
Overall								
Light	47	39	53	45	36	67	33	51
Medium	52	45	58	41	64	55	58	47
Heavy	76	71	81	89	79	63	80	67
Gamma	.30[a]	.32[c]	.31[c]	.40[b]	.49[a]	.03	.44[a]	.13
News								
Light	48	45	52	52	41	50	44	52
Heavy	60	56	64	53	66	60	68	52
Gamma	.19	.19	.17	.05	.43[c]	.27	.32[c]	.07

[a]$p < .001$
[b]$p < .01$
[c]$p < .05$

"medium" level of support—not a single heavy viewer younger than thirty-two was either opposed to the war or uncertain about it.

TV news viewing was less strongly related to how fervently people supported the war, although the relationships were all in the same (positive) direction. Overall, 48 percent of light news viewers and 60 percent of heavy viewers expressed strong support for the war. As seen in Table 18.2, this pattern was consistent across all subgroups, though not always significantly.

Again, almost everyone was watching at least some TV news during the period in which the data were collected; yet even though our measure of TV news exposure did not provide sufficiently fine gradations, the same relationships appeared, albeit less strongly. But given the habitual and ritualistic ways in which most people watch television, it is clear that heavy "general" viewers tended to be more exposed to TV news on a regular basis (and not just very intensely during the first few weeks of the war).

In sum, despite all the coverage, people in the United States knew remarkably little about many critical aspects of the background and context of the war. The more people knew, the less likely they were to support the war; the less they knew, the more strongly they supported the war. People who generally watched a lot of television showed dramatically lower levels of knowledge and were substantially more likely to strongly support the use of military force against Iraq.

Conclusions and Implications

Our findings suggest that the U.S. media failed quite dramatically in their role as information providers. Despite months of intense coverage, most people did not know basic facts about the political situation in the Middle East or about the recent history of U.S. policy toward Iraq. Television, as the "information" source most people depended on, was particularly responsible. Even though support for the war was extraordinarily strong, it was built at least partly on a body of knowledge that was either incorrect or incomplete. Support for the war, though immense, thus looked rather fragile because the more people knew, the less likely they were to support the war.

We cannot blame the Pentagon and the Bush administration for only presenting those facts that lent support for their case—it was not their job, after all, to provide the public with a balanced view. Culpability for this rests clearly on the shoulders of the media, particularly television, which have a duty to present the public with the relevant facts. Our study suggests that they failed quite dismally in performing this duty.

Television's tendency to present a one-sided view is compounded by the economic imperatives of a system funded by advertising. The upbeat tone of the coverage was seen as necessary to retain advertisers because nobody wanted their product surrounded by images of death, pain, and destruction. Unfortunately from the point of view of journalistic objectivity, this upbeat tone played into the hands of the Bush administration's attempt to sell its war policy to the public.

The question raised by our findings is a significant one: If the media had done a better job in informing people, would there have been less support for the war? Our study indicated that the answer to this question is yes. This is not to say that people with awareness of most of the relevant facts about the Middle East and recent U.S. foreign policy could not have supported the Bush policy; our study simply suggested that they would have been less likely to. Fuller knowledge would have made it harder to accept a moral rationale for the war because of all the inconsistent and nonsupporting facts. To support the war in the light of this knowledge would have required additional thought and reasoning—support would had to have been contingent, based on particular judgments and configurations of rationales.

The media also failed in their "duty to be objective" because they largely communicated facts that supported the administration's policy and played down those that did not. Their message consisted of three claims: (1) "The enemy is pure evil incarnate," (2) "We are winning," and (3) "God is on our side." These bore a curious similarity to the message promoted by the Iraqi government and media. Yet in the United States, the government and the media were assumed to be independent of each other and distinct.

The implications of these findings suggest that the U.S. media—if they take their role as information providers seriously—need to reexamine the way they cover foreign policy events such as the Gulf War. As our findings indicate, this means a greater concern with historical fact than with opinion and unsupported "official" interpretations.

These results also suggest greater caution in the use of public opinion polls. Our study implies that these polls did not validate Bush's policy; instead, they simply reflected the failure of the news media to enable the public to reach an informed opinion. In other words, opinion polls did not reflected a citizenry making rational and independent decisions about issues; rather, they largely reflected the bias of the U.S. media system.

This can, unfortunately, become a cyclical process. Once the war began, the political establishment in the United States closed ranks on the issue. The media coverage reflected this narrowing of opinion, which in turn influenced public opinion. The media were therefore able to justify their partiality with the notion that they were simply reflecting public opinion—allowing public opinion to further solidify on the issue. Raising broader issues could have encouraged contingent, rather than moral, positions, thereby avoiding the simplistic misconceptions that characterized public opinion during the Gulf War.

These data do not "prove" that the media "caused" lower levels of knowledge or that ignorance of many basic facts "caused" people to so strongly support the Gulf War. There are many plausible (and non-mutually exclusive) explanations and interpretations of our results. It may be that people who opposed the war went to greater lengths to find out "correct" information (which was indeed available) to bolster their position; that is, their views could have produced their greater knowledge, rather than vice versa. And it may be that people who supported the war simply tended to watch more television because what they saw there tended to confirm and gratify their views. To us, however, the data suggest an ongoing process in which support for the war, lower levels of knowledge, and greater media exposure all interacted and reproduced one another in dynamic and systematic ways.

Beyond the complex and distracting arguments about "causality" in these data, the more critical questions are "Why, in an ostensibly democratic society, were the media so complicit in blurring the lines between independent critical analysis and official government policy? Why did they so stifle the debate and essentially silence opposing voices? And why did they so willingly allow themselves to be skillfully used as weapons of disinformation directed at both the U.S. public and the Iraqi military leadership?"

These questions need to be addressed, despite the accusations from some quarters that the media gave too much attention to antiwar protests and mindlessly disseminated pro-Iraqi propaganda. Some have criticized our conclusion that the media "failed" in their "duty" to provide "correct" information, arguing that they actually brilliantly "succeeded" in suppressing debate and in brainwashing the vast U.S. public into a vitriolic fervor of patriotism. We, however, reject such "conspiracy theories" as the total (or even the primary) explanation of the media's performance.

More plausibly, and more simply, we believe a major answer to these questions can be found in the economic (commercial) foundation of the dominant media structures in contemporary U.S. society. This structure demanded that media decisions about how to present the war were in part driven by fears of being called "anti-American" (and therefore obstructing the erasure of the presumed "Vietnam syndrome") and by the need to deliver audiences in the "proper mindset" to receive commercial messages. Thus, the media needed to minimize any potentially controversial messages that might have unsettled the audience.

Moreover, the news media have for some time also allowed themselves to become highly dependent on government or "official" agencies as the primary sources of "news." It can also be argued that the main U.S. news organizations are vested in the hands of a few giant corporations, some with direct links to the defense industry. This situation can hardly be expected to encourage a selection of diverse and independent views and perspectives.

The media "solution" was to choose the safe option. In this view, it was far better to wave the flag and propagate disinformation (in the name of "military security") than to enhance the debate, risk disturbing audiences with uncomfortable information, and thereby possibly alienate advertisers. The final result was a troubling mixture of support for violent military solutions, happy patriotic audiences, and obfuscations of reality.

References

Anderson, Robin, and Paolo Carpignano. 1991. "Iraqi Dupes or Pentagon Promoters? CNN Covers the War." *Extra!* (May): 12–13.

Bennis, Phyllis. 1991. "The CNN War That Wasn't." *Lies of Our Times* (February): 4–5.

Bernstein, Jonas. 1991. "Press Showing Its Stripes." *Insight,* January 28, pp. 15–16.

Boston Media Watch. 1991. "Scenes from a War: A Study of Boston Press Coverage." Boston: Boston Media Action, March 20, mimeo.

Browne, Malcom W. 1991. "The Military vs. the Press." *New York Times Magazine,* March 3, pp. 26–30, 40–45.

Cockburn, Alexander. 1991. "The Press and the 'Just War.'" *Nation,* February 18, pp. 180, 186–188, 201.

Dennis, Everette E. et al. 1991. *The Media at War: The Press and the Persian Gulf Conflict.* New York: Gannett Foundation Media Center.

DeParle, Jason. 1991a. "Long Series of Military Decisions Led to Gulf War News Censorship." *New York Times,* May 5, pp. A1, 20.

———. 1991b. "Keeping the News in Step: Are the Pentagon's Gulf War Rules Here to Stay?" *New York Times,* May 6, p. A9.

Gelb, Leslie H. 1991. "The Next Surprise?" *New York Times,* February 3, p. E19.

Gerbner, George, Larry Gross, Michael Morgan, and Nancy Signorielli. 1986. "Living with Television: The Dynamics of the Cultivation Process." In J. Bryant and D. Zillman, eds., *Perspectives on Media Effects,* pp. 17–40. Hillsdale, N.J.: Erlbaum.

Goodman, Walter. 1991. "Not Letting TV Do Its Best Job in the War." *New York Times,* February 2, p. A18.

Herman, Edward. 1991a. "Mere Iraqis." *Lies of Our Times* (February): 5–6.

———. 1991b. "Gulfspeak II." *Z Magazine* (March): 15–16.

Hickey, Neil. 1991. "The War Is Over, But the Battle Between TV and the Pentagon Rages on." *TV Guide,* April 6, pp. 2–6.

Index on Censorship. 1991. "Warspeak: The Gulf and the News Media (April-May).

James, Caryn. 1991. "Watching the War: Viewers on the Front Lines." *New York Times,* February 10, pp. B29, 40.

Karem, Brian. 1991. "One Local Reporter's Tale of the War." *Electronic Media,* April 22, p. 13.

Larsen, Ernest. 1991. "Gulf War TV." *Jump Cut,* no. 36 (March): 3–10.

LeMoyne, James. 1991. "Pentagon's Strategy for the Press: Good News or No News." *New York Times,* February 17, p. E3.

Lewis, Anthony. 1991. "To See Ourselves . . . : The Failings of the Press in the Gulf War." *New York Times,* May 6, p. E25.

Nathan, Debbie. 1991. "Just the Good News, Please." *Progressive* (February): 25–27.

Naureckas, Jim. 1991. "Gulf War Coverage: The Worst Censorship Was at Home." *Extra!* (May): 3–10.

Ray, Ellen. 1991. "How to Lie." *Lies of Our Times* (February): 6.

Ruffini, Gene. 1991. "Press Fails to Challenge the Rush to War." *Washington Journalism Review* (March): 21–23.

Schanberg, Sydney H. 1991. "Censoring for Military Political Security." *Washington Journalism Review* (March): 23–26.

Shaheen, Jack G. 1984. *The TV Arab.* Bowling Green, Ohio: Bowling Green State University Popular Press.

Sklar, Holly. 1991. "Buried Stories from Media Gulf." *Z Magazine.* (March): 57–61.

Solomon, Norman. 1991. "War Deaths Mere PR to Media's Eyes." *Guardian,* February 27, p. 4.

Wallis, Victor. 1991. "Media War in the Gulf." *Lies of Our Times* (February): 3–4.

Wines, Michael. 1991. "Years Later, No Clear Culprit in Gassing of Kurds." *New York Times,* April 28, p. A13.

Winter, Jim. 1991. "Media Broom Sweeps Clean" *Toronto Star,* January 24, p. A27.

JOYSTICKS, MANHOOD, AND GEORGE BUSH'S HORSE
Rami G. Khouri

The intensity and scope of the American-led bombing campaign in Iraq, combined with Washington's negative initial responses in the past week to Iraqi and Soviet proposals to end the war on the basis of U.N. resolutions, have triggered deep misgivings throughout the world about Washington's conduct and true aims in the Gulf war and about its future role in the area. While Americans are enjoying the video films of laser-guided bombs and the deceptive emotional highs of their first-ever joystick war, most of the rest of the world is asking very specific questions: What does the civilian casualty toll and destruction of non-military targets in Iraq speak about American political morality? Is the military conduct of the war a prelude to American political behavior in the Middle East and around the world in decades to come? Does Washington really seek the liberation of Kuwait from Iraqi occupation, as stipulated by United Nations Security Council Resolution 660? Or does it seek the military and political bludgeoning of Iraq, a Third World country whose challenge to the British-American imperial order of the twentieth century had to be put down with such brutality that no other country from the South would even contemplate such a challenge for many decades?

The brutality of the war and the horror of civilian deaths were most dramatically captured in the television images of the burnt, charred, and still-smoldering bodies of over three hundred women and children killed in the American missile attack February 13 on the Baghdad shelter. In Arab eyes, as gruesome as the human inferno itself was the American government's attempt to blame the Iraqis for placing civilians in what had been used as a civilian shelter for many years during the Iran-Iraq War.

Iraqi officials this week said their country has suffered twenty thousand dead and sixty thousand injured, of whom up to seven thousand may be civilian casualties, alongside economic damage of some $200 billion. The wholesale destruction of the civil infrastructure of Iraq, including power stations, roads, refineries, industrial plants, bridges, water systems, homes, religious sites, and other nonmilitary facilities, has brought hardship and potential health hazards to virtually the entire population of 17 million

(*continues*)

(*continued*)

people. Everywhere, but most critically in big cities, people live without electricity, clean water, sewage systems, emergency medical supplies, heating oil and gasoline, and other essential goods and services. Cholera and typhoid epidemics are a major immediate hazard.

All this seems largely hidden from the American conscience. In the world of those who fight a joystick war, there is no room for real problems, no reality to burning human flesh, no validity to Third World emotions, and no appreciation of the political or moral consequences of one's actions halfway around the world. In a flag-waving America dazzled by the glare of its yellow ribbons, it seems the mind has no room for the possibility that ninety thousand air sorties and one hundred thousand tons of bombs dropped on Iraq in five weeks can disrupt the lives of ordinary people. In the mind of America, the bombs are smart, the war is moral, and the president is at peace with himself. Laser-guided bombs do not make mistakes. There is no room for human error. There is only the triumph of technology over humanity, of militarism over conscience. Zap the Iraqoids!

This piece was originally published in *Jordan Times,* February 23, 1991.

◆

CHAPTER NINETEEN

Clusters of Reality
Bombed into Bold Relief

Erskine B. Childers

THE GULF CRISIS OFFERS a number of sharp lessons in perception, communication, and democratic consultation. The first lesson is that imperialism is alive and well; it has only changed its clothing and language. But few Western citizens can perceive this because most Western establishment media have themselves behaved for thirty years as though it did end when the independence flags were raised. It has been rather impolite and "extremist" to use the words *imperialism* and *colonialism* ever since. Most Westerners thus live in a fundamentally unreal perception of the total world they share.

National borders that were imposed by colonial powers without any consultation with the indigenous people on either side of them have *not* been accepted, as orthodox Western information has sought to suggest. There is not one endogenously evolved frontier in the entire Arab world, from Morocco to Iraq. Although the Iraqis had disputed the British creation of a separate Kuwait entity since before Saddam Hussein was born, and although Kuwait's achievement of independent status as a member of the United Nations occurred under direct British military protection, the Iraq-Kuwait crisis of mid-1990 burst on the Western world as if it were some sudden machination of the current dictator. The Iraqi territorial and oil grievances that were in fact acknowledged in the first Security Council resolution condemning Iraq's aggression were quickly buried in most Western media by the avalanche of demonization launched by the war powers. The establishment media became the dutiful, passive reporters and active editorial supporters of the entire campaign of demagoguery.

Then, too, the Kurds have been alive and suffering throughout this century. It was, however, only when they rebelled under active encouragement and covert arming from the new world order warriors, but were then abruptly abandoned by them and fled into the mountains, that the Kurds in *Iraq* even came into the vision of the Western world. Even in the midst of the reporting, most Western media demonstrated the usual facile bias: How many Westerners learned that the Kurds in *Turkey*—a favored Western ally—were not allowed even to speak their language, which at least the Kurds in Iraq were allowed, or that the Turkish army had been practicing vicious *ratissage* on their villages for years? Which Western newspaper or broadcasting station told the whole story—how the Kurdish people, totaling now some 20 million, went to the Versailles peace conference to secure their national self-determination and were brushed aside like dirt by the victorious Western powers that had proclaimed such self-determination as a war aim?

Some sixty U.N. member states—more than a third of the total membership—have entirely artificial, colonially imposed boundaries. Most of the genuine national liberation movements had no choice but to accept them because decolonization was geographically haphazard or because ethnic tensions engendered by colonial divide and rule threatened to erupt in the chaos of independence. In other instances, as we have just seen in the Gulf, a colonially imposed boundary was preserved under great-power military protection to maintain Western oil (or other precious resource) interests. None of this is known in the West except by a handful of scholars. Yet our world is laced with these time bombs, and their defusion must not be left to the dubious and thoroughly self-interested machinations of major powers. Communicators who care must now bring these dangers to a just and democratic international peace to public attention and must support increasing U.N. ability to anticipate and help mediate them.

The Gulf crisis also demonstrated all too convincingly that the gross inequities of the continuing, never-reformed imperialist economic system are alive and flourishing. But this, too, the Western world has not been and will not be told by orthodox media. We have seen a feudal family living on top of an oil reserve that by 1990 had created domestic wealth enabling six hundred thousand Kuwaitis not to work unless they wished (free housing, free schooling, free medical care, etc.) and an *external* economy of some $200 billion. Ninety percent of that external wealth was invested in the West, not in the Third World. Meanwhile, in the surrounding Arab world there were tens of millions of desperately poor people, and in the Third World generally there were hundreds of millions of people more living in absolute poverty than twenty years previously. And by 1990, the existing international economic system had produced the ultimate zero equation of disguised imperialism: $50 billion in official northern "development assistance" (most of it actually spent in the North) and $50 billion paid *to* the North *by* the Third World in debt servicing. The zero net was the result of forty years of what most decent Western citizens had been misled into believing was genuine "aid."

Again, this is little known in the Western world except by economists, governments, and corporate leaders who arrange the West's profits from this economic system. The establishment Western media helped kill all proposals for a new international economic order fifteen years ago. It was almost impossible in those years to find in such Western media any reflection of the Third World's well-presented and analyzed argument that a reformed, more equitable international economic system was in the North's own interest because the current economic system was not working correctly for anyone. All such perspectives were buried, with dutifully heavy reporting that Western leaders objected to the proposals for a new international economic order because, they said, talk of a "new international order" smacked of Nazism. The same establishment Western media are now busy hailing the proclamation of George Bush's new world order, which apparently does *not* smack of Nazism.

Imperialism also had as its perceptual and informational foundations every moral double standard imaginable—the leaders of Western civilization extolling their high principles to the majority of humanity kept in economic, social, and intellectual prison. The Gulf crisis demonstrated that the same double standards were alive and well thirty years after the imperial and colonial era was ostensibly over. One of dozens of illustrations of this demagoguery will suffice here.

Several days before the Gulf War began, an entire small nation of 1.7 million people already generally imprisoned by a U.S. ally occupying their land for seventeen years were now imprisoned *in their homes* in a continuous twenty-four-hour curfew. They were forbidden on pain of prison or shooting to go out to produce food, earn any income, or even take sick family members to a doctor. The Western media scarcely reported even the fact of this house arrest of every Palestinian in the occupied territories; they were very busy reporting on the behavior of Iraq as an occupying power in Kuwait.

Israel had been in open violation of the U.N. Charter so often that even a summary list would have run to pages. Indeed, Israel had been in violation even of the explicit terms of its own admission to the United Nations as a member. Israel has emerged from the Gulf cisis with pledges of billions of dollars in more Western military and economic aid and is busy openly violating U.N. resolutions and Geneva conventions in settling more Israelis in the occupied territories. No proposal even for U.N. Security Council sanctions has ever been seriously discussed by the same powers that erupted in outrage in August 1990. In April 1990 the United States had vetoed a U.N. commission to *investigate* how to protect the Palestinians.

Given this long and sordid record, it is absolutely unsafe to trust the powers now proclaiming a new world order and involving such high moral principles and so much international law over Kuwait. Yet they seem to have convinced most of the establishment media that they have suddenly become paragons of international virtue. The notion of the new world order is infinitely dangerous because so many decent Westerners want to believe that their leaders mean what they say and may all too easily be deceived as they were in the Gulf. Those who care must become far more alert and vigorous in demanding an end to the miseries of tens of millions living under the long nightmare of imperialism's double standards. We now have to build altogether new bridges of solidarity between an outraged South and the many decent Westerners whom the South can no longer see through the clouds of resentment and fear that have boiled up out of the Gulf War.

Underlying the Gulf crisis were a thousand years of general Western cultural antagonism toward the Arabs and Islam. To this day, neither the wealthy school systems nor the establishment media of the West have ended the ancient cultural amnesia of their peoples, who were deliberately never informed that Europe's intellectual and scientific achievements were *founded* on Arab intellectual synthesis and knowledge.

Western television audiences were mesmerized by the pictures relayed from cameras mounted on bombs and missiles as they raced to their Iraqi targets. How many of those decent citizens knew that the camera lens was based on the Iraqi ibn al-Haytham's vast tenth-century thesaurus on the principles of optics and perspective, which was still being annotated by Lorenzo Ghiberti in Florence five hundred years later?

On March 27, 1991, in the exuberance and exultation of his "victory," General Norman Schwarzkopf let slip on television that the plan of operations he used against Iraq had been in preparation for eighteen months. The dictator who had been very useful, who had been armed and otherwise supported for a decade while Western realpolitik was trying to destroy the second Iranian revolution, was now dispensable under the new realpolitik. (It was apparently not considered important "background to the news" that Schwarzkopf père went into Iran with the CIA to train the shah's police after the *first* Iranian revolution, led by Muhammad Mossadegh, had been wiped out by the CIA because Mossadegh was bold enough to nationalize the Anglo-Iranian Oil Company.) But to fulfill the plan to destroy Iraq militarily, the Western powers needed the moral cloak of the United Nations.

This was arranged as follows: The sanctions resolutions gained the general support of the international community; under the U.N. Charter, whatever the origin of Kuwait, Iraq had committed an open act of aggression. Western media rediscovered, and hailed, the United Nations as though it had gone away somewhere. Under the screen of this genuine support, every Iraqi offer to negotiate, and the initiative of every head of state or government to mediate, was stifled and deflected while the coalition's military forces were assembling in Saudi Arabia and in the Gulf waters. These Iraqi offers and mediation efforts—and their rapid sabotaging—went virtually unreported in the West, and a picture of the Iraqi dictator refusing to budge was relentlessly built up. The U.S. denial of permission for the Iraqi foreign minister to appear at the United Nations to state Iraq's case went virtually unreported. George Bush's highly personalized obsession—eerily reminiscent of Anthony Eden's over the 1956 Suez aggression when he, too, was smarting from being called a "wimp"—was translated daily by most Western media into the most massive demonization since Gamal Abdel Nasser had been called "another Hitler."

The Hussein regime's detestable human rights record and the Iraqi counter-behavior provided much media material; but the constant official Western disinformation about Iraqi atrocities was never corrected in the media. One has to search high and low, for example, to discover the smallest media correction, tucked into some obscure space, of the story about the babies taken out of incubators in Kuwait.

The war powers arranged to hijack the name and moral authority of the United Nations by ramming through resolutions supposedly "acting under Chapter VII" but not specifying any article of Chapter VII, so that they would not have to secure council approval of a war when their forces were ready. Again, because the Western media had for decades scorned the United Nations, their commentators knew nothing about the charter and Chapter VII; nor did decent Western citizens. The U.N. constitution was temporarily discarded, and Western peoples, among others, were kept in ignorance of what was being done. Meanwhile, the leading government of the new world order, which was suddenly so devoted to the United Nations yet owed it more than $500 million in membership dues withheld as political pressure, expended over Iraq a sum in military expenditures equivalent to the next twelve to fifteen years of the entire U.N. system's global budgets. And the U.N. high commissioner for refugees, whose annual world budget equaled the amount the United States refused to pay in its arrears to the United Nations, criticized for not moving quickly enough to pick up the pieces of the refugee tragedy.

The impoverishment of the Third World that had steadily been increased by Western refusal even to continue a dialogue about reforming the international economic system, and by Western installation of and support for corrupt regimes, was now used to buy off bully government after government to join the coalition or keep silent or else. The U.N. membership was in effect economically recolonized to secure what President Bush proclaimed was "the support of the whole international community." This, too, went all but unreported throughout the Western world. The revulsion of Third World opinion was not reported to the North, the extent of opposition in the North to the war was not reported there, and little about it could reach the South. A Western-dominated media structure contributed to, and then concealed, a massive widening of the abyss between one-fifth and four-fifths of humankind.

And, finally, a war that was neither necessary nor just was itself totally sanitized, by a combination of official Western censorship, media compliance in purveying military doubletalk, and the mesmerizing use of the video-arcade effect in portraying the high-technology assault. Nor was there hardly any comment then or subsequently in the Western press on the strange fact that the so-called war produced more than 100,000 Iraqi military dead for just 150 coalition dead—a kill ratio never before witnessed in the history of warfare. This was not a war; it was a planned and deliberately, brutally protracted high-technology massacre. The Iraqi corpses from what coalition pilots reportedly called "turkey shoots" of troops in open, visible flight have been bulldozed into the sands and with them the moral voice of the Western world.

DANGERS OF THE CULTURAL INVASION?
Mostafa Mahmoud

It was not that long ago that colonial powers came to take spices, slaves, gold, and mineral ores, draining our resources and occupying our land. Now they are returning with considerable cunning to occupy our minds by different means, through science, technology, economy, art, and philosophy. In the press we find the monopoly of the four giant news agencies: Associated Press, United Press International, Reuters, and Agence France Presse. All radio and television networks and every newspaper around the world subscribe to these agencies. Sixty-five percent of the world's news emanates from America. This subtle propaganda, such a lavish gift, is irresistible. It will throttle all cultural and intellectual innovations, impose its sovereignty over the minds of its viewers with the cultural and intellectual examples it offers. In the best of circumstances, the minds on the receiving end will only get a single flavor of information, inspired by a source of information fed by those who plan and shape the viewers' mind from behind closed doors. France offers its national information services for free via satellite to African radio and television stations. They will reap the benefits of this service for free, in political positions that suit their intellectual hegemony.

The age of military conquests and empire is over. This time around, the West will dominate the globe forever through its cultural occupation of the mind. The first crusade was when Saint Boniface fought to bring Christianity to the Saxons from 480–754 A.D. Several centuries later, the Christians marched into Jerusalem. And the same war is still going on today, though with more appealing slogans and tempting loans and grants. The aims are also the same—expunging identity, eradicating local customs and tradition, and remolding modes of thought and behavior. All this is in exchange for gleaming technology, electronic dummies and a paradise of sexual liberty and vain freedoms.

This piece was originally published in *Al-Ahram,* July 25, 1991.

◆

CHAPTER TWENTY

Persian Gulf War, the Movie

George Gerbner

THERE COMES A TIME in the accumulation of quantitative changes when a qualitative transformation takes place. Add heat to a pot of water, and at one point it begins to boil. A confluence of controls, technologies, and power reached that point in the war in the Persian Gulf. The change occurred not just in geopolitics. It also happened in the way we write—and make—history.

A scholar of media technology, Frederick Williams, compared the Gulf War to the first moon landing in 1969: "It was one feat to put two astronauts on the surface of the moon, but another, perhaps just as amazing, to broadcast live that first human step on the moon's surface." Technology-based immediacy, Williams concluded, was a preview of the shape of things to come.[1] In 1991, the preview led to the main event.

When Mao Zedong was asked what he thought about the meaning of the French Revolution, he is reported to have said that it was too soon to tell.[2] Official history, written from the point of view of rulers, is typically the story of the inevitable unfolding of the glorious present. As written by losers, history is tragedy crying for redemption. When roles change, or when long-hidden facts come to light, it takes time to sort things out.

When that other astute observer of the world scene, Saudi financier of Irangate fame Adnan Khassoghi, was asked what he thought about the war in the Persian Gulf, he said that it was "like going to a movie: we

---

An earlier, brief version of this chapter was presented as the first Wayne Danielson Award Lecture for Distinguished Contributions to Communication Scholarship at the University of Texas, Austin, November 13, 1991.

paid our money, we went to the theater, we laughed, we cried, the movie ended and an hour later we had forgotten about it."[3]

Mao's and Khassoghi's observations marked a change that had come about after a long buildup. Cheap parchment had replaced rare papyrus. The printing press had replaced the quill. The telegraph and telephone had replaced the pony express. We had gone from oral to scribal, to literate, to audio-visual-digital-cybernetic mass-produced culture. The quantum leap had occurred when satellites connected them all around the world. The stage had then been set for centrally scripted real-time live global imagery, evoking instant reaction, feeding media events back into an ongoing crisis, and giving the deliberate sorting out of historical meanings a swift kick in the pants.

Historiography is a communicative activity that relates the past to the present and future.[4] But, as with any communicative activity, it depends not only on the events to be communicated about and the communicating parties but also on the means and modes of communication. When the means change, as Harold Innis, Marshall McLuhan, Elizabeth Eisenstein, and others have observed, access to and control over communications change, and the telling of stories, including history, also changes.

The boiling point is reached when the power to create a crisis merges with the power to direct the movie about it. Participation, witness, and confirmation hitherto limited to those on the scene can now be a vicarious global experience, and response, or cooptation, occurs while the event is still in progress. Having achieved the desired outcome, the movie ends, but the images remain in archives and memories.

The convergence of new communicative technologies confers controls, concentrates power, shrinks time, and speeds action to the point where reporting, making, and writing history merge. The "simultaneous happening," in which, as Ien Ang described it, "the whole world presumably participated through the electronic collapsing of time and space,"[5] usually occurs in crises, or tends to precipitate a crisis, as in climactic trials and hearings, disasters, uprisings, and wars.[6] These are situations when, one would think, deliberate speed and careful consideration are needed the most. Instead, however, past, present, and future can now be packaged, witnessed, and frozen into memorable moving imagery of instant history—scripted, cast, directed, and produced by the winners.

Instant History—Image History

Instant history is made when access to video-satellite-computer systems blankets the world in real time with selected images that provoke immediate reactions, influence the outcome, and then quick-freeze into received history. Instant history is a magic lantern projecting images on a blank screen in a temporal void. The show has a clear beginning, middle, and end. It telescopes roles, parts, and outcome into the same act. It appeals to prior beliefs and predilections. It triggers familiar responses. It blends into our repertory of imagery. It is not easily dislodged, reinterpreted, or even attributed to one particular show. We have forgotten the title.

Films of Vietnam took hours or days to reach us after the fact. It may have been the first "living-room war," but not for the first few years and not in real time. Starting with the make-believe incident in the Gulf of Tonkin, it was a long, slow, duplicitous buildup. It lasted eleven years, destroyed three countries, and left behind some 2 million dead and continuing economic sanctions for the living.

"Body counts" were in headlines but did not have public witness. The tide of public reaction turned after victory eluded policymakers and cameras began to record unsettling images: the Tet Offensive, a summary execution of an "enemy" suspect, naked "enemy" children fleeing napalm, thatched "enemy" huts being put to the torch. (When cameras turn to focus on the fallen, the war is lost, or soon will be. The press was barred from Dover Air Force Base, where Gulf War body bags landed.)

Instant history is image history. The crisis unfolds before our eyes, too fast for thoughtful consideration of antecedents, alternatives, or long-range consequences but just in time for conditioned reflex. The show is on, we are in it, and the deed must be done before second thoughts, counteracts, and regrets can derail the action.

The Iraq-Iran War, totally out of sight, dragged on for more than eight years, claimed more than 1 million casualties, and ended in exhaustion. Chaotic *perestroika,* made visible by *glasnost,* rolled into Eastern Europe, where each successive counterrevolution took half the time of the previous one. The long-pent-up Soviet backlash led to the attempted coup of August 1991 or, as the plotters saw it, countercoup, which was intended to prevent disaster. But the plotters lost control. The magic lantern was snatched from their hands. Defiant imagery swamped their timorous stance. A tidal wave of domestic and world reaction swept them from power in seventy-two hours. Instead of victory, they fell victim to instant history.

Speed and controlled imagery give instant history its thrust—and its burden. When emphasis shifts to image, complex verbal explanations and interpretations, if any, switch into supporting and explanatory, rather than alternative, modes. Experiments have shown that dramatic imagery tends to inhibit both complexity and alternatives. Instant history preempts alternatives.

Neil Postman argued that pictures "have no difficulty overwhelming words and short-circuiting introspection."[7] He cited studies that found the complexity of diplomatic exchanges in international crises that ended in peace to be significantly higher than in crises that ended in armed conflict. Research by Tom Grimes concluded that words can influence the memory of imagery.[8] Thus, congruent narration will often be recalled as a part of actuality witnessed on the screen, even if it never occurred there.[9]

If, however, the voice-over conflicts with the image, the former may be ignored. Todd Gitlin recounted his four-hour interview for "The NBC Nightly News" in which he expressed the view that his opposition to the Gulf War did not conflict with donating blood for the troops. The few seconds selected for the news only showed him donating blood, with his opposition to the war briefly noted in the voiceover. Viewers who confronted him afterward recalled only the image of his apparent support for the war. "People who wouldn't be caught dead saying out loud that the news (to use the media's own favorite metaphor) mirrors reality, saw a media image and *assumed it not to be a construction, not a version, but the truth.*" And "when an image comes advertised as actuality, it raises the expectation of accuracy."[10]

Images of actuality appear to be spontaneous and to reveal what really happens. They do not need logic to build their case. Following William's observation, spontaneity and immediacy preclude time for reflection and evaluation. And if the audience response quickly becomes news, the effects of superficial responses to important world events can be exaggerated."

"Image Industry Erodes Political Space" is the title of John M. Phelan's analysis of the uses of new technology. "The image's new role in organizing complex information is increasingly played out in dynamic interactive contexts," he wrote. In the cockpit of the latest automatically controlled aircraft, the pilot punches in his flight plan on a keyboard, and the flight management system on board calculates the route and flies the plane from takeoff to landing while he monitors the scenery. Phelan commented, "There is a running joke among pilots, who do not find it entirely comical, that the modern flight crew consists of a pilot and a dog. The dog's job is to bite the pilot if he touches any of the controls and the pilot's job is to feed the dog." "By a strange process," Phelan observed, "the further one gets from the reality the more processed the information gets, the more authority it assumes."[12]

The Scenario

The war in the Persian Gulf was an unprecedented motion picture spectacular. It crammed into its first month alone the entire imagery—and firepower—of four years of bombing in World War II. But unlike a carpet of explosives leveling cities and setting off firestorms, or of GI's "flushing out" Vietcong from their hiding places, we were shown "seeing-eye" bombs zooming in on their targets, followed by computer graphics tracing the ground offensive against an invisible enemy.

General Norman Schwarzkopf forbade casualty estimates, so sortie counts replaced body counts. Photographs of battle or of Iraqi (or U.S.) dead were censored. Sleek aircraft "sortied" over unmentionable people in unfought battles in an unseen country. The few unauthorized shots of bombs falling on civilian targets were attacked as treasonous or rationalized as "collateral damage." Never before were selected glimpses of actuality strung together with sound bites of photogenic crews, omniscient voice-overs of safari-clad reporters, and parades of military experts with maps and charts at the ready, so mesmerizing, so coherent, and so contrived.

Desert Storm was the first major global media crisis orchestration that made instant history. The Soviet coup six months later was the first attempt that miscarried. A year before the coup, Mikhail Gorbachev had signed a new press law that gave editorial staffs autonomy not known in the democratic West. This move made for a relatively fragmented and leaky communication system that may have saved his life, if not his job. When the coup came, the plotters could not shut down or conduct the increasingly cacophonous media orchestra. What happened then also made instant history, but that is another story.

Opportunities for making instant history may be few and far between, but when they come, they unloose a landslide that shifts the political landscape. ("I came back to another country," said Gorbachev returning from Crimean captivity.) George Bush grasped the opportunity and proclaimed his "new world order."

It takes a crisis and five strategic moves to seize (or possibly provoke) such an opportunity. They are control, orchestration, witness, feedback, and quick freeze. Here are instructions for successful crisis management by instant history as learned in the Persion Gulf War:

1. Gain access to and keep control of real-time global imagery. Speed the action, and develop a sanitized scenario to show how moral, decisive, necessary, and invincible the action is. One brief burst of saturation coverage is all that is possible before unauthorized voices, costly network preemptions, and audiences missing their daily mayhem with happy endings blunt the momentum.
2. Orchestrate the main event with mainstream media events and other signs and symbols. Invent code names and terminology that fit the scenario, demonize the enemy, and wrap jarring realities in playful euphemisms. Encourage integration of supportive signs into

everyday life, sports, and commerce (yellow ribbons on cars and Kent cigarettes, Super Bowl halftime prowar pageant with President and Mrs. Bush on tape and Peter Jennings live giving upbeat reports on the destruction in progress). Promote miracles. (The icon of St. Irene gained worldwide attention when congregants in a Chicago church reported that it wept "tears of grief" on the eve of the Persian Gulf War.)[13] Instant history requires a total environment of actuality, images, talk shows, slogans, and other evocative manifestations.

3. Offer the witness-audience a sense of "being there," including what appear to be spontaneous (but still stage-managed) occasions such as press conferences, panel discussions, "briefings," and interpretations. This will suggest that alternative perspectives have been explored and exhausted. It will simplify and isolate the crisis from distracting complexities and unwanted alternatives.

4. Translate witness and participation into supportive feedback from polls, letters to the editor, driving with lights on, and horn honking. To evoke conventionally cultivated responses, make participation "like going to a movie." Let this feedback reverberate across all media, crystallize in public opinion (i.e., published opinion), and hasten the desired resolution.

5. Celebrate the outcome as the happy ending. Quickly produce and distribute videos, CD-ROM disks, paperback books, and lavishly illustrated texts to saturate the market for instant nostalgia and school use. Use the triumphant imagery to fight political opposition and resist revisionists.

Prologue

The curtain rises on an operation long in preparation. Several U.S. administrations wanted to project U.S. power into the Middle East. Dwight Eisenhower landed troops there. Ronald Reagan landed troops there (only to have 241 Marines killed in one bombing attack), condoned Israel's invasion of Lebanon, and bombed Druse villages from the sea. After building up Iraq's war machine and also secretly arming Iran in its war with Iraq, U.S. diplomacy encouraged the Saudi and Kuwaiti economic offensive against Iraq. Iraq's historic claims, grievances, and offers to negotiate a settlement were ignored, as was Saddam Hussein's advance notice of his intentions. He finally took the bait and struck.

After the invasion, Hussein released parts of a transcript of his meeting with the U.S. ambassador in which she gave him no clear warning against the impending move. Ambassador April Glaspie related before an "informal" Senate committee meeting (not officially a "hearing" so she did not have to testify under oath) that she indeed warned Hussein in no uncertain terms. The State Department backed her up. When, under more congressional pressure, the diplomatic cables were declassified, the facts became clear: she and the State Department had lied.

No attention was paid to Hussein's brutalities until he marched on cue. Media "watchdogs" were still asleep when the U.S. head of Amnesty International complained that "there was no presidential indignation . . . in 1989, when Amnesty released its findings about the torture of Iraq children. And just a few weeks before the invasion of Kuwait, the Bush administration refused to conclude that Iraq had engaged in a consistent pattern of gross human-right violation."[14]

When Hussein invaded Kuwait, however, gruesome atrocity stories filled the media. They were used in six speeches by Bush and were cited by seven senators as a reason for voting for the war resolution (which passed by six votes). A year later it was revealed that the story was hearsay told by the daughter of Kuwait's ambassador, whose appearance was arranged by Hill and Knowlton, the Washington public relations firm representing Kuwait. The *New York Times* also reported on December 20, 1991, "the discovery that the country suffered less damage than originally estimated" and was "recapturing its former affluence.")

The first stage, Operation Desert Shield, was to stop Hussein from marching into Saudi Arabia, although there was no evidence he intended to do so and the United States had no treaty or prior policy to defend the Saudis. The mission of the troops, according to Bush was defensive; they would not initiate hostilities.

Soon, however, the operation became a simple and unconditional offensive to rebuff "naked aggression." The U.S.-led military buildup proceeded swiftly with no consideration of the colonial and recent history of the shifting boundaries of Middle Eastern nonnations or of other invasions, occupations, and repeated violations of U.N. resolutions and international law by the United States and its allies.

The United Nations itself was brought out of media mothballs. The *New York Times,* after spearheading the successful campaign for U.S. withdrawal from UNESCO, and mostly ignoring U.N. actions, now editorially complimented the United Nations on September 11, 1990, for having "provided legal and political armor" for the operation.[15] Vague resolutions authorizing force were rammed through without significant opposition (absent on the world scene since the collapse of Soviet power). The resolutions concealed, but were later used to justify, the allies' ultimate objectives. Having achieved them, the allies exploded the equivalent in bombs of the next twelve to fifteen years of the entire U.N. global budget. Other resolutions condemning the invasion of Lebanon and continuing military occupation by Israel were ignored.

The United States was still withholding $720 million in overdue membership payments. This long-standing pressure tactic drove the United Nations to the brink of bankruptcy. Secretary General Javier Pérez de Cuellar had to report in the fall of 1991 that "it is a source of profound concern to me that the same membership which sees it appropriate to entrust the United Nations Secretariat with unprecedented new responsibilities has not taken the necessary action to insure that the minimum financial resources required to carry out those responsibilities are provided on a reliable and predictable basis."[16]

A loose coalition was patched together, with the United States contributing most of the military might; the Arabs, the location; and the oil sheikhs, Germans, and Japanese, most of the cash. While preparation for war proceeded, diplomacy was faked for the media. Bob Woodward's book *The Commanders* described the panic in the White House when it seemed that the Saudis might "bug out" (in Bush's words) and accept some settlement.[17] King Fahd did not buy the excuse of a Iraqi threat to Saudi Arabia. (Neither did the satellite photos published in the *St. Petersburg Times* on January 6, 1991, which were refused by the U.S. wire services.) But then the White House sent Secretary of Defense Richard Cheney with an offer the king could not refuse, apparently a promise to push for favorable regional settlement after Hussein was safely out of the way. While Secretary of State James Baker went to Baghdad to "negotiate," national security adviser Brent Scowcroft told Saudi Ambassador Prince Bandar that the president had made up his mind and that diplomatic efforts were all exercises.

Exaggerated estimates of nuclear capability, "the world's fourth largest standing army," and Iraq's "crack Republican Guards" were fed to eager media. A vast and sophisticated U.S. intelligence community that five months later was able to warn Gorbachev of the impending coup in his own backyard (in vain, as it turned out) now seemed to be muted. Disinformation, rationalized as "confusing the enemy," confused everybody. Decisionmaking was restricted to a small group headed by former CIA director (now President) George Bush. "It was apparent even before the Gulf War, wrote Maureen Dowd in the *New York Times* (November 22, 1991, p. 1), that "this White House does not have a traditional policymaking process." Dowd cited a "top Administration official" as saying, "It's hard to debate decisions because there is a lot of secrecy."

In the preparation for Desert Storm, even the National Security Council was held at arm's length.[18] Woodward reported that the chair of the Joint Chiefs of Staff, Colin Powell, and other commanders advised "containment or strangulation" and found themselves excluded from decisionmaking.[19] Later they complained of "faulty intelligence." The order to attack came from a White House apparently acting on superior intelligence.

Final planning for the attack was known to have begun in September but was not reported until much later. The *New York Times* published the "news" on March 3, after the war had ended. *Newsweek's* account of the preparations, published on January 28, quoted "one of his closest advisers" as saying, "This is a fight George Bush has been preparing for all his life." Elizabeth Drew wrote in the *New Yorker* on January 25, "John Sununu . . . was telling people that a short successful war would be pure political gold for the President." Reporters who usually rushed on the air and into print with every scoop now held back. "The road from Watergate to the Gulf War is marked by ever greater cautiousness and opportunism on the part of the press," wrote Michael Massing. "Bob Woodward [who saved revealing details for his book] provides a particularly disquieting example of the change."[20]

The full history of the swift and massive military buildup still remains to be told. A nearly Vietnam-size military force was built up over a period of months in the desert. Information, communication, and coordination were key elements. Williams reported that more communications networks were put into full use during the buildup and war than in all of World War II.[21] As late as December 1990, the Pentagon sent out a call for $30 million worth of computers to be shipped to Saudi Arabia in six weeks. A small and little-known Texas company called Compuadd got the contract and did the job. Its full reward came when, ten months later, it shared in the biggest Defense Department computer order ever awarded.

Forming the backbone of the new instant-history-making machine were the portable uplinks, the global satellite network (including the collaborating Soviet satellite), the dedicated direct telephone lines, and the computer links. This tightly guarded system made it possible to provide controlled real-time simultaneous live global coverage in several selected sites, even when nothing much was going on. Suspenseful "live" boredom filled with breathless analysis and photo opportunities gave audiences around the world a realistic sensation of "being there." Donning gas masks enhanced the feeling of spontaneity even, or perhaps especially, when the alarm turned out to be false. At the height of the crisis, CNN's audience share rose more than five times its normal 3 percent.

The prologue ended with the U.S. ultimatum of January 15, 1991. The deception, suppression, misinformation, and disinformation that characterized the buildup overwhelmed and disoriented the public. Many watched in disbelief as the juggernaut assembled in the Gulf was set to strike. When the nonnegotiable ultimatum was about to expire, the public was still deeply divided: four out of ten responding to a *Times Mirror* poll thought sanctions should be given more time. The same number also wanted to hear more about the views of the 41 percent of the U.S. public that did *not* think Bush "did the right thing" sending troops to the Gulf.[22] Even though the congressional authorization had passed by only seven votes, once the war started, dissenting voices fell silent or were silenced, and the media-driven instant history blitz kicked in.

The Main Event

"As the skies cleared . . . an American officer proclaimed it 'a beautiful day for bombing,' " wrote R. W. Apple, Jr., in the *New York Times* on February 12, 1991. Before the day was over, 750 bombing missions had been completed. " 'There is more stuff up there than I'd see in 20 lifetimes,' said an Air Force pilot."

What may have been happening on the Iraqi ground could only be surmised from a safe distance. A British defense expert calculated that in the first month "the tonnage of high explosive bombs already released has exceeded the combined allied air offensive of World War II."[23] But the military terminology that permeated the reporting was more sports than slaughter. "Our team has carried out its game beautifully," exulted a military expert on NBC. "We ran our first play, it worked great," said a pilot interviewed on CBS. "We scored a touchdown."[24] Secretary of Defense Cheney told U.S. Air Force personnel that they had conducted "the most successful air campaign in the history of the world."[25]

The precision-bombing spectacular was, in fact, the dumping of the equivalent of five Hiroshimas on a small country of 18 million people. The targets were the life-sustaining infrastructure of water, power, and transportation facilities. When the bombing was over, the carnage of hunger and disease began. Western health authorities estimated 1 million children malnourished, and child mortality quadrupled within a year. Middle East Watch, an affiliate of the international Human Rights Watch organization, reported that allied decisions to drop unguided bombs in daytime over populated areas without warning civilians of imminent attacks violated generally accepted practice and international law "both in the selection of targets and the choice of means and methods of attack."[26]

The memorable Patriot missiles, costing $700,000 each, missed eight out of ten times. When they found their targets, the resulting debris caused more destruction than the Scuds might have done. MIT weapons expert Theodore Postol told the House Armed Services Committee that thirteen Scuds that fell unchallenged near Tel Aviv caused no deaths, fewer injuries, and less than half the property damage than the eleven Scuds in the same area that were intercepted by Patriots. Marc S. Miller, senior editor of *Technology Review* magazine, called Patriot "the anti-truth missile."[27] Roger N. Johnson concluded in his study of war damage that the Patriots were "successful mainly as psychological weapons used to fool the public."[28] Their public relations success was shown in the survey by Michael Morgan, Justin Lewis, and Sut Jhally (see Chapter 18): 81 percent of the respondents knew about the Patriots, while only 42 percent could identify Colin Powell.

The mighty armies that brutalized Kuwait and were supposed to march on to Saudi Arabia, if not beyond, could not be found. Poorly equipped and demoralized troops sitting in trenches, caves, bunkers without air cover were napalmed and "fuel-air bombed" to deprive those inside of oxygen, and then they were bulldozed; dead and alive alike were buried in some seventy miles of trenches. (Bodies of soldiers who "suffocated in their bunkers after U.S. tanks plowed them under" were still being discovered nine months after the war.)[29] Defenseless convoys fleeing in panic were bombed and strafed into oblivion in what pilots called a "turkey shoot."

There was much media concern expressed about Iraqi chemical and missile threats. The erratic Scuds and the even more erratic Patriots got extensive coverage. Missing were signs that the roughly four-week, $61 billion massacre inflicted on Iraq was more lethal than any nuclear, chemical, or biological warfare had ever been.[30]

One may question, as Noam Chomsky does in this book (Chapter 4), whether there really was a war, if by war we mean a conflict in which an enemy shoots back. The slaughter, as it is more properly called, claimed more than 100,000 lives in direct casualties alone. That is the official figure. In a secret report, former navy secretary John Lehman revealed a Pentagon estimate of 200,000.[31] The kill ratio of even about 100,000 to 150 U.S. soldiers, at least 35 of them, as it later turned out, killed by "friendly fire," was unprecedented in military history.[32]

The main facts of cost, casualties, and damage were carefully kept out of the briefings and were censored from the reports. U.S. and allied reporters were rigidly controlled, and few other journalists were even admitted into Saudi Arabia. The few independent reporters who managed to obtain information on their own, and the analysts who might have contributed more diverse perspectives, were excluded from the media mainstream.

NBC first commissioned, then refused to broadcast uncensored footage of heavy civilian casualties. (The broadcast was vetoed by NBC president Michael Gartner, who had led a media crusade for freedom of the press in the 1980s.) The video was then offered to CBS. The night before it was to air on the "CBS Evening News," the show's executive producer was fired and the report was canceled.[33]

Roger N. Johnson monitored CNN for the climactic twenty-seven-hour final prewar period when Iraq proposed conditional withdrawal and Soviet and Iranian peace initiatives were advanced.[34] His study revealed that thirty military experts but no peace experts were interviewed. George Bush, the most frequently shown, brushed aside peace talks. Others interviewed included mostly right-wing hawks, such as Oliver North, Robert McFarlane, Jeane Kirkpatrick, Pat Buchanan, Richard Allen, Richard Perle, Dan Quayle, and Ronald Reagan. And CNN may have been the most open to a diversity of views. (NBC is owned by General Electric, a supplier for every weapons system used in the Gulf. Major military contractors sponsor news programs and sit on the boards of directors of other networks and leading media, such as the *New York Times* and the *Washington Post*.)[35]

Instead of full and accurate reports and documentaries, network "docudramas" shot in sync sound on location and in Hollywood studios took audiences to the Persian Gulf War movie. Realistic shots of training, tanks maneuvering in the sand, simulated trench warfare, attacks on the enemy lurking in the darkness, scripted scenes of camp life and the "home front," patrols on a mission firing into the darkness, a full sequence of mission control launching a Patriot and scoring a "hit," and even "hostages" being beaten alternated with promos of *Die Hard 2* and *Terminator 2*. Spectacular explosions lit distant horizons, hurled vehicles, and blasted bodies in all three movies.

Deborah Amos, who covered the Gulf War for National Public Radio, scoffed at the adage that truth is the first casualty of war. "In this war," she wrote, "truth was more than a casualty. Truth was hit over the head, dragged into a closet, and held hostage to the public relations needs of the United States military." The docudrama's happy ending showed jubilant faces, while the voice-over spoke of "an outpouring of joy not seen since World War II." The real documentary footage of the conflict was locked in Pentagon vaults.[36]

The Cult of Violence

"It was a colossal failure of politics that plunged us into the war," said the *New Yorker* (January 28, 1991, 21). Then how did this failure become a triumph? How was the engineering of a vast and unnecessary human catastrophe made to seem not only acceptable but also politically advantageous, even triumphant? How did the war become a virtual breeding ground for presidential prospects?

The buildup, orchestration, saturation, and fabrications of the war provide only part of the answers to these questions. Another part comes from those characteristics of instant history that isolate critical events from their broader historical context and throw the spectator-witness back on conventional conceptions of how things work in the world. In our culture many of those conceptions stem from what we should recognize as the cult of violence.

Violence has many faces. Wholesale mass executions of people, otherwise known as war or genocide, have become increasingly technical, scientific, and deadly but no more precise.[37] They have killed an ever-increasing percentage of civilians, eventually far outnumbering military casualties. For instance, the German terror-bombing of the small Spanish city of Guernica provoked worldwide outrage and Pablo Picasso's antiwar mural. But by the end of World War II—thousands of large-scale air raids and a genocide later—the calculated destruction of Dresden's historic center, the firebombing of Tokyo, and the pulverizing of Hiroshima and Nagasaki for little, if any, military advantage (but more likely to impress Joseph Stalin before the agreed-upon entry of the Soviets into the war in the Pacific), numbed our senses.

The Vietnam War witnessed further escalation of firepower and the chemical poisoning of Vietnam's countryside, both which were met with rationalization. The trend toward increasingly skewed kill ratios has culminated, so far, in the Persian Gulf War. Recounting such facts of "cultural evolution and war," Roger N. Johnson observed that political bombing of civilians is no longer considered an act of barbarism.[38] Wholesale violence against basically innocent people is seen, if at all, as potentially embarrassing information to be sanitized and wrapped in euphemisms.

Retail violence is not far behind. The United States is the undisputed homicide capital of the world. We also lead industrialized countries in jailing and executing people.[39] Our streets, our schools, and our homes have become places of fear and brutality, widely publicized and profitably dramatized. Killings in the workplace doubled in the 1980s over the previous decade.[40] And yet the cult of violence is neither simply a reflection of these trends nor just a stimulus for them. It is more like a charged environment affecting many aspects of social relations, control, and power.

The facts of violence are both celebrated and concealed in the cult of violence that surrounds us. There has never been a culture as filled with images of violence as ours is now. We are awash in a tide of violent representations. There is no escape from the massive invasion of colorful mayhem into the homes and cultural lives of ever-larger areas of the world.

Of course, there was blood in fairy tales, gore in mythology, murder in Shakespeare, lurid crimes in tabloids, battles and wars in textbooks. The representation of violence is a legitimate cultural expression, even necessary to balance tragic consequences against deadly compulsions. But the historically defined, individually crafted, and selectively used symbolic violence of heroism, cruelty, or misanthropy has been swamped by violence with happy endings produced on the dramatic assembly line.

The violence we see on the screen and read about in our press bears little relationship in volume or in type, and especially in consequence, to violence in real life.[41] Yet much of it looks realistic, and we tend to project it onto the real world. This sleight of hand robs us of the tragic sense of life necessary for compassion. "To be hip," wrote Gitlin, "is to be inured, and more—to require a steadily increasing boost in the size of the dose required."[42]

Our children are born into a symbolic environment of six to eight violent episodes per prime-time hour alone (four times as many in presumably humorous children's programs) and an average of at least two entertaining murders a night. Children are "the first to react to the environment around them," wrote playwright Steve Tesich.[43] "Unless we are willing to change that environment, we must accept the verdict that our children have become the victims of choice for most Americans."

The dominant portrayals of mayhem and crime misrepresent in important respects the actual nature, demography, and patterns of victimization of real-life violence. Contrary to promotional hype, most uses of cable, video, and other new technologies make the dominant patterns penetrate even more deeply (but not more cheaply) into everyday life. No historical, esthetic, or even commercial rationalization can justify drenching every home with images of expertly choreographed brutality.

Movies exploit the cult and increase the dosage. Escalation of the cinematic body count seems to be one way to get attention from a public punch-drunk on video mayhem. *Robocop*'s first rampage for law and order in 1987 killed 32 people. The 1990 *Robocop 2,* targeting a twelve-year-old "drug lord," among others, slaughtered 81. The sick movie *Death Wish* claimed 9 victims in 1974. In the 1988 version, the bleeding-heart-liberal-turned-vigilante disposed of 52. *Rambo: First Blood,* released in 1985, rambled through Southeast Asia leaving 62 corpses. In 1988, *Rambo III* visited Afghanistan, killing 106. *Godfather I* produced 12 corpses, *Godfather II* put away 18, and *Godfather III* killed no less than 53. The daredevil cop in the original *Die Hard* in 1988 saved the day with a modest 18 dead. Two years later *Die Hard 2* thwarted a plot to rescue "the biggest drug dealer in the world," coincidentally a Central American dictator to be tried in a U.S. court, achieving a phenomenal body count of 264.

The decade's record goes to the 1990 children's movie and tie-in marketing sensation and glorification of martial arts, *Teenage Mutant Ninja Turtles.* Released as the Gulf War buildup began, with 133 acts of mayhem per hour, *Ninja Turtles* was the most violent film ever marketed to children. Undaunted by the outrage of trapped parents and overworked psychiatrists, *Turtles II,* appropriately subtitled *Secrets of the Ooze,* followed the success of the Ninjas (and of the Gulf War) as another nonstop punchup and kick-in-the-teeth opera in which the martial artists continued their rampage.

The infamous "Faces of Death" videos, withdrawn from circulation in 1987, were quietly rereleased in the fall of 1991.[44] The October 14, 1991, international edition of *Variety* featured 123 pages of ads for new movies, with pictures of shooting, killing, or corpses on every other page and a verbal appeal to violence, on the average, on every page. Leading the verbal procession were "kill," "murder," "death," "deadly," and "dead" (thirty-three times) and "terror," "fatal," "lethal," and "dangerous" (twelve times). Bringing up the rear were "rage," "frenzy," "revenge," "gun-crazy," "kickboxer," "maniac," "warrior," "invader," "hawk," "battle," "war," "shoot," "fight," "slaughter," and "blood."

Terminator 2 dominated the list of box-office blockbusters from fourteen major movie markets around the world. Its leading actor, promoter, and role model, Arnold Schwarzenegger, chaired the President's Council on Physical Fitness and Sports. The National Coalition on Television Violence named Schwarzenegger "the most violent actor" of 1987 and found that ten of Schwarzenegger's twelve movies averaged 109 often graphic and gruesome violent acts per hour.

Growing up in a violence-laden cultural environment cultivates aggressiveness in some people and desensitization, insecurity, mistrust, and anxiety in most people.[45] These are highly exploitable sentiments. They set up a scenario of violence and victimization in which some take on the role of violents but in which most adopt the role, and psychology, of victims. They demand protection and condone, if not welcome, violent solutions to domestic and world problems purported to save them from aggressors. This scenario contributes to the appeal of punitive and vindictive action against dark forces in a mean world, especially when the action is quickly and decisively presented as enhancing a sense of control and security.

The cold war is over, and the cultural props for imperial policy are shifting from anticommunist rationalizations to sharp and selective offensives against real and concocted terrorists, narco-terrorists, petro-terrorists, unauthorized aggressors, and other unfriendly (as opposed to friendly) demons of the Third World. The cult of violence is the ritual demonstration of brute power and its projection into sex, family, job, politics, and war.

An overkill of violent imagery helps train the military mind and mobilize support for taking charge of the unruly at home and abroad.

Bombarding viewers with violent images of a mean and dangerous world without illuminating the real costs of violence and war is, in the last analysis, an instrument of intimidation and terror. It was indispensable to the triumph of instant history in the Persian Gulf. It is a preview of the shape of things to come in a unipolar world with no effective democratic opposition or geopolitical counterforce.

Epilogue

What was represented as a clean, swift, surgical strike to punish aggression, get rid of Hussein, and secure cheap oil, petrodollars, peace, jobs, and democracy became, in fact, a human and ecological disaster of "cataclysmic proportions" (in the words of the U.N. inspection team) that achieved few of its purported aims. The war "changed almost nothing," concluded *Newsweek* on June 28, 1991. "Most of the same faces and the same tired policies remain. . . . Internally, the regime's capacity for repression seems undiminished." Hussein was riding high. U.S.-inspired revolts of Kurds in the north and of Shiites in the south were crushed. A Palestinian settlement was as far from manifestation as ever.

At year's end, Human Rights Watch issued a comprehensive report saying that Washington had sacrificed principle to political interest, promoting rights "only when it is cost-free." "When competing interests arose," the report observed, ". . . maintaining warm relations with Saudi oil sheiks, . . . or avoiding politically embarrassing questions about why the United States went to war to restore the Kuwati Emir—human rights took a back seat at the White House."[46]

The war and its global imagery traumatized many Third World countries. It paralyzed the already weakened Nonaligned Movement, which "had done absolutely nothing to stop the war," observed the *Christian Conference of Asia News* in its November-December 1991 issue. "It is a cruel irony," the *News* noted, "that it took the blood bath of the Gulf War . . . to bring these cold realities home to the Non-Aligned Movement members." The disruption of trade and travel and the shutting of Iraq's pipelines deepened the Third World's economic distress and political paralysis.

The Middle East was left in turmoil, with Iran and widespread fundamentalist backlash gaining power. Arabs versus Arabs were arming faster than ever. (Saudi Arabia alone was getting twenty new Patriot batteries at the cost of $3.3 billion.)[47] Syria, invader of Lebanon and newfound U.S. ally, spent the $2 billion earned for good behavior in the Gulf on North Korean Scuds, Czech tanks, and Soviet MIGs.)[48]

The full scope of nuclear disinformation was still unclear. Although Third World nuclear proliferation (generally unreported) was by no means limited to Iraq, and twenty Iraqi nuclear facilities were destroyed by U.S bombers, the *Bulletin of Atomic Scientists* estimated in its March 1991 issue that Iraq was five to ten years away from producing a usable nuclear device. Since then, commission after commission has released widely publicized—and divergent—reports on hidden nuclear plants. The "nuclear story," not the story of misery the continuing blockade was inflicting on the people, became the largest single topic of postwar coverage. And yet the salient facts of even that story were missing from the sweep of instant history.

Not reported was the fact that the International Atomic Energy Agency (IAEA) had inspected the Iraqi facilities in November 1990 and had found them to be in compliance with IAEA safeguards, meaning that nuclear fuel was not being diverted to weapons use. Not reported were the further facts that Article 56 of the Geneva Protocols explicitly forbade the targeting of live reactors; that both IAEA and U.N. General Assembly resolutions had called for a ban on attacks on nuclear facilities; and that the IAEA had declared any such attack "a violation of the Charter of the United Nations and of the Statutes of [this] Agency." Many proliferation experts considered the targeted reactors to be of dubious military value and the bombing of operating reactors with probably "hot" cores to be potentially more harmful than either necessary or effective.[49]

The Western alliance had been strained. U.S. arm-twisting of Japan to contribute troops, in contradiction to the latter's U.S.-dictated constitution, divided Japan (which resisted, though agreed to contribute mine-sweepers and $13 billion) and started a political backlash. The backlash in the Muslim world led to the defeat of the Turkish government. The loss of trade and increased energy costs added to the trauma of the Third World. Kuwait's oligarchy was restored and proved more repressive than before. The Kurds had been abandoned again, as had the democratic forces in Iraq, which apparently posed a threat to the new world order.

The day the war ended, the Bechtel Corporation, from which U.S. secretaries of state and defense had been recruited, announced a multi-billion dollar contract for the reconstruction of Kuwait. Stock prices rose, but the economy slumped, and consumer confidence declined. The high costs and mounting deficits incurred to pay for the war and its aftermath contributed to recession in the United States. After an initial rise in the price of oil, friendly Gulf states boosted oil production. By year's end, falling prices (and revenues) plunged OPEC into a crisis and further postponed serious discussion of an effective U.S. energy policy.

The only clear successes have been the extension of U.S. power into an increasingly troubled region, the renewed flow of petrodollars propping up increasingly shaky economies, and the domestic "political gold." The quality of political (or any) thinking behind the celebration was suggested by George Bush's response to a question a year later: "If I had had to listen to advice from the United States Senate leadership, the Democrats—or from the House, the leadership over there—to do something about the Persian Gulf, we'd have still been sitting there in the United States, fat, dumb, and happy, with Saddam Hussein maybe in Saudi Arabia."[50]

Within weeks of the victory, Time Warner completed in record time the collection and compression of imagery that would fill five hundred floppy disks into a single CD-ROM history of Desert Storm and its speedy distribution to stores and school libraries. (The job ordinarily takes several months.) *CNN: War in the Gulf,* advertised as an "authoritative chronicle of the world's first 'real-time television war,'" was published soon thereafter. Pentagon-aided victory parades, the ABC-TV docudrama "Heroes of Desert Storm" (with a thirty-second introduction by President Bush), and the first deployment of Gulf War imagery in an election campaign rounded out the triumphant quick-freeze stage of instant history.[51]

In a fitting and perceptive tribute, *Time* magazine named CNN owner Ted Turner its Man of the Year for his influencing the dynamic of events and for his making viewers around the world into instant witnesses of history. (Time Warner is also one-fifth owner of Turner Broadcasting System.) A review of the year in *Modern Maturity,* the largest-circulation magazine in the United States, was titled (appropriately to the promised "gentler, kinder nation") "The Gentle Giant." Sent to 32 million "mature" readers, the review summarized the war as "a stunning success in the Gulf" and concluded, "The Bush Administration's conduct of the crisis had been in the purest American spirit of respect for international law, winning the widest international support for joint action and the use of minimum force. It was a model of successful modern diplomacy."[52]

Anatomy of Triumph

Let us now consider how this model of success played out on the home front. Once the saturation bombing had started, dissent had been marginalized, challenge had been suppressed, and the tide of saturation coverage had risen, most respondents to the *Times Mirror* poll were swept up in the flow. Their responses became news and sped the rush of events. Half the respondents, most of whom wanted more diverse views before, now said they heard too much opposition.[53]

As the operation entered its second full week, instant history found its true believers. Nearly eight out of ten believed that the censors were not hiding bad news; 57 percent wanted increased military control over reporting. Martin Shaw and Roy Carr-Hill report in Chapter 13 that in a

British poll 82 percent agreed the sorties were "precise strikes against strategic targets with minimum civilian casualties."

The effect of television coverage can be gauged from the differences between responses of light and heavy viewers of otherwise comparable groups. The Morgan, Lewis, and Jhally survey showed that less than half (47 percent) of light viewers, compared to three-quarters (76 percent) of heavy viewers, "strongly supported" President Bush's decision to use military force against Iraq.

A panel study conducted as part of the 1991 American National Election Study also revealed some gender differences. During the buildup, 61 percent of male light viewers but 71 percent of male heavy viewers approved "the way George Bush is handling the crisis in the Persian Gulf," a highly significant ten-point difference. For women, who were less supportive to begin with, viewing made no difference: About 50 percent of both light and heavy viewers "approved." After the war, however, with even the "light viewers" saturated with the images of the war, the approval rate for light and heavy male viewers rose to 83 and 86 percent and for light and heavy female viewers to 78 and 85 percent. Instant history almost closed the gender gap.

Heavy viewing also boosted the percentage of those who would vote for George Bush, especially among those who were otherwise the least likely to vote for him: Only 31 percent of low-income light viewers but 51 percent of low-income heavy viewers expressed an inclination to vote for Bush in 1992. And as Morgan, Lewis, and Jhally demonstrated, the more viewers saw, the more they remembered the misleading imagery, but the less they knew about the background and facts of the war.

Two months after the war, the public rated the coverage, military censorship, and general information about the war even higher. The *Times Mirror* percentage of "very favorable" rating of the military rose forty-two points from 18 to an unprecedented 60 percent. Secretary of Defense Dick Cheney's rating jumped from 3 to 33 percent (extraordinary for a secretary of defense). Desert Storm commander Norman Schwarz-kopf's 51 percent was the highest "very favorable" score in more than 150 *Times Mirror* public favorability surveys conducted since 1985, stimulating instant speculation about his political future.

The war in the Persian Gulf is fading to a few flickering images: Scuds streaking through the sky and Patriots rising to intercept them, or so we thought; bombs falling down factory smokestacks with deadly accuracy, or so, too, we thought. But that was no movie. Its consequences will linger in the real world for a long time to come. When the balance sheet of critical events of the 1990s is finally tallied, the world will marvel at the mischief wrought by the new scenario of instant history.

262 ◆ George Gerbner

Global immediacy gives us instant history, which is simultaneous, global, mass, living, telling, showing, and reacting in brief and intensive bursts. Image driven and violence laden, as compelling as it is contrived, instant history robs us of reflection time, political space, and access to alternatives. The horror of a holocaust can now be managed with glorious efficiency.

This is not an isolated problem that can be addressed by focusing on media violence or crisis coverage alone. It is an integral part of a global cultural condition that increasingly permeates, and poisons, the mainstream of the common symbolic environment. Only a new international cultural environment movement, dedicated to democratic participation in cultural policymaking and an alternative media system, can do justice to the challenge, and terror, of instant history. But that, too, is another story.

Notes

1. Frederick Williams, "The Shape of News to Come: The Gulf War as an Opportunity for TV News to Show Off, and to Raise Questions," *Quill* (September 1991): 15–17.

2. Cited in Timothy Garton Ash, "Poland After Solidarity," *New York Review of Books,* June 13, 1991, p. 57.

3. Cited in a book review by Tom Masland, *Philadelphia Inquirer,* September 1, 1991, p. 2F.

4. Ernst Briesach, "Historiography," *International Encyclopedia of Communications,* vol. 2 (New York: Oxford University Press, 1989), p. 280.

5. Ien Ang, "Global Media/Local Meaning," *Media Information Australia* (November 1991): 4.

6. Disaster relief has been particularly vulnerable to the vagaries of instant history. A 1991 report to the United Nations concluded that "far too often, thousands who are starving and uprooted in one part of the world receive the minimum of relief and succor, while aid pours forth for those who are suffering at the focus of international power politics and media attention." The highly politicized aid to the Kurds in Iraq was one case in point (*New York Times,* November 13, 1991, p. A9).

7. Neil Postman, *Amusing Ourselves to Death: Public Discourse in the Age of Show Business by Neil Postman.* (New York: Penguin Books, 1985), p. 103.

8. Tom Grimes, "Encoding TV News Messages into Memory." *Journalism Quarterly* 67, no. 4 (Winter 1990): 757–766.

9. The Tianenman Square massacre, which many claim to have witnessed on television, did not take place on Tianenman square; only the cameras were there, recording the clearing of the square by troops and tanks. The massacre took place off camera in another part of town.

10. Todd Gitlin, "On Being Sound-Bitten," *Boston Review* (December 1991): 16–17.

11. Williams, "The Shape of News to Come."

12. John M. Phelan, "Image Industry Erodes Political Space," *Media Development* 38, no. 4 (1991): 6–8.

13. The story of the weeping icon took on a life of its own when it was extensively described, then reported stolen, then recovered, and finally called a hoax and a publicity stunt. (See, e.g., *New York Times,* December 29 and 30, 1991, January 1, 1992; and Associated Press stories during that time.)

14. Cited by Deborah Amos, "When Seeing Is Not Believing: Desert Mirage—the True Story of the Gulf War," *Nieman Reports* (Winter 1991): 61.

15. George Gerbner, "UNESCO in the U.S. Press," in George Gerbner, Hamid Mowlana, and Kaarle Nordenstreng (eds.), *The Global Media Debate: Its Rise, Fall, and Renewal* (New York: Ablex, 1992).

16. "U.N. Asks Billion for Peacekeeper Fund," *New York Times,* November 25, 1991, p. A3.

17. Bob Woodward, *The Commanders* (New York: Simon and Schuster, 1991).

18. John B. Judis, "Twilight of the Gods," *Wilson Quarterly* (Autumn 1991): 55.

19. Woodward, *The Commanders.*

20. Michael Massing, "Sitting on Top of the News," *New York Times Review of Books,* June 27, 1991, p. 11.

21. Williams, "The Shape of News to Come."

22. "The 1990–91 Panel Study of the Political Consequences of War," *in American National Election Study* (Center for Political Studies, Institute for Social Research, University of Michigan, 1991).

23. Reported in the *Philadelphia Inquirer,* February 5, 1991, p. 6A)

24. For these and more examples, see Michael Parenti, "Media Watch: Now for Sports and Weather," *Z Magazine* (July-August 1991): 104.

25. *Philadelphia Inquirer,* February 9, 1991, p. A1.

26. Melissa Healy, "Group Faults U.S. on War Deaths," *Philadelphia Inquirer,* November 17, 1991, p. 9A. The law is a 1977 international treaty that has not been ratified by the United States.

27. Marc S. Miller, "Patriotic Blindness and Anti-Truth Weapons," *Index on Censorship* (November-December 1991): 32.

28. Roger N. Johnson, "Cultural Evolution and War: From Science to Social Science," *Bulletin of the International Society for Research on Aggression* 13, no. 2 (1991): 7–10.

29. Associated Press dispatch from Nicosia, Cyprus, November 5, 1991.

30. Pentagon estimate reported in the *Philadelphia Inquirer,* November 6, 1991, p. 3A.

31. *People* magazine reporter Dirk Mathison crashed the highly confidential Bohemian Grove encampment in northern California, where each year top male U.S. policymakers, including media chiefs, assembled. Mathison's story of what he heard (before he was discovered and ejected by an executive of Time Warner), including the Lehman speech entitled "Smart Weapons," was killed by *People* magazine, owned by Time Warner. It was published under the title "Inside the Bohemian Grove: The Story People Magazine Won't Let You Read," *Extra!* (November-December 1991): 1, 12–14.

32. David H. Hackworth, "Killed by Their Comrades," *Newsweek,* November 18, 1991, pp. 45–46.

33. Dennis Bernstein and Sasha Futran, "Sights Unseen," *San Francisco Bay Guardian,* March 20, 1991, p. 23.

34. Johnson, "Cultural Evolution and the War."

35. See, for example, Martin E. Lee, "Arms and the Media: Business as Usual," *Index on Censorship* (November-December 1991): 29–31. Lee recalled that on the day U.S. bombs killed four hundred men, women, and children in a Baghdad shelter, *Newsweek* (owned by the Washingon Post Company) featured a stealth bomber on its cover with the caption "How Many Lives Can It Save?" (30).

36. Deborah Amos, "Seeing Is Not Believing," *Nieman Reports* (Winter 1991): 61.

37. Wars in the twentieth century have killed 99 million people (before the Gulf War), twelve times as many as in the nineteenth century and twenty-two times as many as in the eighteenth century. Other hostilities, not counting internal state terrorism, are resulting in an estimated one thousand or more deaths per year (*World Military and Social Expenditures* [Washington, D.C.: World Priorities, 1986]).

38. Johnson, "Cultural Evolution and the War."

39. One of every 133 Americans will become a murder victim. (*U.S. Bureau of Justice Statistics Technical Report,* NCJ-104274 [March 1987]). The U.S. rate of killings is 21.9 per 100,000 men fifteen through twenty-four. The rate, for example, for Austria is 0.3; for England, 1.2; and for Scotland (highest after the United States), 5.0 (National Center for Health Statistics study published in the *Journal of the American Medical Association* and reported in the *New York Times,* June 27, 1990, p. A10). Between 1985 and 1989 the number of homicides nationwide increased 22 percent (congressional hearings reported in the *Philadelphia Inquirer,* August 1, 1990). The U.S. rate of incarceration is 407 per 100,000 citizens. This compares to 36 in the Netherlands, 86 in West Germany, and 100 in England. While the prison population in the United States doubled in the 1980s, the crime rate rose 1.8 percent, suggesting that the "need to incarcerate" is out of proportion with the actual crime rate but is a political response to culturally generated insecurity and demand for repression. There is no evidence that capital punishment is a greater deterrent than a life sentence or that it relates to lower crime rates.

40. Associated Press dispatch by Fred Bayles reported in the *Philadelphia Inquirer,* November 15, 1991, p. 3A.

41. See, for example, Ray Surette, *Media Crime and Criminal Justice: Images and Realities* (Pacific Grove, Calif.: Brooks/Cole, 1992).

42. Todd Gitlin, "On Thrills and Kills: Sadomasochism in the Movies," *Dissent* (Spring 1991): 247.

43. Steve Tesich, "The Watergate Syndrome: A Government of Lies," *Nation,* January 13, 1992, p. 13.

44. *Variety,* October 14, 1991, p. 61.

45. See, for example, George Gerbner, "Violence and Terror in the Mass Media," *Reports and Papers in Mass Communication,* no. 102 (Paris: UNESCO, 1988).

46. Paul Lewis, "New U.N. Leader Is Taking Over at a Time of Great Expectations," *New York Times,* December 30, 1991, pp. A1, 6.

47. Eric Schmitt, "Saudis to Buy 14 More Batteries of Patriot Missiles from the U.S.," *New York Times,* November 9, 1991, p. 3.

48. Matthew d'Ancona, "All Eyes on the Armourer," *Index on Censorship* (November-December 1991): 2.

49. For more details, see Mel Friedman, "Too Little, Too Late: How the Press Misses the Proliferation Story," *Nuclear Times* (Winter 1991–1992): 27–32.

50. Andrew Rosenthal, "Bush Returns the Democrats' Fire, Pointing to Success Against Iraqis," *New York Times,* November 9, 1991, pp. A1, 9.

51. A "test run" by the National Republican Congressional Committee in a November 1991 race in central Virginia yielded positive results. A thirty-second spot superimposed a photo of the Democratic candidate over an antiwar demonstration showing a "Victory to Iraq" banner. Although it was acknowledged (after the election) that the candidate did not attend that rally, she lost the election 37 to 63 percent.

Although by year's end the alternative press and more searching examinations had begun to challenge the instant history of the war, they were not likely to thaw the massive quick freeze of the mainstream media. The first "revisionist" book to appear was Martin Yant, *Desert Mirage: The True Story of the Gulf War* (Buffalo, N.Y.: Prometheus Books, 1991).

52. John Keegan, "The Gentle Giant," *Modern Maturity* (December 1991–January 1992): 52.

53. "The People, The Press and the War in the Gulf" (Washington, D.C.: Times Mirror Center for People and the Press, releases of January 10, January 31, and March 25, 1991).

About the Book

THE TRIUMPH OF IMAGE over reality and reason is the theme of this book. New communication technologies have made possible the transportation of images and words in real time to hundreds of millions of people around the world. We thought we witnessed the Gulf War as we sat, mesmerized by the imagery. But the studies from the many countries assembled for this book suggest that it was not the war in the Persian Gulf that we witnessed but rather imagery orchestrated to convey a sense of triumph and thus to achieve results that reality and reason could never have achieved.

The book offers contributions from thirty-five authors in eighteen countries, including short samplings from the media of several regions. The authors explore the social, economic, and political context of media coverage in their countries, the domination of one image in most of them, and the struggle for alternative perspectives. The authors probe the dynamics of image-making and pose some challenges for the future as well as provide us with a unique glimpse of how the world outside of the United States (as well as many Americans) viewed the war in the Persian Gulf and how the dynamics of image-making and information control operate.

Triumph of the Image will be useful to scholars and students in communications and mass media, international relations, political science, cultural studies, propaganda, censorship, and contemporary history as well as to the general public.

About the Editors
and Contributors

Asu Aksoy is on the faculty of the Centre for Urban and Regional Development Studies, University of Newcastle upon Tyne, England.

Naiim Badii is an assistant professor and the director of the Department of Social Communication Sciences, College of Social Sciences, Allameh Tabatabai University, Tehran, Iran.

Héctor Borrat, who is from Uruguay, is a professor of journalism, Autonomous University, Bellaterra, Barcelona, Spain.

Roy Carr-Hill is a senior research fellow and research coordinator, School of Social and Political Sciences, University of Hull, England.

Erskine B. Childers is an Irish writer and broadcaster and a former senior adviser to the United Nations Director-General for Development and International Economic Cooperation.

Noam Chomsky is a professor in the Department of Linguistics and Philosophy, Massachusetts Institute of Technology, Cambridge, Massachusetts.

Farrel Corcoran is the dean and professor in the School of Communication, Dublin City University, Ireland.

Richard A. Falk is Albert G. Milbank Professor of International Law and Practice, Princeton University, New Jersey.

Andre Gunder Frank is a professor of political economy at the University of Amsterdam, the Netherlands.

George Gerbner, editor of the *Journal of Communication* from 1964 to 1991, is a professor and former dean of the Annenberg School of Communications, University of Pennsylvania, Philadelphia, Pennsylvania.

Kamel S. Abu Jaber, formerly a political science professor, is currently the foreign minister of Jordan.

Sut Jhally is on the faculty of the Department of Communication, University of Massachusetts, Amherst, Massachusetts.

Rami G. Khouri is a writer and contributor to the *Jordan Times.*

Tetsuo Kogawa is a social critic and media activist from Tokyo, Japan.

Justin Lewis is on the faculty of the Department of Communication, University of Massachusetts, Amherst, Massachusetts.

Heikki Luostarinen is an assistant professor in the Department of Journalism and Mass Communication, University of Tampere, Finland.

Mostafa Mahmoud is an Egyptian writer and scholar.

Khawla Mattar is a Bahraini journalist and a Ph.d. candidate at the University of Durham, England.

Eugeni Mikitenko is a Soviet journalist.

Mehdi Mohsenian-Rad is on the faculty of Imam Sadegh University and is a communication researcher at the Iranian Research Organization for Science and Technology, Tehran, Iran.

Michael Morgan is on the faculty of the Department of Communication, University of Massachusetts, Amherst, Massachusetts.

Kazem Motamed-Nejad is a professor of journalism and mass communication in the Department of Social Communication, College of Social Sciences, Allameh Tabatabai University, Tehran, Iran.

Hamid Mowlana is a professor of international relations and the director of the International Communication Program, School of International Service, American University, Washington, D.C. He is also vice president of the International Association for Mass Communication Research (IAMCR).

Zaharom Nain is on the faculty of the Communication Programme, School of Humanities, University of Sains Malaysia, Penang, Malaysia.

Masanori Naito is an assistant professor of social studies at the Hitotsubashi University, Tokyo, Japan.

Stig A. Nohrstedt is on the faculty of the University of Örebro, Sweden.

Omar Souki Oliveira is on the faculty of the UFMG-Federal University, Belo Horizonte, Brazil.

Rune Ottosen is a member of the International Peace Research Institute, Oslo, Norway.

Kevin Robins is on the faculty of the Centre for Urban and Regional Development Studies, University of Newcastle upon Tyne, England.

Haluk Sahin is a columnist, the secretary general of the Turkish Press Council, and the president of the Foreign Press Association, Istanbul, Turkey.

P. Sainath is the deputy chief editor and foreign editor of *Blitz,* Bombay, India.

Herbert I. Schiller is professor emeritus, University of California, San Diego, and editor of the Westview Press series Critical Studies in Communication and in the Cultural Industries.

Martin Shaw is a senior lecturer in sociology and the director of security studies, University of Hull, England.

Richard C. Vincent is on the faculty of the Department of Communication, University of Hawaii at Manoa.

Index